WHEN THE LIGHT GOES ON

THE LIFE-CHANGING
WONDER OF LEARNING
IN AN AGE OF METRICS,
SCREENS, AND DIMINISHED
HUMAN CONNECTION

MIKE ROSE

BEACON PRESS ■ BOSTON

BEACON PRESS
Boston, Massachusetts
www.beacon.org

Beacon Press books
are published under the auspices of
the Unitarian Universalist Association of Congregations.

Many names and identifying characteristics of people
mentioned in this work have been changed to protect their
identities.

26 25 24 23   8 7 6 5 4 3 2 1

This book is printed on acid-free paper that meets the uncoated paper
ANSI/NISO specifications for permanence as revised in 1992.

Text design and composition by Kim Arney

Library of Congress Cataloging-in-Publication Data is available for this title.
ISBN: 978-0-8070-0853-9
E-book: 978-0-8070-0854-6; audiobook: 978-0-8070-0832-4

CONTENTS

FOREWORD

E ducation matters. It matters for health and quality of life, for democracy and a civil society. Mike Rose understood this deeply. For Mike, education is about nurturing intelligence, a blending of the practical and experiential, the cognitive and analytic. It is also about the potential in individuals and for humanity. Mike was masterful at showing us the different angles of how and why education shapes growth and opportunity. His perspectives on educational possibility and inequality in our society are understood through the careful telling of stories of people's lives, including his own. Through his writings you learn of the power of a good education and of the various ways in which smarts are inspired, developed, and articulated in everyday, commonplace teaching and learning. At his core, Mike was a teacher. He was also a writer.

While working to publish this book, my dear friend and colleague passed away. Most deaths feel untimely, but Mike's felt particularly so, as there were no indications of fatally ill health. The loss of Mike Rose was immense for the many who care about education, and particularly for those of us who knew him well. His intellect along with his thoughtfulness made him an endeared colleague and friend, one who lifted spirits with his humor and kindness. His dedication to his craft was in humility and without pretension, even while he earned vast national recognition for his work.

Mike Rose joined the faculty of the School of Education and Information Studies at UCLA in 1994, having already published on central issues in education, including perhaps his most well-known and praised book *Lives on the Boundary: A Moving Account of the Struggles and Achievements of America's Educationally Underprepared.* In all of his writings, Mike challenged prevailing narratives and national conversations that seemed to drown out the subtleties and lived realities of education. They were an antidote to the wholesale, broad-brush portrayals that denied the humanity and very real experiences of its participants.

Arguably one of the most important modern-day scholars of education, he was at once master of literary technique and rigorous in his research approach—meticulous documentation, thick description, and reflexivity. Through literary imagination and ethnographic depth, he brought the vibrancy of classrooms and the workplace, and the teaching and learning that transpires within these spaces, to life. Equally importantly, he was a champion of the promise of quality, public education for all.

When the Light Goes On is Mike's final major work. The writing and publication of this book was so important to Mike. He had been working on it for several years, conducting interviews, engaging in focused discussions with colleagues and friends, questioning his insights and the tensions he was observing, iteratively testing his hypotheses, and constructing every sentence with a delicate exactness. This was his process.

Here, Mike examines education as a complex human endeavor. Guiding us through his own and others' personal experiences, he shares with us the power of the moment. He aims to make what is good and right in education, and often invisible, visible. He brings us close to the person, the student, and the teacher—while also revealing much about himself, an intimate look that helps us better appreciate the complexity of contemporary educational and social issues, as we come to understand these issues through a story of a human experience. His prose is sophisticated, and he writes so that his words are meaningful to those about whom he is writing. In the end, we appreciate the ways in which education excites curiosity, struggle, love, and joy.

One day, when I was drained by the stressors of being a university administrator, I followed the suggestion of Mike and walked across the UCLA campus to our laboratory elementary school. And just as he knew it would, my brief observations of the children and their teachers brought a renewed sense of purpose to my work, and not only for that day. At its best, education is transformational, and not just for the student. It is this marvel that Mike Rose brings to us in this book, the extraordinary in the ordinary. Enjoy this, his last gift to us.

—Christina A. Christie

PREFACE

E ducation is human work with human beings. Therein lies its power and its beauty and most everything we are at risk of losing. We have been converting education into a vast assessment, scoring, and ranking enterprise; a laboratory for magic-bullet reforms; a platform for high-tech utopians and entrepreneurs; and a fiercely competitive arena of advantage and status that grinds the poor and propels the middle class into debt and frenzy. The justifications behind some of these developments have merit in the abstract—accountability, rigor, innovation—but as so often happens in our time, the technology or procedure we establish to attain a worthwhile goal becomes an end in itself, the focus of effort and expense. Education's vibrant human core fades from policy and public discussion, diminishing the imagination of our school boards and the joy in our classrooms.

To reclaim that joy and imagination, I take us in close to the lives of a wide range of Americans, exploring with them those times when education broadened what they knew about the world and about themselves, in some cases changing their lives. What better way to gain insight into education at its best, a view both empirical and intimate? Their stories span the primary grades through graduate study, involve mathematics and history, literature and dance, occupational programs and GED classes. Various assessments, technologies, and the like are often part of these stories, but are secondary, in the service of people's engagement with ideas, books, experiments, and tools that matter to them. We witness how learning is lived, the foundation for a more humane and generous vision of education.

There is a personal dimension to this project, for, as with a number of people I interviewed, a teacher had a profound effect on my young life. I therefore include my story, for without that teacher, I wouldn't have been able to write this book, wouldn't know in my bones what can happen when education takes hold, and wouldn't have spent a lifetime in classrooms thinking about the transformational possibilities of these everyday places.

WHEN
THE LIGHT
GOES ON

WHEN THE
LIGHT GOES ON

I am tutoring a tenth-grade boy in basic geometry—the properties of angles. He is having a hard time, and it shows. His jaw is tight with anger and defeat. I ask him again to tell me what he's doing, unsure myself of how to help him, but something in what he says clues me into another way to explain the concept underlying the calculations. He listens, immobile. Then his eyes widen. He shifts forward, up over the worksheet, and solves the problem without any further assistance from me. His jaw eases. His shoulders relax. We do a few more problems to be safe. As I'm getting up to go to the next student, he grabs my forearm. "Thanks," he says, looking right at me. "Thanks a lot."

You see it in their faces. A brightening. Compressed within this boy's shift from frustration to knowing, there is a rich story of education that opens up onto the human condition. In its basic structure, the boy's success offers a familiar snapshot of insight, a *eureka* moment. But there's more going on here than the intellectual click of solving a problem, which is why this brief encounter has stayed with me after thirty-five years: the grasp of my arm, the emotion in the boy's voice and across his face. At least in this moment, geometry is a little less distant and impenetrable; it makes sense to him. In this moment, learning emerges out of close interaction with another human being, adding warmth to the formal elegance of mathematics. And in this moment, solving a geometry problem has an effect on how this boy thinks about himself and what he is capable of doing. If this boy has more experiences like this, in geometry or in other subjects, they could change his life.

That is what happened to me. I was drifting through high school until landing in a senior English class taught by a young guy with an Ivy League reading list for our blue-collar campus. My classmates and I were stunned by Mr. McFarland's assignments, but something about them—and him—caught and directed my meandering curiosity. As he told us the backstory on books I never cared about, I wanted to know more. And I worked on his essays with a level of effort I didn't know was in me, sparking my first interest in writing. Mr. McFarland's class changed the direction of my life, so I have thought about that year often. What combination of chance, my teacher's talents, his books, my classmates, the educational opportunities of the time, and my own nascent desire—what mix of all this led to such a sweeping change in behavior, to a commitment to school with everything I had? Because there are so many young people who resemble me before my transformative year, exploring my time in senior English could lead to some broader understanding of what makes the light go on for a kid who doesn't see a clear path, or much of a path at all.

Seven years after senior English, I would be teaching children in a White and Latin American working-class elementary school, then two years later adapting what I learned from Mr. McFarland to prepare Vietnam veterans who wanted to go to college. I have been teaching ever since, participating in other people's lives, young and not so young, developing over the long haul an ever-deepening appreciation of the wondrous nature of learning, the meaning it can have, both in the moment—as with the boy and the geometry problem—and down the stream of one's life, as has been the case with me.

For much of the time I've been doing this work—the final decades of the twentieth century and the first few of the twenty-first—our national education policy and a good deal of our mainstream discussion of schooling has not reflected this view of teaching and learning. Nothing close to it. Education, like many spheres of our lives, from healthcare to the pursuit of happiness, has been significantly influenced by the concepts and language of high technology, economics, and schools of management. We've gained a certain efficiency, perhaps, a methodical way of thinking about, even quantifying, complex human phenomena—but at what cost? Our often-stated justification for education, the fundamental reason we send our kids to school, is to secure individual advantage and maintain global economic prominence. Finding one's place in the economic order is important, of course, but education is about more than a ledger sheet and a paycheck. Can you remember a time when federal policy makers, let alone local school boards, championed the cognitive and emotional pleasures of discovery—what tools enable us to do, what ideas enable us to see—or the value of students exploring their limits, taking intellectual risks, learning to tolerate uncertainty; or the importance of imagining the good life and the good society and how to work toward them? Teaching itself is defined as a technical and managerial activity, shrinking its human core: to do one's damnedest to bring what one knows into the lives of others. Schooling has become an extended and engulfing institutional rite of passage, marked at many points with segmented assessments and benchmarks. This is an immensely consequential but largely procedural endeavor that leaves parents and their kids exhausted. We have lost our way.

After all my years in classrooms, I'm convinced that one way to reclaim education as a vital and vitalizing human activity is through studying those experiences when the light goes on, when a person is not regulated and regimented in school but finds it meaningful and is drawn to it. We are not relying on a static measure of learning like a test score or the end result of motivation like a grade or certificate but rather are witnessing what learning does to people's lives.

I begin with my own experience in Mr. McFarland's class, for it not only put me on a path to college but also had a powerful influence on the way I teach—my life's work—and on my beliefs about human potential and the value of education. So I have personal and professional reasons to dig deep into that year. And I was fortunate beyond belief to be joined in my inquiry by the man who made that year possible.

I am still in touch with Jack McFarland, and we set out on our exploration by rereading together the books he assigned, hoping that revisiting Homer, Virgil, and the rest would spark some recollection of what happened to me intellectually and emotionally in senior English. Miraculously, I kept the papers I wrote—brown at the edges, covered with my teacher's red script—so I have something of a record of my adolescent self-struggling with that stack of intimidating classics. And because my high school awakening is bound up in the life I was living and the place I lived it, I went back again and again to my old neighborhood in South Central Los Angeles, standing before the weathered house where I read those books and wrote those papers, trying to understand what needs and desires I brought to Mr. McFarland's classroom and how he tapped into and directed them.

As I was investigating what made the light go on for me, I was also interviewing a wide range of people about their educational histories, adding to my understanding with each encounter. They were referred to me by other teachers or educational researchers or were drawn from my own network of friends or my former students. And sometimes the people I met referred me to a friend or relative.

In all, I would interview one hundred people of diverse backgrounds. They ranged from high schoolers to sixty- and seventy-year-olds, people who grew up in well-to-do neighborhoods and people who grew up in neighborhoods like mine—in a few cases *in* my old neighborhood. Approximately 45 percent identified as White and 55 percent as persons of color. Gender had a similar ratio, with a few more women than men. Approximately 10 percent identified as LGBTQ, with two people self-designating as transgender. Collectively, the one hundred individuals come close to representing the United States today, a portrait of America learning.

I encouraged people to begin by telling me what stood out when they thought about their time in school. As they spoke, I might ask them to offer additional details, or to describe as best they could how they felt, or to tell me what else was going on in their lives at the time. There was a predictable rhythm to most of the interviews. An initial formality, even a self-conscious reserve that moves into a more relaxed give-and-take as both of us begin to feel more comfortable with each other and as I learn more about the person's life that I can refer to and weave into the flow of conversation. When people believe they are heard, they want to tell their story.

For those who were still attending school, at times in the ripples of a transformative experience, our conversations had an exploratory cast to them. These young people were commenting on their development from the middle of the stream. Those recalling events past, sometimes long past, had a clearer understanding of how pivotal events and people affected their lives. But even in mature recollection, there were connections made as we talked, discoveries, surprises of anger or sadness or gratitude.

Some of those I interviewed had been doing well in school and then encountered a teacher or a subject or something outside of school that led to a qualitative change in their involvement—a change in interest or focus or intensity of effort. More often, the people I spoke with were like me, falling somewhere between modest achievement and marking time. A smaller number were barely hanging on or had left school, and, in a few cases, were incarcerated or ravaged by personal trauma. Getting back into school saved their lives.

People generously opened up their lives, and as I was on my own quest, I was given access to the memorable journeys of others. There was a supermarket checker whose job wore away his soul, leading him on a path that began with remedial math and took him to architecture school. A high school junior abandoned gang life and threw herself into history and English because she didn't want to end up "an ignorant little girl." A single mother working in a truck stop found through a GED not only a better job but also a reassessment of her own intelligence. An introductory astronomy course at her community college captivated a young woman who became an astrophysicist, and a young man badly injured in a motorcycle accident found both gradual rehabilitation and a career in a welding program. A transgender youth's odyssey to self-definition extended though courses in social sciences and campus advocacy groups. A Native American athlete found in graduate study a way to use her celebrity to articulate the needs of her people. And, reflecting back over their careers, a woman in social services recalled the satisfaction she felt in kindergarten translating for Vietnamese refugee children, and a writer noted "a change in the way I saw myself" when her third-grade teacher collected her poems into a little mimeographed volume.

These stories inspire, but they also instruct, are full of information about the beautiful human intricacy of teaching and learning and what should be the goal of education in our time: to open the mind and explore in a baffling world who one is and the possibilities for shaping what is yet to come.

Questions about the purpose of education and about the very operation of schooling itself gained sudden urgency in the early months of 2020 as mass education in the United States and around the world was upended by the global pandemic of COVID-19. The everyday realities of schooling in our country that are not always evident were thrust into wide public view, and for most parents thrust into their kitchens and living rooms. The demands of teaching and the services students require became strikingly evident and overwhelming. The public and politicians alike grew quickly aware of the vital social and communal role played by the traditional school. COVID-19 also cast a cold spotlight on the destructive economic and racial inequality that runs throughout our society—in housing, employment, healthcare, education—and yet the degree to which schools also function as a kind of social service agency, providing food, safety, internet access, screening for neglect and abuse, and more.[1] And though a lot of creative and heroic work was done online that will undoubtedly be carried over to regular instruction, the strong contemporary claims about the superiority of online learning, even utopian visions of virtual learning replacing the brick-and-mortar classroom, were diminished by human need. Coursing through all these disruptions and reconfigurations were the core issues of this book, from the interpersonal substrate of learning to the purpose of education in an open society—issues that will remain, intensified by the pandemic but lasting far beyond it.

———————

Throughout the five years of this project, my former teacher and I continued to read the books and review the assignments from his class, looping back to them multiple times as new ideas or further recollections struck us or something said in an interview offered a new perspective on an issue we thought was settled. There were times when the books I was reading, my visits to my old neighborhood, and the interviews came together, each enhancing the other. I would be living in the fantastical Spain of Cervantes one day and a few days later be lingering in the narrow stacks of the first public library I knew, touching the worn spines of books I discovered long ago. Then soon after, I'd be interviewing someone who was telling me about the corner of the cafeteria where her group hung out and the teacher who sensed that things were not good at home. The desire to plumb the origins of my own growth combined with a rich participation in other people's development, walking with them through the schoolyards and classrooms of their memories, dwelling on those times when they knew that their young minds and hearts mattered.

We can't understand learning through test scores or course outlines or certificates alone. Learning involves all of these, of course, but it also has a backstory and a story unfolding in the present, and these stories are laden with the messy particulars of our lives. In chapter 1, "Anatomy of an Awakening," I present my history before entering Mr. McFarland's English class, trying to convey the immediacy of the needs and events that precede and contribute to my awakening. The telling of my tale provides a way to think about the stories of others to come, some of which bear similarity to mine, some of which are quite different. Most, however, share several basic elements: a core subject or activity; a catalyzing person or event, usually a teacher; and an emergent or intensified student ability and engagement. And there is a general pattern or movement: from need, searching, or stagnation to a change in behavior and the meaning one finds in education.

The kinds of transformative experiences depicted in my story and others involve not only desire and a change in attitude but also the acquisition of knowledge and skill, for there is an intricate relationship between knowledge and identity. In chapter 2, "Learning to Do Things with Books," I discuss with illustration how I learned to read carefully and critically and how to write effectively about what I read. Doing things with books led me to libraries—and all their resources—as well to new friends and new social worlds that contributed to my developing literacy and sense of self. Through print I became less of a faceless adolescent. As people become adept at what they are learning—from mechanics to poetry—their proficiency affects who they are.

The orientation to teaching and learning displayed in my story is elaborated in chapter 3, "What Teachers See," and illustrated with a number of cases, from young writers and debaters in the elementary and middle grades, to students in nursing and welding programs, to a lawyer and a doctoral student. As different in background and style as the teachers in these cases are, they share a nuanced and generous perception of student potential. And the diversity of these stories, which continues throughout the book, demonstrates the wide range of lives and circumstances in which the light can go on. A democratic compendium of achievement.

One broad difference among the stories is whether the initial spark of transformation occurs in or out of school, which can affect the interpersonal and institutional resources you have available to you and your pathway toward them. The impetus to change can come from the encouragement of loved ones, or events that disrupt your life, or a job that kills your spirit, or exposure to a subject or activity that captivates you. In chapter 4, "From Life Lessons to the Classroom," we meet people for whom the journey to a meaningful education began outside the schoolhouse. Once inside, though, these people were fortunate to find teachers who nurtured the lessons life taught them and advanced the new lives they were creating for themselves.

Some of those I interviewed were doing well in school, and several were at the top of their class, but then they encountered a teacher or a subject—perhaps even a book or vexing problem— and academic business as usual was no longer adequate or satisfactory. In chapter 5, "Expecting More of Yourself," their revelatory experiences play out in K–12, college, and professional school across a range of pursuits: literature and writing to mathematics and physics to surgical pathology and Native American studies. An interest becomes a passion.

As opposed to those we meet in chapter 5, the people in chapter 6, "Becoming Smart," had a hard time in school—it was a source of pain and diminishment—or if they did well, there were limitations on what they could achieve because of their place in the social order or because of race, ethnicity, gender, or social class. Their stories involve a discovery of what they can do—the emergence of ability at times unknown to them—initiated by a teacher or counselor or educational program. Learning to be capable, becoming smart, affects not only their performance in school but also the way they think about their ability and move through the world. And in their stories, as in the stories before, we witness further consequences of the light going on: from the emergence of intellectual and aesthetic pleasures to the development of social and political commitments.

The light doesn't go on in a vacuum but depends on the presence of educational opportunity in the environment—the sites of learning and the teachers and programs that make a difference in the lives of people like myself and the many others we meet. My old community and the many low-income communities that run through the center of the Los Angeles Basin provide a vivid setting to explore the social and economic conditions that help or hinder an educational awakening. In chapter 7, "Finding Educational Opportunity," I travel with young people coming of age today where I grew up in Central and South Central Los Angeles, visiting their homes and schools, walking their streets, and talking about their educational histories. We get an intimate view of where opportunity is found and how it is generated. We learn about the teachers or family members who were instrumental in shaping their education. And as we travel, memories of my own history on this landscape blend with the lives of my traveling companions, reading and writing their way into their own beckoning future.

The journey of discovery that began with my life-changing year in senior English and continued through the transformative experiences of a wide range of other people affords a picture of education at its vibrant best, those times when the mind stirs and schooling is infused with meaning. In chapter 8, "How the Light Goes On," I draw from the book's diverse stories—not hypotheticals or abstractions, but lives lived in school—to reimagine education, to liberate ourselves from the bloodless policy narrative that has dominated our lives for a generation. Collectively and cumulatively, the lessons learned from these stories help us think in more accurate and generous ways about ability and achievement, about teaching, learning, and motivation, and about the structure of school and the purpose of education itself.

CHAPTER ONE

ANATOMY OF AN
AWAKENING

The person I would become evolved over nine months of my
senior year in a spare, cream-colored classroom on the perimeter of our small Catholic high school. As is the case with so many
kids, then and now, I was drifting along, not headed any place in
particular, but I had found a comfortable—at least familiar—rhythm
to my days. I had friends and entertainments and a brimming reservoir of adolescent longing. My grades were so-so, my investment in
school was somewhere between tepid and lukewarm, and as I ambled
into my senior year, I had no plans beyond the upcoming weekend,
hiding a half-pint of drugstore vodka in my pants for a night of big
talk and revelry with my buddies.

The English curriculum for the first two years at my high school
was drawn from unimaginative textbooks of American standards:
nineteenth-century poetry, a Hawthorne story, an early poem by
Frost, Carl Sandburg's "Chicago." For our junior year, we had a
teacher who was obviously bright but put little time into our course.
We read only two short books, *Animal Farm* and a sentimental religious novel titled *Mr. Blue*, and wrote brief papers on each, returned
with minimal feedback: a grade and a single comment like "A little

12

more thought," or "Pretty fair work." In terms of effort, he and I were on the same page.

Neither I nor my classmates were in any way prepared for what came next. Three thousand miles away, a young guy named Jack McFarland took leave from graduate study at Columbia University and came back home to Los Angeles. Needing a job and lacking certification to teach, he took over senior English in our high school—a place that didn't require a standard credential. He gave us what he knew: with some creative modifications, it was the mid-century Columbia Western Civilization course, starting with *The Iliad* and *The Aeneid* and over nine months hauling us all the way through to the existentialists. We wrote papers every two weeks that he covered with comments. Except for a few gifted students, we were confounded and out of our league, but, to my surprise, Mr. McFarland hooked me, guiding me off my meandering path to nowhere. School began to matter in a way it hadn't before.

I had several good and caring teachers in the elementary and middle grades, and high school biology and world history held my interest, but I never developed a sustained connection to school. My father was ill during most of my school years, and my mother supported us by waiting tables. An only child, I had to stay close to home to care for him, and in retreat from the sickness and hardship around me, I lived a good deal in my head, not engaging much with my classes. I could read well, which saved me, but learned little of mathematics beyond arithmetic, went through the motions in social studies, couldn't figure out grammar to save my soul, and developed into the kind of average, nondescript, semi-out-of-it student I would later teach and write about.

Such kids, particularly from families who aren't knowledgeable about school and not able to be forceful within it, fall through the cracks when they hit high school. My high school story is a too-typical one—not the drama of a young person in big trouble, but rather the story of someone loitering anonymously in the vast academic midlands. I flunked algebra, got stuck in low-level courses (the coach who taught civics honest-to-God could not read aloud the textbook), was absorbed with my poor father's slow death—and then, *wham*, senior year and I'm sitting in the front row of Mr. Mc-Farland's English class (commanded up there because I was acting the fool in the back of the room), being challenged to read and write in a way I had never been before.

Here's an observation from a one-page paper I wrote the previous year on *Animal Farm*: "I cannot go into any detail in the explanation of the story. But it was a fabulous plot and story, one of the best I have ever read." In addition to my affinity for the superficial, I wrote sentence fragments and run-on sentences and made a slew of agreement and reference errors. My pronouns didn't line up with the objects or people they referred to. And spelling? In an essay on *Othello* for Mr. McFarland, I dimwittedly misspelled the word *villain* throughout my discussion of Iago as the perfect villain. Fortunately, Mr. McFarland wasn't big on ridicule. He marked all our blunders and kept track of them, but they did not slow him down from directing us through increasingly demanding papers, pushing the quality of our thinking forward in fits and starts. One day, he started talking to me about going to college.

Mr. McFarland's class opened up a new world for me. What I didn't know at the time was that his work with us also was opening up a new world for him. Jack McFarland grew up in a middle-class neighborhood about six miles west of where I lived. His father was an accountant for the movie studios, a connection to Hollywood that perhaps contributed to young Jack's early desire to be a writer and director. Jack went to college at nearby Loyola University (now Loyola Marymount University), writing for the newspaper and forming part of the small college's literary circle. From there he traveled across the country to Columbia University, where he devoured classes in American and European literature and history. He came back home to Los Angeles the summer after that first year of graduate study, an opportunity for him to begin his master's thesis, but he decided that he "had enough schooling." It was time to write that novel.

Jack found work as a maintenance mechanic in a nearby electronics factory and eventually decided to try his hand at teaching, interviewing after his factory shift in a gray uniform at my high school. He taught us during his second year, and midway through the semester he began to realize that he didn't want to be the next great realist film director Elia Kazan, but instead wanted to teach. So in this class where a future was opening up for me, several futures were closing down for Jack McFarland. From Columbia's point of view, he had failed to complete his master's program, was a dropout. And his dreams of being a writer and director were quickly fading. But another future was shaping itself week by week as he wrote on the blackboard in bursts of chalky script what he had learned about Greek tragedy, and Cervantes, and *Othello*, taking us somewhere we hadn't been before. *This is made for me*, he thought.

Here are the books we read for the two semesters of Mr. McFarland's senior English, an old-school Western literary canon. We began with two epic poems, Homer's *The Iliad* and the Latin poet Virgil's tribute to the founding of Rome, *The Aeneid*. We also read Sophocles's *Oedipus the King*. Then came the second book of Dante's *Divine Comedy*, *The Purgatorio*, assigned because Mr. McFarland liked a new translation that had just been published. Three Elizabethan tragedies followed: Christopher Marlowe's *Doctor Faustus* and Shakespeare's *Macbeth* and *Othello*. We read the first half of Cervantes's *Don Quixote*, but in an abridged edition, perhaps indicating a momentary pang of guilt about the heft of our reading list. Guilt quickly resolved, however, for then came two French neoclassical plays, Racine's *Athaliah* and Molière's *The Would-Be Gentleman*. We headed toward the modern age with Anton Chekhov's *Three Sisters* and Joseph Conrad's *Heart of Darkness* and closed with Aldous Huxley's *Brave New World* and Graham Greene's *A Burnt-Out Case*, released in paperback a short while before. All Western, all White, all male. Jack's reading would, over time, grow widely, as would mine, but as I list these books, I'm struck by how many of them deal with striving, destiny, identity, and the search for meaning—themes central to the journey I was beginning in senior English.

We had quizzes on the books, mimeographed sheets of blurred blue type testing our recall of key names and events. We wrote eight essays, often combining several books in one essay—for example, a comparative analysis of melodrama in *Doctor Faustus* and *Macbeth*. And we wrote two more papers: a critique of a newspaper opinion piece and a commentary on a news story in *Time* magazine. Ten in all. We would turn them in on a Monday—ruining my weekends—and get them back the following Monday, folded lengthwise with a grade under our name and plenty of comments inside. One more thing. To build our vocabulary, Mr. McFarland gave us quizzes drawn from a then-popular book, *30 Days to a More Powerful Vocabulary*, also typed in mimeograph blue. Like a boxer in round ten or a marathoner at mile twenty, we were operating somewhere between peak performance and exhaustion.

As my senior year was drawing to a close—somewhere between Chekhov and Conrad—Mr. McFarland succeeded in getting me admitted as a probationary student to his alma mater, Loyola University. He mentored me through a bumpy freshman year and continued to teach at our high school for several years after that. Then he returned to graduate school, but this time up the coast at the University of California, Santa Barbara. From UCSB, he moved north to Sacramento to begin a long, rich career teaching history at a community college. He met his wife, Joan, a faculty member in sociology, and they had a daughter, Cathy. He found a life both in and beyond the classroom.

I started teaching at about the same age as did Mr. McFarland and since then have spent tens of thousands of hours with other human beings—from kindergarteners to graduate students to minimum-wage workers in literacy programs—teaching or tutoring them or studying how they learn. Over the last few years, I've become more and more interested in those times in school when we see signs of the mind stirring, of people beginning to get a sense of what education can make possible for them. Obviously, this interest has deeply personal significance for me, but such experiences also reveal crucial psychological and social elements of teaching and learning that get lost in our current discussions of education. A number of school reformers, for example, view teaching as essentially a technical problem to be solved with technical remedies. Effective teaching is defined as raising scores on standardized tests of the basic school subjects, mathematics and reading. Other factors can come into play, such as student perceptions of teacher effectiveness, if these factors can be reliably measured. This technocratic approach is further applied to teacher education. Are there techniques we can isolate—how to bring a class to order, how to ask a question—that correlate with increased test scores or other metrics? All this affects the way we think about education itself, amplifying its procedures and techniques over its complex intellectual and interpersonal dynamics. There certainly is nothing wrong with trying to add some precision to our judgments about teaching or to help young teachers acquire tricks of the trade. But the kind of thing that happened to me in Mr. McFarland's class—and that in some fashion happens to many of the other people you will meet in this book—isn't readily measurable. There's no simple scale for it.

Yet these periods of awakening take us to the heart of teaching, to an appreciation of knowledge and what it can do in fulfilling need and capability in others.

I wanted to understand the experience of the light going on as thoroughly as I could, in my own life and in the lives of others, other backgrounds and circumstances, other grade levels, other subjects. My own exploration was a tenuous memory experiment—trying to determine what in a bombardment of dense prose and poetry tapped some vague desire in me to achieve—but perhaps with my teacher's help, I could get a glimpse of that distant fork in the road that would have such consequence for my life.

It all started with *The Iliad*, Homer's account of the volatile hero Achilles and the long, bloody siege of Troy. Fortunately for us, Mr. McFarland assigned a prose rendition; "plain English," the translator promised in his brief preface. The spine of my original copy of *The Iliad* is cracked and the cover torn, evidence that I read it, but there is not a single mark on the pages. Mr. McFarland had explained to us the features of the classical epic poem, so I would have been primed for the heroic exploits, the interventions of the gods, the epic catalogue—that is, long lists of warriors or spoils of war. He also told us about the ancient Greeks' beliefs concerning honor and morality, the afterlife, and more. I don't remember any previous English teacher setting so full a cultural context for something I read. I had some helpful lenses to wear as I read *The Iliad* but evidently saw no need to highlight anything in nearly three hundred pages of crammed, small print. Like so many young people with backgrounds like mine, I had little training on how to read a difficult book. Rereading *The Iliad*, I'm struck by the number of characters and events that, to be honest, I find wearisome now. I bet I skipped over entire battle scenes, boasting speeches, and, for sure, those epic catalogues.

Mr. McFarland paired *The Iliad* with *The Aeneid*, Virgil's celebration of Aeneas's torturous journey from Troy to found the city of Rome. We read *The Aeneid* in verse, which demanded more of us than reading *The Iliad* in prose, and perhaps that's why I marked some sections of the book and scribbled a few words here and there. These annotations give me a little more of an idea as to how I might have read it.

I remember lying across my bed concentrating with all I've got on *The Aeneid*. A faint television show plays in the next room. Our small house has only one bedroom, and I do my homework at the table where my mother and I eat or in this room, either on the bed where my father died the year before and where I now sleep or at the small metal desk my mother bought for me at Sears. That desk is wedged between my bed and my mother's, a single box spring and mattress close to the bathroom, so she can get up before sunrise to make it to the breakfast shift at a chain restaurant across town.

I read *The Aeneid* propped up on my elbows, a pencil in my right hand, shifting now and then to mark with wobbly underlines names and events that I think might be on Mr. McFarland's quizzes. I'm hoping I'm right. We just finished *The Iliad*—which Virgil drew from—and the quizzes shocked us into reading more carefully, not the gliding half-steps we were used to. I don't have any specialized technique to help me, so I mentally grunt, bear down a little harder, and use this pencil, something I didn't do with *The Iliad*.

Thinking about the quizzes, I mark some of the places where gods intervene in the lives of the characters—a constant in *The Iliad* and here in *The Aeneid*. There's frightful omens: A swarm of bees shape themselves into a buzzing sheet hanging from a tree while nearby a young maiden's hair bursts into flames. And I mark high drama. Queen Dido, her heart broken by Aeneas, impales herself on his sword atop her moonlit funeral pyre.

I can zero in on stuff like this. But a good deal of *The Aeneid* is less accessible to me. As with *The Iliad*, I am awash in names I have trouble sorting out, let alone pronouncing: Anchises, Cloanthus, Philoctetes. But I do underline some of them, not all of which turn out to be important. I'm still learning how to make that distinction.

Long passages are not holding my attention—Aeneas's endless trials and tribulations and the winding geography of his journey. I had read in the tenth and eleventh grades the standard poetic fare of the mid-century American curriculum: Longfellow and Poe and Whitman's "O Captain! My Captain." But *The Aeneid* is nearly ten thousand lines long, translated into a highbrow English verse by C. Day-Lewis, Britain's poet laureate (and, it would turn out, the father of the actor Daniel Day-Lewis):

> *The wind blows fair, and we leave palm-fringed Selinus behind*
> *To skirt Lilybaeum's waters, tricky with reefs submerged.*
> *After which, we put in at port Drepanum, a landfall*
> *Of little joy; for here, after so many storms weathered,*
> *I lost, alas, my father, him who had lightened my cares*
> *And troubles—lost Anchises.*

I push myself off the bed, my shoulders stiff, and move to my desk. Sitting upright gives me a second wind. My underlining and notation are straighter, clearer. Aeneas is iron-willed through a journey of storms, and battles, and a descent into the tormented shadowland of hell. He is fierce in combat, driving his sword deep into his enemy's heart. My father was frail in this house, slowly succumbing to arterial disease before there were medications and treatments that could have saved him. A year earlier, he slipped into a coma and died.

Rereading *The Aeneid*, I am surprised and moved by Aeneas's devotion to his father, at one point carrying him beaten and grieving on his shoulders out of the burning ruins of Troy. In high school, I didn't mark those passages. Perhaps at that point in the book I was so focused on just making my way through the pages upon pages of verse that I only superficially registered the meaning of what I read. I was counting the pages I'd read so far and the number I had to go, figuring that if I really concentrated, I could finish by the time my mother had to go to bed.

————

My mother and father came to South Central Los Angeles in the early 1950s searching for a house they could afford to rent. We weren't the only people having a hard time of it, but overall our neighborhood was solidly working class with some middle-class families sprinkled in. A lot of our neighbors owned their modest houses, sustained by industrial and service jobs that have long since disappeared. The street we lived on, Vermont Avenue, now bisects two South Central neighborhoods. Vermont Vista borders Vermont on the east. It is 52 percent Latin American, 45 percent Black, with a median annual household income of just over $31,000. Westmont borders Vermont on the west with a median income about the same as Vermont Vista's, but the demographics shift to 39 percent Latin American and 58 percent Black. Westmont is unincorporated, so it suffers even greater political isolation than other neighborhoods in the region. While some pockets of South Central have undergone modest economic development, this area is marked by all the signs of long-term poverty and neglect: houses in disrepair, empty storefronts, mini-marts rather than markets, liquor stores, check-cashing joints. It has one of the highest violent crime rates in the city.[1] A subtle but eerily telling indicator of neglect is the number of faded commercial signs that remain on old buildings decades after businesses have closed. Within a few blocks of my old house, there remain pale script or metal remains for Gil's Auto Body, a drugstore, a mortuary, the hardware store Million Article Thompson, the outline of a cartoon bear for Behr auto products. Ghosts of commerce from my childhood, and a symbol of how little redevelopment has happened in the last half century.

On this early Saturday morning, I pull into the parking lot for Launderland, on the corner of 92nd Street, where the father of my best friend, Keith, owned a small television and radio repair shop. I remember standing just inside the back door with Keith, marveling at the innards of the old consoles, a puzzle patch of tubes and wires hooked up to his dad's monitors, needles flicking across their screens. Then Keith and I would go upstairs to his home, one of two apartments right behind the shop, to listen to records and be given cookies or sandwiches by his mother. The shop is gone now—the space is part of the laundromat's parking lot—but the twin apartments are still there, peeling and gouged. The stairs look unstable, and the stairway, the landing, and the windows are all covered with black metal bars.

Three or four women are in the laundromat, talking, folding clothes, one standing by a big washer reading a magazine. As I walk down Vermont, a few people are setting up shop. Several of the old storefronts are dark shells; others have makeshift repairs and a fresh coat of paint. The street is still pretty empty, but outside of the Rios mini-mart an older woman sits alongside a folding table with jewelry, handbags, and flip phones on display. Next is Jayleen's Beauty Salon, dim light inside with one chair turned toward the front, a woman getting her hair cut. Another empty storefront, then my old house and the house next to it. When I lived here, they were small clapboard structures with two windows and flower boxes facing Vermont. Now they are trim stucco rectangles, no hedges, no greenery, surrounded by a chain-link fence. Two men who look like they might be from Southern Mexico or Guatemala are wheeling out used appliances, furniture, and auto parts from the backyard. Starting almost at the front door there are stoves, washers, vacuum cleaners, kitchen cabinets, chairs, tables, tires, and tire rims cascading right out to the edge of traffic. In a part of South Central with little economic opportunity, these men are creating a pop-up secondhand store, trying to make a few bucks to add to their wages as busboys or construction workers or gardeners in other parts of the city. We exchange a greeting, and I continue on, rounding the corner at 91st Street and walking down to the alley that ran behind my house. The sun is warm on my face. I close my eyes. This alley led to the back of our house, a small yard behind the bedroom and the desk where I spent so much time working on Mr. McFarland's assignments.

A nagging question for me as I read again *The Iliad* and *The Aeneid* is simply why I put forth the extraordinary effort to read them in the first place. I can understand my commitment later on in the school year, once Mr. McFarland and his books and a sense of achievement captured me, but right out of the gate? I knew the usual school-based smattering of Greek and Roman lore—Zeus and his thunderbolts, Helen of Troy, the Trojan horse, Cyclops—but had no particular interest in any of it. Why did my academic throttle so quickly go from idle to full combustion? Mr. McFarland got to something vital but hidden to others and probably, to some degree, hidden to me.

—————

My elementary school was four blocks to the north on Vermont Avenue, and a few of my classmates would come to play at my house before my father got too ill. I also made good friends among the few kids in my neighborhood, like my buddy from the corner TV shop. The telling thing, though, is how few memories of this time are social—no school events, or birthday parties, or group outings, or sleepovers. There's a feeling of being alone—not lonely necessarily, but a suffusion of aloneness in the house, the backyard, on the street outside our front door. I get a very different sense from those I interview who grew up in neighborhoods like mine, or poorer ones, but were heavily into sports. For them, recollection, though it may involve sadness or threat, also includes the vibrant human scramble of the soccer field, the basketball court. My world was more physically and experientially constrained.

The center of this small world was my father's illness. He was sick most of the time I knew him. At first he would lie down in the afternoon. My mother said, "Your father is resting," but eventually I somehow knew this wasn't just a nap. He kept a dark, pharmaceutical-sized bottle of pills on the dresser and took two pills at a time. One evening at dinner he passed out, falling face first into his plate, the fork and knife clattering to the floor. I got so scared it was like being ripped out of my body and watching the whole thing from the ceiling, rocking frantically in my chair asking if he was okay. Later in the hospital my mother told me that food had gotten stuck in his throat, but I would realize later that it was a stroke—the first of many. The stroke led to tests and an eventual exploratory surgery. Thus began a life in hospitals, the benches in bare corridors or waiting rooms thick with TV and helplessness.

I found escape through a series of solitary pursuits that provided both enjoyment and solace from the quiet suffering in our house. My mother bought me a microscope and then a small chemistry set, and I spent hours observing, mixing, imagining, but not much time consulting the accompanying manuals, which, in my excitement, I found tedious. When I got fascinated with the solar system and space travel (I was nine when test pilot Scott Crossfield flew twice the speed of sound), she bought me a telescope. Other hobbies followed, including model cars and airplanes. And as I began to test myself physically, much of that played out alone in my backyard, hurdling over a broomstick laid across two old chairs and heaving an eight-pound shot from a circle I inscribed in a grassless patch of dirt.

To prod the memory of my time with that telescope, I checked out of the UCLA library old, bound copies of the magazine *Sky & Telescope*.[2] Thanks to odd jobs in the neighborhood, I was able to afford a subscription. Though dulled with age, the pictures in the magazine are still impressive, from the phases of a lunar eclipse, diagonal across the night sky, to the vast, wispy arms of a spiral galaxy. But it is the ads—some full page—that most catch my attention. I suppose it was the ads that represented something new to me; after all, I had already seen photographs of planets and galaxies in the astronomy picture books I checked out of my elementary school's meager library. The funny thing is that the ads with their technical details are the most prosaic part of the magazine. Gray or white telescopes float above unadorned text with an occasional bespectacled man in a suit or woman in a formal dress standing stiffly nearby. Still, these ads trigger a trace of early excitement, a brave new world of mirrors and lenses and magnifying power.

I turn the pages slowly as if with a rare book, more photographs, more ads—then a two-page advertisement that I remember. The Edmund Scientific Company in Barrington, New Jersey. There are dozens of different items and illustrations here, lots of war surplus goods: lenses, eyepieces, cameras, film. Though the ad certainly contains technical specs, the writing is lively, inflected with a sideshow hustle: "Bring the thrills and wonders of outer space right into your home." That would have set my little stargazer's heart aflutter.

I'm reading these ads one by one when I come across a three-inch Astronomical Reflector that brings me to a full stop. There it is. The telescope my mother bought for me. "Assembled—ready to use!" Three-inch reflecting mirror, 60x to 180x power. Sturdy hardwood tripod. Priced at $29.95, "an unusual buy." Let's see: $29.95, what would that be in today's dollars? Over two hundred bucks. How could my mother afford it? Maybe she purchased it through an installment plan.

Having *Sky & Telescope* appear in my mailbox every month made me feel like I was part of some big astronomers' club. Its presence in our home announced: *This is serious stuff.* And, like all kids, I wanted to be taken seriously. The telescope and magazine enabled me to participate in my way in something beyond myself, something of consequence. People doing exciting and powerful things.

What is curious about my pursuit is that I couldn't do more than the basics with this technology that meant so much to me. I had a star atlas that baffled me. I also had a map of the moon but couldn't use it to locate anything; it was a jumble of Latin names and craters. My telescope had a smaller telescope attached to it, a "view finder" with low magnification that yields a broader visual field so that you can aim the larger instrument to the proper area of the sky. I wasn't very good at using it either—simple as the device is—so I would move the larger scope back and forth, back and forth until Mars—was it Mars?—would dart into the center of the lens. I was enchanted with the technology but barely able to use it. And I wasn't connected to anyone in the neighborhood who could help me match map to object or be methodical with my instrument. The one candidate, my friend Keith's father, who owned the TV repair shop, was monosyllabic and distant. To be sure, I continued to learn about the heavens, but, as was the case with my chemistry set and the microscope before that, what I learned was exciting but not coherent, little cat-eye marbles of knowledge.

My interest in building model cars and airplanes began with the unexpected opening of a hobby shop right next door to our house. The north end of our lawn extended smack up against the wall of an old wooden commercial building that had once housed a record store but had been vacant for some time. Then one day a couple of workers started hammering and sawing inside. They built a display case, covered the walls with pegboard, put in new lights . . . and soon were hanging a large, colorful sign over the peeling logo of the defunct record store.

The owner, a ruddy-faced, quietly friendly man named Harry, had the reddest hair I had ever seen, orange-rust, combed back in deep, shiny waves. He sat on a stool behind the counter, arms folded over a generous belly. Around him the walls were lined with model kits while assembled biplanes and fighter jets dangling from wires overhead. I had never built a model in my life, so this was another new world to me. The Ford Fairlane. The Corvette. The British Spitfire. The German Stuka. And, yes, the Bell X-1 rocket plane that broke the sound barrier.

I wasn't drawn to model building the way I was to the telescope, but on this street of repair shops and few children, an emporium of youthful pursuits appeared almost overnight, and I yearned to be a part of it. So I browsed the kits, asking whatever questions I could think of about plastic car assembly or World War II combat planes. And when the questions dried up, there were the Coke machine and a rack of pretzels and potato chips right inside the door. These gave me yet another excuse to come by every day, running down the incline of our front yard and curving into the shop. It wasn't long before this easygoing guy was saying, "You again?"

Back inside the house I was sprinting from, my father's illness had progressed into the last awful years of arterial disease and intermittent strokes. I'm not sure how attuned I was to it at the time, but our home must have been dense with fear, my father's unspoken pain and terror at what was happening to him, and my mother's mix of exhaustion and anxiety. For years she had cared for him as the rug was slowly being pulled out from under her feet. No wonder I craved the bright hobby shop, all those new kits to build—the same hobby shop where I was jeopardizing my welcome.

I started with the simpler models, but still it didn't come easy: glue smudges on the fender, gaps in the chassis, a wrinkle where the decal curves along the fuselage. The wooden pieces needed to be cut just so, assembled with a routine set of procedures. I met the hard pushback of physical reality. Slowly I got better, graduating to small balsa wood planes powered by a tiny engine. Harry started organizing weekend gatherings of customers who flew model airplanes. I wanted badly to be part of that crowd, so I saved up the earnings from my little jobs and bought an ambitious kit, way bigger than anything I had yet attempted.

Around this time, my mother made friends with one of her regular customers, a laundromat repairman named Lou, and he began visiting us, helping to care for my father and helping me with this confounding airplane. We took over the dining room table, laying out the plans, cutting the fuselage formers and the ribs for the wings, gluing thin strips of balsa wood into these elements, pinning everything while the pungent glue dried. I have before me a kit for a plane somewhat like the one I built. It is detailed and elaborate, and as I handle the many pieces and read the plans, nothing enjoyable comes to mind. The plane provided access to Harry's flying club, and that was it. My mother good-naturedly served dinner alongside the fuselage. As the plane slowly began to take shape, I receded, letting Lou do more and more of the work, especially covering the long wings with thin paper, a frustrating task for me. The finished product was more his than mine.

Flying a model airplane, I learn now through reading the instructions in my kit, involves a fair amount of preparation: testing the plane, balancing it. I must have known some of this, but likely gave it inadequate attention. I had my plane and was eager to fly it. I rode out to the lot with another customer one early Saturday morning that I remember as clear and brisk and still. Good flying conditions, the others said.

Our planes had two long wires running from under the wing and attached to a handle. Turn the handle downward and the wires activate control flaps taking the plane into descent; turn the handle upward and the plane ascends. Simple. What I've also learned now—and this should have been plain as day then—is that in addition to balancing the plane, you need to test your controls, possibly adjust your lines, get a feel for the plane's reactivity. As far as I can remember, I did little such testing. I had joined the Academy of Model Aeronautics. I was out on this Saturday morning with fellow flyers. My analytic abilities stopped right at the edge of my belonging.

Flying that plane is the most vivid memory of my whole hobby shop experience. When it is my turn, I bring my control handle out to the center of the field and lay it down, the wires extending straight to the wing. Back then to the plane. I attach battery clips, prime the engine, flip, flip, flip the propeller. Finally, the high-pitched buzz of ignition. One of the other hobbyists holds my plane as I run out to pick up the handle. I'm ready. In the circle. My partner releases the airplane and it scoots quickly along the ground, nice and smooth, and as it ascends it begins to wobble. I try to correct it, and the plane cuts sharply upward. Turning to my left, I correct again to level the plane, but there's no finesse to my wrist, and from its high point, the plane jerks downward, diving at full throttle into the ground.

––––––––––

I never went flying again. A year or so later I would enter Mr. Mc-Farland's English class, an intellectually curious kid who through his hobbies developed an imaginative orientation toward the world that was both pleasurable and protective. But in a way, that imaginative transport released me from the disciplined involvement that would have brought real competence. The writer of children's books Kwame Alexander makes the compelling observation that the mind of an adult begins in the imagination of a child.[3] To be sure, there are certain ways my mind works that are traceable back to the interior life I created as a boy. But it is also true that my refuge in imagination shielded me from the hard engagement with the world that yields skills and dispositions that make possible further engagement with the world.

Looking back on those interests of mine, I see how easily they could have connected to school subjects, mostly with the sciences. Several people I've been talking to who also grew up in households beset by physical or mental illness found refuge, or at least distraction, in school, a place where they had friends and the rewards of achievement. "In the chaos of my childhood," one woman said, "school was something I could control, a way to provide order." But while certain of my teachers covered the basics—the solar system, simple biology, and the like—we didn't have a formal science program in my eight grades of Catholic school. Other than drawing a lot of rocket ships in the middle grades, I don't remember bringing to any significant degree my hobbies or the difficulties at home into the schoolhouse.

As is the case with many working-class families then and now, there is not always an open pathway between school and home. But to be fair to my school, I kept things to myself, especially as my father got sicker, for, much to my shame now, I felt embarrassed and wanted my family to be normal so as not to scare away potential friends. And knowing my mother, she put the best face on things she could—both out of pride and for privacy. I can imagine her smiling at the nun during parent–teacher conferences, perhaps explaining why her work made it difficult to attend those meetings, perhaps adding that my father was too sick to work. . . . But that's it. We're doing okay, Sister. Thank you for telling me about Michael.

I wanted what most kids want: to be liked and to matter. My hobbies, fanciful as they were, still featured artifacts of worldly and weighty endeavors: beakers and bubbling flasks, a telescope. I got what attention I could in class with bush-league quips that had me leaning out from my desk to poke another snorting knucklehead, but not the kids at the top of the social order. Among the many things I learned subliminally from my mother was to hide hurt or embarrassment. After a classmate held me flushed and helpless in a headlock at recess, I told him and anyone listening that I let him do it to learn how it felt. I outdid my mother on that one.

As I moved through the grades, I increasingly became aware of who was popular, who was in and who was out: the good-looking kid, or the really smart one, or the athlete. All this amps up preposterously for most of us when we arrive in high school. One of my dear friends today was also a student in Mr. McFarland's class, but in those days, our paths hardly crossed, except as we were bumping our way toward our seats. He earned varsity letters in three sports and dated the homecoming queen. We laugh about it now, but at the time I might as well have been looking at him and his world through that telescope my mother bought for me.

My father was dead. I no longer had the insular comfort of my hobbies, my last one ending in humiliation. The hormonal changes of adolescence were hitting like a sledgehammer, driving my buddies and me all over the teenage landscape of early 1960s Los Angeles, from downtown burlesque houses to a sprawling amusement park by the beach. High school for some of the men and women I interviewed was where they found a defining interest—science or dance or literature or sports—or at least found that school was their road out of poverty or a troubled family. Others were more like me, and I know now from decades of teaching that there are many of us. We show up but are unfocused and vaguely unfulfilled; no goals call us forward. Yet young people's inner worlds are churning with explorations and defeats. There is so much that can be tapped. I think back to the need webbed into those hobbies of mine, the yearning of the classroom antics, that desperate, curving sprint into the hobby shop. This is what I carried into the first week of senior English and to its teacher, young enough to be my older brother, maybe an uncle, smart, quick, knowledgeable as all get-out, and, to my seventeen-year-old eyes, masterfully assured and in control of this ungodly mix of dorks and football guards and tackles. He's lucky I didn't bulldoze him in a rush to grab onto all he represented. Instead, I threw myself into the first chapter of the first book he assigned:

"An angry man—there is my story: The bitter rancor of Achilles . . ."[4]

My story is set in its time and place, but the storyline, the arc of the tale, plays out in the educational histories of a number of people I interviewed: there is drift and boredom, desire kept under wraps, the adult who draws out and directs that desire—and the resulting change in outlook and possibility. Consider Dorie Mendoza.

Dorie had a lot of friends in high school. She rode on the bus with them, sat with them at lunch, exchanging gossip, talking music. But privately Dorie wondered how tight these bonds really were. Her school was the standard urban comprehensive high school, an anonymous mass of adolescents. Without her friends, Dorie would be an atom, a nameless speck. Yet with them . . . did these girls really know her? Or care that much? Dorie "felt alone a lot of the time."

School itself offered little connection either. She describes remedial English classes that dealt with the parts of a sentence or gave students a list of words that they spent the balance of the period looking up. Dorie was bored with school and felt "mediocre at everything." Her mother worked in a small manufacturing plant and her father installed refrigerator systems. Neither graduated from high school, so Dorie did set that one goal for herself, but otherwise "had no clue as to what I was going to do with my life."

Ms. Barker taught at another high school in the district and transferred to Dorie's school in the mid-1990s, right before Dorie entered senior English. Suzanne Barker wasn't an imposing figure: middle-aged, about 5'3" or 5'4", a pleasant face, shoulder-length blonde hair. But she had a strong, no-nonsense classroom presence; she took over a room. She assigned novels and short stories and had the class write papers on them. She gave weekly quizzes. Students gave presentations. She asked questions and expected intelligent answers. She didn't care what you had done or didn't do before, what skill level the school said you were at. She made her own assessments. After reading Dorie's first essay, she yanked her out of that remedial English class she had been consigned to for three years. Dorie has a low-key, wry demeanor that animates as she describes the liberation she felt. Ms. Barker saw no reason why her students couldn't do good things; everyone started with an A, she announced, and she expected you to maintain it. Beyond the walls of her classroom, there were fist fights and gang skirmishes, security guards crisscrossing the campus on bicycles, drugs galore, no doors on the stalls in the boys' or girls' bathrooms. "You got used to the violence," Dorie said, shrugging her shoulders. But inside Ms. Barker's room, the teacher created a class where, in Dorie's words, "the buzz was no longer about the class clowns or the gangsters—it was about the work."

Dorie was ready. She had felt detached, adrift—and increasingly afraid as she saw her friends get suspended, fail classes, rush into a dead-end life that Dorie did not want for herself. She grew up poor—twelve people in a two-bedroom house—and knew she "didn't want to live like that again." Yet here she was at the end of high school, facing "the finality of this last year . . . I'd never been good at anything, and school is going to end. How," she wondered anxiously, "am I going to support myself?" Ms. Barker provided a way out by appealing to an intellectual curiosity in Dorie that had not been recognized before: "I enjoyed reading and thinking about what we read, synthesizing it, making connections, finding patterns. I had never been challenged that way." Ms. Barker saw how Dorie was coming to life and upped the ante. She had Dorie help those students who were having a hard time with the readings, and this peer tutoring lit Dorie up, making her feel both confident and competent—not feelings she typically associated with high school.

And something else was going on. "We were reading these books and had to think about them and write about them—you know, 'What does this really mean?'" Dorie pauses, reaching for the right words. "It was sort of the practice of reflection. We were taking the time to do that, and I started thinking 'What the hell's going on with *my* life?'" Dorie's examination of imagined worlds carried over to an examination of her own.

This shift in awareness and agency had important consequences for Dorie's as-yet-unrealized future. She started applying herself in her other classes, "no matter how much I hated the subject or what I thought of the teacher." And then *those* teachers started treating *her* differently as well. "I was sure my government teacher thought I was a loser," she laughs, "and, you know what, she gave me her 'Most Improved Student' award!"

One of Ms. Barker's assignments was to have the class write the personal statement for college applications. It was the first time Dorie gave more than a passing thought to college. As she worked on the essay, college became increasingly real, within reach. She felt unsure and apprehensive, but also felt an energizing curiosity, cautiously hopeful. She wrote about the life she had and the life she was beginning to picture for herself—a possible life that a year before she could not have imagined.

Dorie Mendoza was the first of the hundred people I interviewed while I was exploring my own pivotal year in senior English. Stories like mine, hers, and many to come give us hope about reaching the large numbers of students who are in school but not thriving and, more urgently, reaching those who are disconnected from school and have poor prospects in the world of work. And as the stories accrue, they collectively change the way we see, demonstrating in different settings with different branches of knowledge, with different life histories and social locations the mystery and majesty of human potential, of people forging new goals and developing skills and knowledge—at times beyond what they and others thought possible—redefining themselves and creating a future through education.

CHAPTER TWO

LEARNING TO DO
THINGS WITH BOOKS

B ook by difficult book, I was creating a future by learning how
to read deeply and carefully. Sure, I could read pretty well long
before I plunged into *The Iliad*, thanks to my mother reading to me—
dog tired from work, I know from her diaries—and the efforts of
the Sisters of Charity in the primary grades. I had a solid foundation
and got good grades in reading throughout elementary school. As
a child, I was hooked on comic books and went on a science fiction
binge when I was eleven or twelve, but I wasn't a consummate reader.
"I lost myself in books," says one person I interviewed. "I wanted to
figure life out and loved what books had to offer." I lost myself, too,
in Superman's world-saving heroics and on a rocket ship bound for
the moons of Jupiter, but my deliverance was sporadic, with years
of laxity in between.

Aside from schoolwork, I infrequently consulted books for information—how to effectively use that telescope, for example. And it
wasn't until Mr. McFarland's class that I went below the surface of
the fiction I read or did much more than react quickly and viscerally
to any written claims or arguments that might come my way, in
school or out. The line I drew under a sentence or the check mark
I made beside it, my scribble in a margin or on a note card began

to change all that, enabling a more deliberate reading of books, then writing from them, and eventually teaching them to others. To repurpose a phrase from the philosopher of language J. L. Austin, I was learning to do things with books and make something happen with them.[1]

The knowledge and skills acquired once the light goes on are central to many of the educational histories people shared with me. Their stories are also stories of welding or nursing, of mathematics or history or literature—and of what their developing competence enabled them to do, both in school and beyond. And some accounts, like mine, are stories of reading and writing. Over the nine months of senior English, I was developing the skill of annotating what I was reading, progressing from those few wobbly lines in *The Aeneid* to checking and underlining ten passages in the seven-and-a-half-page foreword Aldous Huxley wrote for *Brave New World*. Huxley reflects on the book's themes years after its initial publication, and I used those reflections in an essay I was writing on the idea of freedom in *Brave New World* and *A Burnt-Out Case*.

I don't want to claim that the only way to dig deep into a book is to mark it up, on paper or electronically on a screen, but taking a pencil or pen to the page helped me think about and remember what I was reading. Great Books champion Mortimer Adler advocates marking a book as the best way to make it "part of yourself."[2] Taking the longer view, the author of a history of marginalia—yes, there is such a history—observes that marginal marks and comments "may be as old as script itself, for readers have to interpret writing."[3] Rereading the books from senior English in the order we originally read them gives me a sense of how I was gradually finding my way into a long tradition.

Another skill I was starting to acquire was analyzing *how* something was written, its style. One way Mr. McFarland turned our eye to style was through several assignments where we had to imitate one of our writers—for example, Joseph Conrad. Conrad's *Heart of Darkness* is the story of an agent for a Belgian company traveling deep into the Congo to find an ivory trader named Kurtz who has abandoned the company to become a powerful figure among an African tribe.[4] The journey is a highly symbolic one, blending criticism of European colonialism and a meditation on humankind's primordial barbarism. In the years after my first encounter with Conrad, I became more attuned to the complexity of Conrad's beliefs about colonialism and to his demeaning portrayals of those colonized, but in 1962 my attention was on his long sentences of description. As with the other books I read, I suspect that I skimmed or skipped over entire passages—in this case, stretches of the narrator's interminable trip up the Congo River. But there are a few places in the book where I underlined words as I had never done before. I had to carefully consider word by word the author's choice of vocabulary, otherwise how could I imitate Conrad's style?

The following comes as the narrator seeks refuge from the sun in what turns out to be a "grave of death" populated by terribly sick African laborers:

> At last I got under the tree. My purpose was to stroll into the shade for a moment; but no sooner within than it seemed to me I had stepped into the gloomy circle of some Inferno. The <u>rapids</u> were near, and an <u>uninterrupted, uniform, headlong, rushing noise</u> filled the <u>mournful stillness</u> of the grove, where not a <u>breath stirred</u>, not a <u>leaf moved</u>, with a <u>mysterious sound</u>—as though the tearing pace of the launched earth had suddenly become <u>audible</u>.

I picture myself bent over the book at my desk in the bedroom, zeroing in on sound and motion. The analysis is pretty crude. I'm underlining a lot and not differentiating very well. But I imagine myself pleased with what I was doing, using my pen to consider each word, assuming that Conrad was up to something and that I was going to figure it out. I was being led to read in a new way. Mr. McFarland's choice of *Heart of Darkness* makes sense. For though the book is difficult, the novel's gloomy, ominous language is thick as fog in a horror movie, discernable and available for imitation by a youngster with a rudimentary set of tools.

––––––––––

Reading and writing for Mr. McFarland led me to another set of tools in my local library. There was a tiny library in my elementary school, and during my space travel days I checked out science fiction and a few books on astronomy. But that was it. Mr. McFarland's class got me into the library at my high school and to the public library on Figueroa and 96th Street, about ten blocks away from our house. These were the places where I discovered resources I could use to help me read Mr. McFarland's books and write those papers for him: bigger dictionaries than I had ever seen, encyclopedias, guides to mythology or history or philosophical concepts, companions to literature. I would pedal my bike east on 92nd Street, past Bret Harte Junior High School, past bungalows and small apartments, then turn south on heavily trafficked Figueroa with its motels, auto shops, and family markets and restaurants. Today, I drive my car, taking the same short route. A few blocks after turning onto Figueroa, I see a boy, barefoot, white T-shirt, maybe eight or nine, running across 94th Street and into a bright orange mini-mart. I think about sprinting across our yard and into the hobby shop, and then pull into the parking lot behind the library.

The current incarnation of the Mark Twain Library was built in the early 2000s and is in the same location as the one I frequented but looks to be a bit larger, with a bright wall of windows in the rear and a raised ceiling in the central room. Tables and chairs are arranged across the floor, with the children's stacks on one side and adults' on the other. To your right as you walk in there is a display of "Popular and Best-Selling Black Authors" that includes Alice Walker, Terry McMillan, and the hip-hop crime novelist K'wan. On this summer day, five or six men and women sit in the main area relaxing with magazines or using the library's computers. A cluster of middle schoolers is reading at a round table. A college-aged Asian fellow tutors two younger children, one Latina, one African American. Back in the stacks where I settle, a middle-aged Black man has two GED prep books open and is intently taking notes. I look up behind him and see a packed shelf of GED materials. Around us, there are general interest books on everything from managing finances to eating disorders. Fiction ranges wide, from Cervantes and Charlotte Brontë to Stephen King and Sandra Cisneros's *The House on Mango Street*. Matching the changing demographics in South Central—the area is now majority Latin American—there are several long shelves of books in Spanish that include Pablo Neruda and Octavio Paz.

I realize the building is new, but I swear the wood-paneled stacks themselves came from the former library—as have the older books. I get up and slowly walk through the stacks, reading the titles of the books I remember using: Bulfinch's *Mythology*, Will Durant's *The Story of Philosophy*. I find reference books for Greek and Roman literature, for Shakespeare. The poet Rita Dove has a lovely tribute to her childhood library in which she reminisces, "I could walk any aisle / and smell wisdom."[5] These books have a distinctive scent, musty and floral. I open one of them and suddenly remember standing in these stacks and practicing the pronunciation of the word *epitome*, which I was up till then mispronouncing *epi-tome*. The stacks feel old and solemn—one of the editions of *Don Quixote* was translated hundreds of years ago—but I also remember a sense of the new, something unexplored.

I round the corner, headed for the next row of books, and almost bump into a young Black guy, maybe fourteen or fifteen, wearing a

Cal Berkeley T-shirt. We quietly excuse ourselves and move on. I go back to my seat and scribble some thoughts about Mark Twain: how vitally important these local libraries are, what this one opened up to me, what resources and services it is daily making available to children and adults living along this stretch of the Figueroa corridor. And I think about those worn reference books. Who gets the opportunity to learn how to do things with books? If it weren't for Mr. McFarland's senior English, it is unlikely I would have gotten that chance. When I leave an hour later, I see the fellow in the Cal T-shirt talking with the librarian, pointing to something on her computer screen, which she has turned halfway toward him.

During the summer following senior English, with college looming, I used the library to help me read on my own contemporary books and plays that Mr. McFarland only had time to mention during our last few weeks of school: I bought Albert Camus's *The Myth of Sisyphus*, a meditation on the meaning of life in a world without God, and Samuel Beckett's absurdist play *Waiting for Godot*. Heavy lifting for any eighteen-year-old, let alone someone who was still analytically wet behind the ears. Although there would be no quizzes or papers on these books, I carried over the annotation techniques I had developed for senior English, adding stars to my repertoire to indicate magnitude of importance and writing neater and much longer notes of summary and interpretation in the margins, though still flecked with my trademark misspellings. Cut loose from Mr. McFarland's guiding instruction, I somehow knew I had to step up my game. Something else occurs to me, and given my previous school history, it is significant: whatever barriers I once had between the classroom and my private pursuits were gone.

––––––––––

Before senior English, the few papers I wrote about books were an assemblage of clichés, run-of-the-mill observations, loosely supported opinions, and quotations lifted from the back covers of the very books we were reading: "As the *New York Times* said about *Animal Farm* . . ." In addition to the ten essays for Mr. McFarland's class, I wrote seven essays, two short stories, and, of all things, a ballad for an elective he offered during our second semester—a mix of what today we would call honors English and creative writing. In line with Mr. McFarland's insistence that I raise my grades in order to have a shot at college, I also ratcheted up my effort in my other classes, especially civics, which was taught by Brother Gallagher, a young man in the religious order that ran the school. I wrote six essays for him, carrying over to the national and world politics of the time the skills I was learning from Mr. McFarland. These papers collectively give the most reliable evidence of my intellectual growth during my senior year.

Jack McFarland, in an undertaking that qualifies him for sainthood, read again the twenty papers I wrote for him, paying attention to my development as a writer over nine months. He sent the packet back to me with extended observations in fresh green ink, adding to his original thick red comments, sometimes agreeing with and elaborating on his red script, and sometimes disagreeing with his twenty-four-year-old self. Then we had a number of long conversations about what we read.

In the many years that have passed since Jack McFarland first deployed that red pen, time has rounded him out—full trousers, suspenders—and his hair has grown wildly beyond the Brylcreemed formality required by our high school. But his intellectual snap remains, and in retirement his reading is voracious in its depth and reach. Within the same few months that he was telling me about a graceful translation he found of *Orlando Furioso*, one of the chivalric romances mentioned in *Don Quixote*, he was also recommending *The White Boy Shuffle*, a novel by a then little-known contemporary writer named Paul Beatty who, two years later, would win the

National Book Award for *The Sellout*. Books for Jack offer a life of continual discovery and renewal: "It's new knowledge sitting on the horizon that keeps me alive and thriving." He brings this vitality to our investigation, and there are moments when I can almost conjure the feeling of my first encounter with this man. What he did for me extends like an embrace across time.

————

Laid side by side, my essays yield a time-lapse record of me learning to write for college. My development is uneven, falling back into old mistakes or leveling off at a plateau, for development in just about any domain—from writing to athletics to social interaction—is not smooth and linear. Still, Jack and I see that over nine months there is growth in the syntactic complexity of my sentences and the organization of my paragraphs along with a decline in certain grammatical errors and a refinement of word usage and phrasing. I am also trying out more ambitious ideas and arguments and supplying supporting evidence for them. These are measurable improvements writing teachers would hope to see over the course of a school year.

Reading the essays with the benefit of my archaeological dig into senior English, I see a lot else evolving with and through the development of these linguistic and rhetorical features. They are less easily measured but are significant examples of the further benefits of acquiring knowledge and skill. I'm increasingly invested in writing, gaining satisfaction from it and internalizing my teacher's criteria for improving it. I'm acquiring habits of mind that will contribute to my urgent adolescent desire to make sense of the world. And my improvement in writing ripples into the social world of my classroom, generating new friendships. All this, in turn, further encourages linguistic growth by giving it added meaning beyond the page, embedding it in my young evolving life.

The first-order conclusion that Jack and I come to after looking at the full sweep of my essays is that I was learning to live and work with ideas—learning to better express them, to combine and connect them, to critique them, and, perhaps most important, to be comfortable with them. Five days a week for just under one hour per day, I sit in my assigned front-row seat watching this slim, animated man in a crummy brown coat move quickly from blackboard to podium to blackboard, watching and listening as he, with hard strokes of the chalk, writes on the board key concepts and definitions and lists of characteristics related to epic poetry, or the Elizabethan worldview, or Hegel and Marx. He asks questions, smiles or turns serious, says, "Oh, I like that," or, "I hadn't thought of that," pivots to the board to draw a quick arrow from one idea to another, chastises us for thinking sloppily, asks more questions, reads something to us, his book folded open in one hand. Every night I go home and recopy my notes, something I have never done before. This is all new material to me, heady stuff, and I don't want to lose any of it. What I am less aware of at the time—but see clearly now—is how much I am learning about thinking by observing my teacher think out loud.

Mr. McFarland gave us a while for all this to sink in before he assigned the first of his many papers, a comparison of the three epic poets we had read up to that point in the first semester, Homer, Virgil, and Dante. His lectures and our class discussions guided us toward ways to write this paper. Using Mr. McFarland's notes, I defined epic poetry, then compared the different ways our three poets used several features of the epic poem. Formulaic but effective. We later wrote other papers for which I could use this comparison strategy, for example when Mr. McFarland had us discuss the elements of melodrama in *Doctor Faustus* and *Macbeth*.

Another kind of assignment required us to critique a commentary or opinion piece: New York City's powerful city planner Robert Moses on the condition of American cities or historian Christopher

Dawson's lament about the narrow goals of modern education. And yet other assignments provided us with a claim about a novel or play that we had to support or refute or qualify—the approach we took was up to us. For example, we had to consider the claim that there is a conflict between love and honor in Racine's *Athaliah* or that the mysterious Kurtz in *Heart of Darkness* functions as a symbol.

My attempts at these papers had their structural flaws; in Jack's words, "Your ability to think outruns your ability to organize." But in my papers for civics, it's clear that I'm using my newfound comparison and critiquing strategies to good effect. Brother Gallagher gave me A's on those papers, and in his contemporary reading of one of them—a comparison of differing positions on US–Latin American relations—Jack writes: "this could be taken as an index of how far you had advanced as a thinker . . . you could dash off an assignment like this with ease." Well, Jack, thank you, but I guarantee there was no dashing here. I can see that I neatly recopied the paper in my best handwriting, and there is but one spelling error in the whole thing. Furthermore, the multiple sources I used point to time spent in the library. I wrote this paper late in the school year; I'm carefully applying what I learned in a class other than the one where I learned it, a strong indication that I've truly acquired a skill.

A further development in my stack of papers is the use of evidence. Mr. McFarland demanded evidence. You don't just make a claim or express an opinion, you back it up with a passage from what we're reading, or information and examples, or a quotation from a "secondary source," from someone who has studied the issue. Discovering the library opened up for me the world of secondary sources. Mr. McFarland modeled the use of evidence for us every day in lecture and discussion, providing illustrations from *Oedipus the King* or Shakespeare when he talked about the Greeks' ideas concerning destiny or about the notion of order and disorder in *Macbeth*. And as he engaged us in discussion, he pushed us to supply evidence for what we said. All this materialized in his comments on our papers. "Your beliefs need support," he wrote alongside a paragraph in one of my essays. And in other papers he scribbled "Example?" or "Fact?" or "Quotation?" by a claim that floated anchorless on the surface of the page. When I did provide evidence, which I increasingly did as his message sank in, then I'd get his verbal pat on the back: "good documentation," or "again you're using sources," or "this time you used research the way it should be used, combining facts with a theory." I was developing an evidential cast of mind.

Not only did we need to support our claims, but our claims had to make sense, be logical, and they needed to hang together, a real challenge for writers like me who would sometimes leap from one thought to another without taking the reader carefully along. Again, our time in class, week by week, month by month, clued us in as we listened to Mr. McFarland explain things and play out a line of thought—how does Cervantes use satire in *Don Quixote?*— and then he'd question us as we tried to think our way through an assertion of our own. It was on the papers that this push for careful reasoning was brought home. "This is a pretty illogical jump," he wrote on one of my early essays, and "Doesn't logically follow," on another, and, simply and pointedly, "HUH?" on a third. Making and supporting a claim in print is a high-level, difficult literacy task involving everything from transitional words and phrases (which Mr. McFarland frequently supplied in his comments) to an awareness of an audience beyond the page—which our teacher engendered through those comments. Somebody was reading what we wrote and taking it seriously.

My ability to make a logical claim was also related to my ability to find the right words for the new ideas I was stretching to use, qualities I was trying to define, distinctions I was trying to make. Often it felt like those right words were just beyond my fingertips. One of the things Jack notices as he now looks at my papers is that over the year, I'm taking on more complex topics, more elaborate analyses—though not always succeeding. The writing "got away from you here," or "you were out of your element, but trying something a little more sophisticated." This reach beyond what one can do with assurance is central to cognitive growth, yet, as many commentators have pointed out, students, especially in high-pressure schools, are socialized to avoid this kind of risk.

Consider a sentence Jack and I find in an essay I wrote responding to a critique of modern versus classical, or Shakespearean, tragedy: "To understand what is wrong with modern tragedy, one must see that no fault lies in technical prose." *Technical prose?* I think I was trying to say that if there are problems with modern tragedy, they have nothing to do with the quality of the writing itself—which could be skillful—but with other factors: weak characters or unedifying plots. I'm pursuing a decent idea here, but I didn't have the right phrasing at my disposal, and I lacked a rich enough understanding of literature to articulate exactly what I meant. So I used the word *technical*, referring to the nuts and bolts of the modern playwright's language, the words chosen, the phrasing, the figures of speech. Writing researchers refer to core ideas in disciplines as *threshold concepts*, and in my essay I am sniffing around a significant one: the relationship between a writer's language and the themes and values expressed through that language. The relation between style and content.[6] I wasn't there yet, but I was on the hunt. (I'll say more about the assignment shortly.) In one of the last papers I wrote for Mr. McFarland, he observes, "Your ideas, despite some awkward presentation of them, . . . are intellectually at college level." I bet I read and reread that sentence.

What about the nuts and bolts of my writing? Though I was a superficially adequate writer when I came into Mr. McFarland's class, I made my fair share of spelling and grammatical errors. I was never a diligent enough student to master this kind of detail. I just didn't care. It is also the case that as a writing task becomes more complex—writing on difficult material, like a threshold concept, or to an unfamiliar audience, or in a new form—it is likely that errors in grammar and sentence structure will increase, for the writer's skills are being pushed to the limits. My papers for Mr. McFarland are adorned with corrections for pronouns not aligning with their antecedents and subjects not agreeing with verbs, with loads of misspellings (*defination, steriotype, streched, applys*), and with sentence fragments. In Mr. McFarland's collegiate experience, one sentence fragment in an essay for freshman English would trigger an automatic F, so he was hawk-like in correcting and commenting on them. "Five fragments," he wrote on one of my papers. "You would have flunked five times in college." Ouch. My other problem with sentences was the run-on, fusing two sentences together without the proper punctuation or connective words. I would be on the trail of an idea in an essay, trying to articulate it as best I could with the resources I had at the time, and I'd run right over the boundaries of sentences in the chase:

> Take Dr. Faustus for example, he very easily falls under the devil's influence, perhaps too easily to be plausible.

Though I am still an embarrassing speller, I would eventually get most of these problems under control—but, it turns out, not without pitching a fit on the back of one of my early essays. Rereading my papers, I find a snotty note to Mr. McFarland, challenging his judgment for correcting my run-on sentences!

> I went over this essay & cleared up what *you* refer to as "run-ons." I personally think that this makes the essay dry. It resembles the "Dick saw the dog. *period* Jane saw the dog. *period* They both saw the dog. *period*" type of 1st grade primer writing. In the essays I have seen by famous authors, there appears many so called run-ons?????

I remember myself as awed and diligent in my teacher's presence, but here I am wagging a rhetorical finger at him—underlining *you*, for God's sake—and slamming home five question marks at the end to underscore how clueless he is. Jack tells me how much he liked teaching high school seniors, for they are "flip and irreverent," just like himself. Lucky me. His written response under my note speaks volumes about how he saw his work and regarded his students: "Mike, the rule is used in college, so I am insisting on it. As for its value, little can be said. Run-ons abound, esp. in literature. Hemingway, Sinclair Lewis, Faulkner, F. Scott Fitzgerald all use them." He again invokes the college experience he knows—the image of college hung over our classroom like both a hangman and redeemer, even for (maybe especially for) people like me who entered senior English without much thought as to what to do after high school. Mr. McFarland considers my note and grants me my point about run-ons. Never one to miss a teachable moment, however, he continues and points out that the writing in a first-grade primer has nothing to do with punctuation, but with children's linguistic capacity and reading level—so, he wonders, is a primer the best analogy to use? He's being both tough-minded and respectful.

My quarrel with Mr. McFarland demonstrates a genuine argument about subject matter—and therefore represents another developmental shift. In addition to sending my papers to Jack McFarland, I showed some of them to people who are experts in the teaching of writing. One of them said a quality that stood out to her was the "earnest tone" of my papers, by which she meant a "seriousness" about the task at hand, whether it was comparing two works of literature or critiquing an essay on a social issue. Three or four months into senior English, I'm having an aesthetic disagreement with my teacher; I care enough to pick a fight about language.

As Jack and I reviewed my papers, we couldn't help but reflect on his teaching. What shaped it and what made it work? A more primal way to pose the question is this: What kept that crew of forty-six boy-men from eating this novice teacher alive? The previous year, a member of our school's religious order with twelve years of teaching experience was pretty much run out of senior English halfway through the semester. He was replaced for the second semester by the just-hired Mr. McFarland. Into the lion's den he went. Perhaps that prepared him for us.

I spoke to several people who were in my class to get a reading other than my own on the young Jack McFarland. One fellow would go on to get a degree in business, the other in geology. Though Mr. McFarland certainly didn't enthrall all his students and managed to seriously piss off a few (one insisted on calling him Mr. McFart-land), neither of these men remember much grumbling or resistance from our classmates. One appreciated that Mr. McFarland always explained why we were doing something, such as being diligent about sentence fragments. They both remember a classroom lively—even boisterous—with discussion, some of which continued among students out in the hallway. As for the amount of work, one said, "I didn't really enjoy it, but there was a certain satisfaction to it. He made me want to be a better student." The other shrugged his shoulders and mused that he and his buddies thought this was what it meant to be a senior. Yes, all the reading and writing was "mind-boggling," but he "liked the challenge . . . It made your brain work. It wasn't that rote shit we typically had to do." He added that before senior English he had never read an entire book, but afterward he was never without one—in his truck, on his nightstand.

Mr. McFarland's success in the classroom came from his command of literature and literary history and his orderly way of presenting it. He was passionate, and we could see the extraordinary amount of work he put into his teaching and in giving us all that feedback on our papers—hard as it was to swallow. There were times when Mr. McFarland's inexperience was reflected in these assignments. At one point, he had us applying to the plays or novels mid-twentieth-century philosophical or sociological theories about alienation and the loss of tradition—for example, that assignment on modern tragedy. Most of us didn't have the background knowledge or life experience to write much of anything substantial. Looking at those assignments now, he runs his hand through his shaggy hair and says, "I was just asking too much."

My classmates both mention lively discussion, and in retrospect I think the quality of talk in Mr. McFarland's classroom was a key element of its success. It's talk based on subject matter that both challenges you and draws you out, that expects and invites response. There is both bounce and heft to it. Jack says that he likes such discussion because that's where learning happens. Students have to articulate an idea, make connections, respond to questions they might not expect—and sometimes raise questions of their own. In college I had several professors who were "personalities." A lot of students loved them; they gave the speeches for parents and alums; they were the public face of the liberal arts. Witty, super-articulate, sonorous delivery. I couldn't stand them. They carried their practiced spontaneity into our classrooms, didn't prepare, made minimal comments on our essays, and didn't engage our questions but used them as a launching pad for a burst of cleverness. My father would have called them bullshit artists.

Participating in the kind of discussion Mr. McFarland required of us isn't easy, so it's interesting that so many of the people I interviewed from a variety of grade levels and subjects respond positively to it. Some used the word *respect* when talking about such exchange: a teacher is genuinely asking you what *you* think, which confirms your intelligence. Jack refers to it as "taking students seriously." I had not experienced anything quite like it before.

There is an ethic to this kind of classroom talk. It emerges from a deep belief in the importance of teaching and belief in the ability of your students, a belief in their ability that holds even in the face of evidence that might suggest otherwise: previous test scores, or performance in other courses, or, more generally, characteristics like socioeconomic class. When Mr. McFarland came to our school to salvage that rowdy English class, he gave his students a brief survey and discovered that only 4 percent of their parents had any kind of college degree. It was pretty much the same for our group. "I was teaching in a working-class high school," he says, "and I wanted you all to be able to go out and compete in the larger arena. I figured you'd need to know certain things and be able to write well."

Jack pauses then adds, with sudden emphasis, "I also was trying to be the teacher I wished I had in high school." I had always assumed that Jack McFarland could speak in rhymed couplets by the fourth grade, had mastered the Russian novel by the eighth. Not so. He was expelled from one Catholic high school for challenging his religion teacher in class and ended up in a newer, harder-nosed Catholic school where the priest teaching world history began the semester by holding up the course's thick textbook and asking the class: "Do you know why I picked this book?" After a few half-hearted answers from the students, the good father whacked a guy in the front row alongside the head with the book, explaining that he chose it "because it hurts." So much for the quality of Jack's high school education.

Jack McFarland entered college with "little training and struggled during my first year," for many of his classmates had "read authors like James Joyce, and I had never heard of him." But he read furiously and got in with some of these more literate students and learned from them too. He found his way. The class he created for us emerged, at least in part, from a deep disappointment with his own education. There have been many moments of surprise in the journey I've been taking with my former teacher, but none matched this one: my seemingly omniscient guide through thousands of years of Western literature had an academic background that was not unlike my own.

————————

Whether or not I knew it in these terms, I had been wanting to get good at something for a long time but couldn't sustain the effort. Early on, Mr. McFarland picked up on my fumbling eagerness, remembers me "wanting to participate." But given my pattern of initial enthusiasm followed by drift when a task got challenging, I could have easily glided off the rails. The routine of Mr. McFarland's assignments with his continual targeted feedback kept me focused, and the five-day-a-week surround-sound of talk about our books and essays became a kind of verbal scaffold. Mr. McFarland was dedicated and energetic but not warm or chummy. He was the teacher, which was what I needed—another adult in my life who was looking out for me. Harnessed, directed, my enthusiasm eventually led, as Jack put it, to "wanting to know how things worked," a sharpening of my attention, a commitment to a kind of effort I hadn't exhibited before.

One more thing happened that would keep me on those rails. The kind of extended achievement we're talking about here and in the stories to come rarely happens in isolation. My competence was developing in a classroom, amid other people, witnesses. I was slowly becoming a different person among my peers. A woman I interviewed nicely captured this public redefinition when reflecting on her performance in a pivotal math class: "I wasn't an anonymous person. I had a name. I got to raise my hand and give answers. I publicly had proof that I was getting the math." Because of my gradually noticeable accomplishments in Mr. McFarland's class, I made some new friends with students who had read way more and wrote much better than I did. Art Mitz and Mark Dever both came from modest middle-class backgrounds. Art lived in a nice residential neighborhood a few miles southwest of me; Mark came from San Pedro, one of Southern California's seaport communities, far to the south of our high school. Though our friendship included all the obsessions of our age—sex, music, a new pair of jeans—our camaraderie was built on books. We hung out at school; they came by my house to pick me up for movies. We talked about our readings and our papers. These are the kinds of transformations in high school friendships that can have a big impact on a young person's life.

Art was tall, slim, wore glasses, and had a perennial wisp of hair falling across his forehead. He looked like Hollywood's image of the high-achieving student he was. He excelled on the debate team, edited the student newspaper, was voted "Most Likely to Succeed." Art was articulate and assured and had his sights set on college long before he entered Mr. McFarland's class, so he recognized immediately the opportunity this teacher was setting before us. I learned about achievement just by being around him.

There is a good chance you wouldn't know how smart Mark was unless you taught him, for he kept to himself, didn't speak up in class, wasn't involved in any of the school's activities. But my God, he was a beautiful writer. For an imitation assignment, Mark went in search of the monumental, and difficult, French novelist Marcel Proust and pulled it off, capturing the qualities of the Frenchman's style. Mark's reserve was reflected in his appearance—unassumingly handsome, neatly pressed, every hair in place—but once you got to know him, you found a complicated mix of traditionalism and profanity. He had strong opinions about literature, was almost a classicist in his taste, and was quick to label anything he didn't like *caca*, colloquial Spanish for *crap*. Later on when I started reading on my own contemporary experimental writers, Mark would proclaim them *caca*, with this half-smile that signaled both disdain for the literature and a playful invitation to fight back. And I did, bringing that solitary reading of mine out into open public debate.

These were the guys I had the good fortune to fall in with. In addition to all the specific things I learned from them, they helped me imagine something in myself that I probably couldn't have imagined alone.

———————

Whatever one might think of my senior English curriculum today—and over the years, I've taught one similar to it and many quite different from it—the way Jack McFarland taught it provided for me an indispensable set of intellectual skills to prepare me for college. And what I learned would lead to something else, both during and beyond college. My home was filled with love and sickness and gnawing worry. The world from my front door looked narrow, and my understanding of the social order—of economics and politics, of race and gender, of what it meant to be a man—was composed of whatever filtered in from the street or circulated within my family. My year in senior English equipped me to look more widely at the world around me, to seek information, to question, to analyze, and eventually to turn my learning back onto the world and work within it.

My attempts to read and write in a new way began early in senior English with my attraction to Mr. McFarland and the challenge he laid out before us. As the months passed, the positive response I received from my teachers and my peers stoked effort, sparked a desire to learn more, which itself becomes motivating—a cognitive momentum I've witnessed in others I've spoken with, from welders to dancers to astronomers. Eventually, the thing you're pursuing becomes part of who you are.

In the old folders that held my papers for Mr. McFarland, I found a four-page list of the books I read in senior English and subsequently up to the point of typing, which I can estimate to be around the end of my freshman year of college. I am a poor typist today; back then I would have been hunting and pecking with my two index fingers, heavy, deliberate keystrokes resulting in the dark and thick letters I read on this erasable typing paper, turning tan with age. There are over one hundred titles. Some are books I read for class and some are books Mr. McFarland mentioned in his historical overview, Jane Austen's *Pride and Prejudice* and Albert Camus's *The Stranger*. There are books from my first year of college: W. Somerset Maugham's *Of Human Bondage*. And there is the experimental fiction I was consuming with shaky comprehension and that Mark was labeling *caca*: Marguerite Duras's *The Square* and Fernando Arrabal's *Baal Babylon*. It would have taken me a long time to type this list.

I did some odd things related to that English class of Mr. McFarland's: keeping all of my essays, typing this labor-intensive list. I had long forgotten the list, but as soon as I found it, I understood the motivation behind it. I was cataloguing my wealth in the way someone might catalogue collectables, rare books, or vintage dolls or trading cards. The list is an inventory of achievement, but I think, too, it served as a kind of mirror: this is who I am. Books have weight, heft; you can hold them, stack them, line them up alphabetically. I'm not kidding myself, not half-stepping or living in a fantasy. *I actually did this!*

I've been mentoring several students at a Central Los Angeles community college where I did some research a few years back. One of them, Joanie Contreras, was in her late thirties when she reluctantly enrolled, taking one class to test the waters. Then, still with doubt, she signed up for the next semester. And the next. Joanie had a hard life and expected little from it. She kept the brakes on her hope. But semester by semester, the momentum built and she accumulated an impressive record. She is preparing to transfer to a state university to pursue social work. Joanie speaks and writes with strong emotion about how her life has changed. "It used to be sad to go home," she says. "I felt like I was at the bottom . . . But school has helped me make sense of things. It's real. Nobody can take it away from me."

Last month she sent me two photographs to show what she's done to her small apartment. One photograph is of a bookcase she just bought; the second is of her desk. There are books from her classes: biology, psychology, *The Penguin Book of English Verse*. Other books: Mandela, Gandhi, *Enrique's Journey*, an account of a Honduran boy's dangerous migration to the United States, and Nobel Peace Prize–winner Malala Yousafzai's memoir. Over Joanie's desk there are handwritten quotations from Confucius and Socrates. Under them are stacks of notebooks, some pencils and pens and yellow markers, an orange paper flower. "I wake up wanting to read," she writes in the card accompanying the photos. "I have a purpose. I can't believe this is me." Joanie doesn't know how deeply I understand these pictures. They are a visual inventory of the artifacts that contribute to her becoming.

CHAPTER THREE

WHAT TEACHERS SEE

Teachers who foster an educational awakening have a sense of their students' potential and a knack for bringing it forth. Having experienced this growth-fostering attentiveness myself and, I hope, having exercised it at times in my own classroom, I am intrigued by the many ways it occurs in the lives of others. What a teacher does can be relatively small in scope but ripple downstream, growing in importance and influence. Two writers I interviewed remember specific events in elementary school that had a formative effect on their sense of themselves as authors. Clare Walker's third-grade teacher made a little mimeographed book out of her poems and distributed it to the class. "This changed the way I saw myself," Clare said, taking, as she put it, her creations out of her head and sending them into the world. When Nicki Macias was in the sixth grade, she was so drawn to the adolescent novel *The Westing Game* that she worked and worked on a long essay analyzing each of the book's many characters. Her teacher wrote across the top of her paper, "When are *you* going to write your first novel?" Nicki, who was bused to this school, had felt terribly out of place, but her teacher's comment made her realize that "somebody sees me." The same teacher submitted a haiku Nicki wrote to a district-wide contest, and it was selected for the resulting anthology. Nicki began to keep a journal, produce more poetry, and gain increasing pleasure from writing. The brief comment, the submission of a haiku, the mimeographed booklet stand out in these women's memories as shaping their developing identities as writers.

For Clare and Nicki, their teachers' actions strengthened interests already evident, but sometimes the move a teacher makes comes from an observation or hunch that remedies a problem and, as a consequence, yields further avenues to achievement. Lydia Moreau was a dedicated student, a hard worker, but, looking back on it, admits that she "didn't know the ins and outs of heavy-duty academic achievement." She did well in English and history but had a hard time with mathematics and with languages. In her first year of high school, she studied and studied for her Spanish class, "but just couldn't get it. I was spinning my wheels, and I guess it showed." Her teacher, Ms. Clifford, saw something . . . A kid in distress? A determined girl getting poor grades on her tests? Lydia can only guess, but Ms. Clifford took her aside and told her that she got to school early and could tutor her. Lydia chokes up telling me this story fifty years after it happened—Ms. Clifford's intervention was that powerful in young Lydia's life.

To have some help with a subject that is confounding is, of course, a big deal, especially if doing well in school is important to your sense of who you are. And then there's having someone in authority paying attention to you, to *you*, during your vulnerable first year in high school. But the thing that stands out for Lydia most is that through the Spanish tutorials, Ms. Clifford was teaching her "an approach to studying something I didn't know." Lydia was learning a way to think that took her beyond blunt cognitive exertion to strategies that she was then able to carry over to other subjects. What Ms. Clifford taught Lydia during those early mornings of ninth grade would positively affect her performance in later grades, shaping who she would become in high school.

And there are times when a teacher goes out on a limb and takes a chance that opens up for a student a whole new world. An example I love comes from a radio interview with the English actress Emily Blunt.[1]

The young Emily had a stutter so severe it nearly shut down her ability to communicate. Her parents tried all sorts of therapies, to no avail. One day, her teacher out of the blue asked her if she wanted to be in the class play. You can imagine her reaction and predict her response, a resolute shaking of the head: *No!* It turns out that her teacher had been watching her in the schoolyard, where Emily would do impersonations for her friends and speak in silly voices—and didn't stutter. He suggested that she try an accent or a silly voice in the play. She did, and it worked. Emily Blunt's teacher had looked beyond his student's disability for clues as to what she could do. He was observant and attuned—I like the metaphor of *antenna* here—as he worked with the young people in his charge.

Come with me now to a community college welding program for a very different but equally revealing story of a teacher's antenna and a student's voice. Janice Villanueva was one of two women in a class of twenty-five. The instructor, André Watson, is a big man with a forceful presence, his pedagogy heavy with banter and challenge. He likes to start the semester by messing with his students, testing their mettle. André violates a truckload of maxims about good teaching, but the students respond positively, some crediting André with their success. He strategically converts the classroom into a jobsite, stripping away the propriety of school, a place that for many in the course was an arena of failure and shame. Day one comes and André calls on Janice, purposefully mispronouncing her name *Jan-ese*. She corrects him. Okay, he says, acting the jerk, but how about I call you Jan-ese anyway? "Fuck that," Janice shoots back, "it's Janice." André later told me that he knew in that moment Janice had some special quality. Fearlessness? Sassy determination? He began working on her to do something far-fetched: to run for student government, for, what the hell, student body president! Janice had never given a public speech in her life and had no experience whatsoever with student government. Her reaction was not unlike Emily Blunt's, an are-you-out-of-your-mind disbelief. André let his suggestion sink in and revisited it with both jibes and entreaties. A year and a half later, after developing a platform and an effective stump speech, after mobilizing (with André's help) her welding peers into campaign foot soldiers, and after one failed attempt, Janice was elected student body president of her community college. Along the way, she received a political and oratorical education and developed institutional savvy and leadership skills, a public self she would have never imagined when she first signed up for that occupational program.

For all the differences between the stories of the actress and the welding student, their teachers, like the other teachers we're meeting, possess a fortunate blend of beliefs about ability and an alertness to signs of that ability, signs that can be faint, possibly distorted by school routines, societal biases, or a cloud of anger or defense generated by students themselves. There can be an element of intuition here, taking a chance on someone.

It is telling how often students—and teachers too—will use a visual metaphor to describe the impact of this sensibility. Both writers, Clare and Nicki spoke of being seen or altering the way one sees oneself. Juliet Truman, a student who entered a licensed practical nursing program after completing her GED, praised an instructor she would go to when she felt overwhelmed. This instructor told Juliet that "she could see it in me that I was meant to do this," and encouraged her not only to complete the LPN program but also to continue toward a registered nurse's degree, which Juliet eventually did. Hazel Chua, a teacher in a community college automotive technology program, reflected on the woman who taught her: "The thing I loved about Ms. Marovich is that when she looks at you, she sees the finished product." This is a special kind of seeing, an act of perception that helps bring another person's future self into being.

When he was in the sixth grade, Enrique Diaz was horsing around with one of his buddies during PE and shoved him, and the boy fell and broke his arm. For punishment, Enrique had to empty classroom trash cans after school. One of the teachers, Ms. Rodriguez, started talking to Enrique—What happened? What'd you do? What are you interested in?—and finally offered him a proposal. She and a few other teachers had just started a debate club—an unusual thing in a working-class middle school like this—and if she could get the remainder of his detention time channeled into the fledgling club, would he be interested. As he put it to me, he thought, "Sure . . . it beats taking out trash all the time." Enrique flourished in debate. By the eighth grade, he was winning trophies. He went on to the high school team, which took him around the state, opening his eyes to huge differences in educational resources and to how few debaters looked like him. "Before these competitions, I never knew anything outside of my community." A senior now at a university in the same region where he grew up, he goes back to his high school to help the younger members of the debate team that had such an impact on his life.

Ms. Rodriguez remembers her early encounters with Enrique. She had the sense—later confirmed—that he regularly got himself into trouble with some teachers. He clowned around but was also a talker and asked a lot of questions. She knew kids like this; "they're not docile, and they will push you." When she first talked to him, she could see that he was outgoing and that he was "hungry." I asked her how she knew that, and she said, "by talking to someone and answering their questions. You can see it in their eyes."

Talking to someone. If seeing, watching, observing is crucial to a teacher's perceptual acuity, so, too, is talking and listening. In her initial interactions with Enrique, Ms. Rodriguez is gaining information and formulating a sense of this boy in front of her. Her talk has a diagnostic element to it. But for it to be successful, Enrique, who undoubtedly has his own antenna out during those first exchanges, has to sense that her interaction—her questions, her answers to his questions—are authentic. A number of people I interviewed spoke, sometimes at length, about the importance of real speech between teacher and student, straightforward, not patronizing and not superficial. "It's really something," one man told me, "to be taken seriously as a young person." Such interaction was praised even by those being disciplined. A girl who had a troubled senior year reflected back on her dean of students who even in anger "always treated me like a human being."

Timing also matters. As a community college student put it, two of his instructors gave him "the right words right at the moment" he needed to hear them, urging him to complete his associate degree and transfer to a four-year school. Timing requires an alert sensibility, knowing someone, knowing their circumstances, sensing when to intervene, when something you'll say will be heard.

But it is also possible that those community college teachers said those just-right words to that fellow many times before . . . and he finally *heard* them. I have been focusing on the qualities the teacher brings to these transformational encounters, but there's two (or more) people in this educational tango, and the student needs to be in some way receptive. It could be that other things in their life need to settle down or shift, family or finances or relationships. Sometimes more growing-up needs to occur, or more life experience accrued. And then there are times when we run up against a human brick wall, no matter how keen our insight or skillful and impassioned our appeal. A student's pain or anger might be too intense or their boredom too numbing—or the student simply desires to be *anyplace* but school. There can be a time delay; you run into a former student who tells you that something you said hit home years later. And sometimes a student's transformation happens incrementally, over a long stretch of time. One teacher has an impact, but it weakens against internal doubts or barriers in the environment. Then another class or another teacher. And slowly more permanent change takes hold, a new life unfolding across the fuller arc of a young person's development.

———————

A fuller arc of development can reveal, as it did in my story, the complex difficulties in students' lives outside of school and the negative effects they have on engagement with school. But these difficulties can also create an opening, a flailing desire for a way out. Teachers and their subject matter can play a powerful role in redirecting such a life—literature or mechanics, history or physics becoming the medium for transformation, saving a young person from a bad end.

Tiffany Gamboa was headed for big trouble. During middle school she was involved in gang life and had a run-in with the law. She wasn't interested in school, missed a lot, never really paid attention when she was there. As one of her teachers put it, "she was a mess."

But in tenth grade, she was placed in an English class that caught her attention. The teacher, Mr. Fowlie, gave the class readings on social issues—the gender wage gap, for example—and engaged the class in serious and prolonged discussion about them. These issues became the topics for writing assignments. Tiffany told me that she had never had a class like that, all that discussion. And it was the first time she read about issues like wage discrimination. I asked her why she thinks these issues mattered to her. "They affect us directly. They affect women, people of color, especially people of color in less affluent communities. It's like I'm being told stuff about myself I didn't even know."

I spoke with Tiffany by phone during the summer between her junior and senior year in high school. She lives with her mother and stepfather, who is a mechanic. All are undocumented but are applying for legal status. Tiffany is soft-spoken, attentive, and as our call progressed, she became a bit more animated, though still low-key, her voice rising, a soft laugh punctuating the ends of some sentences. I asked a further question about her teacher's assignments: what effect it had on her to be told things about yourself you didn't know. Why did that matter? "Well, it changed the way I think. Before, it was like my life was only about me. But then I began to think about the community as a whole and why it's the way it is . . ." Tiffany was becoming aware of social change and the kind of knowledge change demands. "I can't make a positive impact in my community if I'm an ignorant little girl."

Fortunately, Tiffany's tenth-grade English teacher, Mr. Fowlie, went on to teach eleventh-grade English, and her US history teacher, Ms. Garza, also took an interest in Tiffany. "During the first week," Ms. Garza told me, "I knew there was something special about this girl. She had strong opinions, and she spoke them with lots of 'shits' and 'fucks' interspersed in them, but she was obviously very smart." One of the early things Ms. Garza did with Tiffany was talk to her in private about the wisdom of "code-switching," of trimming the street talk, but not her ideas or passion, from her classroom speech. Ms. Garza helped Tiffany develop a distinctive public self.

Ms. Garza was a good match for Tiffany. The first in her family to go to college, Erica Garza did well in school, went to community college, and transferred to a top-flight university. But she "never really knew what [she] wanted to do." She majored in political science but found it dry. She wasn't particularly interested in history either, but got curious about American histories she hadn't studied in school and began taking classes in women's studies and in Chicano and African American history. The classes captivated her and opened up entire new worlds to her. "I was falling in love with history." Erica then happened onto a course on racial and economic inequality in our schools taught by a charismatic professor. Before this class she "had no interest in education at all," but during it she realized "this class is calling me somewhere." Those history classes and this class in education opened up a career for Erica Garza. She began to pursue teaching and "never looked back."

From her own experience Ms. Garza understood Tiffany's awakening. It wasn't that long ago that she, too, felt the excitement and the focusing of the mind that comes with learning about the world you live in, the histories that affect *your life* and the lives of those around you. Ms. Garza brought the knowledge she had gained in college to the US history course Tiffany took and tried to reproduce as well the engaging pedagogy of that education professor who so inspired her.

Tiffany caught fire in Ms. Garza's class. "I feel like I was kind of living in a little bubble." She prides herself on developing the ability to think critically, to not just accept something she sees on television, but "to question it and research it on my own." She seeks out challenging material and difficult classes. "I love learning new things, understanding them . . . It's something that makes me feel good, the satisfaction I get from it."

It was Ms. Garza who got Tiffany thinking about college, and Tiffany is now working hard to raise her grade point average, compensating for her earlier academic record. She has her eye on a local state college or, as a backup, one of the community colleges in the area. Her hope is to be able to come back to her neighborhood and work to improve the schools and be an advocate for students like she was. "You can't just simply grow and not help others grow too. There wouldn't be much meaning in life. I want to make some kind of impact before I die."

"I would like to be there when Dionysus returns to Thebes," Mr. Johnson told the student reporter writing a lighthearted piece on the one place teachers wish they could be.[2] Some named famous historical sites—the signing of the Declaration of Independence—or legendary events in sports, a Super Bowl or final game in the World Series, and some went for pure pleasure: sunrise on Maui. Not Mr. Johnson. He then drove his answer home with this tagline: "And if you don't know why, then you don't care."

Chris Kurosawa had Mr. Johnson for eleventh-grade physics and respected him, but that comment about Dionysus and not caring seemed so arrogant it pissed Chris off. So he catches Mr. Johnson after class and asks him what it was that happened at Thebes. Mr. Johnson asks if he read the rest of his quotation. Chris says he did. Mr. Johnson looks at him blankly and says, "Well?" Then the teacher turns on his heel and walks away.

Chris was tracked into his high school's honors and Advanced Placement classes, but his behavioral record was a disaster. He missed as many classes as he attended. He was drinking and smoking marijuana. On his sixteenth birthday, he stole his parents' car and crashed it. But he was a bright kid and did well enough in his classes, even with horrible attendance, to get by. The one teacher's classes he didn't miss were Mr. Johnson's.

William Johnson was known as a demanding teacher, held in high regard, but approached with propriety. As Chris explained it to me, Mr. Johnson maintained a clear role as teacher; he was not your friend or confidant. Chris had him for three years but had few personal conversations with him—though Chris did tell him about his stealing and crashing his parents' car. The relationship Mr. Johnson fostered was an intellectual one. He had an advanced degree in physics as well as a background in the Greek and Roman classics and in the arts, and he taught chemistry and physics and a senior humanities course that he created. His courses were rich in discussion, and, particularly in the humanities course, there were long conversations about higher education, for Mr. Johnson was preparing his students, most of whom came from modest means, for both the rigors and the pleasures of college. As Chris summarized it: "It's like there's a lot of cool stuff out there, but you'll have to work to dig it out."

Chris Kurosawa was walking a thin line through much of high school. He had agonizing conflicts with his father. His buddies were disconnected from school and drinking and smoking dope. And Chris was angry about the situation at home and diving into trouble. Yet there was the pull of Mr. Johnson's classes, "one of the few places you could mine intellectually," and Chris craved that stimulation as much as the reckless kind. Which takes us back to that moment when, in response to Chris's question about Dionysus and Thebes, Mr. Johnson turns and walks away. I could imagine that being an explosive *fuck you* moment for Chris, his question dismissed with such haughtiness. But Mr. Johnson's response had the opposite effect, and I can't help but wonder about the strategy here, given that by that point, Mr. Johnson had known Chris for a year and a half. Chris explained that Mr. Johnson wove references to the classics into all he taught, so though the reference to Dionysus and Thebes was certainly obscure, if you took courses from Mr. Johnson, you would at least be primed to find out its meaning. So rather than increasing Chris's irritation with his teacher, Mr. Johnson's curt answer stunned Chris into the recognition that "I never wanted to be ignorant again. I never wanted to be left out."

Chris still had bumpy times through his senior year, but overall got into less trouble. He threw himself into Mr. Johnson's humanities course, which had students read about theater and then produce a play, study the principles and manifestos behind a school of modern art and then try to create a work of art in that vein—a blend of theory and practice that was unlike anything Chris had encountered before.

To be sure, some of it just seemed "weird" to Chris, but it challenged him, and intellectual challenge was the surest counterweight to his bad behavior. "My transgressions," Chris told me, "were completely inconsistent with how Mr. Johnson was and who he was." William Johnson created a world that demanded intellectual commitment and provided an intellectual code of conduct—exactly what the careening young man needed.

Chris would graduate, attend a nearby community college, transfer to a university, and eventually earn a law degree. "I don't know what I'd be doing now without Mr. Johnson," Chris reflected. "He propelled me someplace that no one else could have taken me."

––––––––

I first met Tomás Herrera in the student lounge of a university I was visiting. I ducked into the lounge to get a soda from the vending machine and saw across the otherwise empty room a big man with a long, faded tattoo on his arm hunkered down in a stuffed chair intently reading the German philosopher Hegel's *The Phenomenology of Spirit*, a pen in his free hand poised lightly in the air. I've got to meet this guy, I thought. A few more steps across the room and I introduced myself and asked about the reading, confessing that I had found Hegel pretty tough going. Thus began a conversation that has continued for years and that reveals how many layers there can be in finding one's way, the external barriers one encounters, the internal demons. More than a few people will need to touch such a life along its winding journey. School plays a complicated role here, at times a place of nurturance and growth, and, sadly, at times a place of limitation, blunting, even cruelty.

Born in the housing projects of a large Southwestern city in the early 1970s, Tomás characterizes himself as a "War on Poverty" child, a "Head Start boy," and a beneficiary of desegregation, for his school district was involved in an important civil rights lawsuit.

Tomás's early school memories are richly positive, from Head Start through fifth and sixth grade. His classrooms were multiracial—Mexican American, White, Black, Vietnamese, and Native American—and he frequently uses the word *love* to describe how he felt about being around these other children and about his teachers, White and Black women who were "good-hearted" and gave "a lot of love" to their students. Tomás, who is fluently bilingual, read and wrote a lot—he still remembers an ambitious story he wrote for Halloween—and one of his teachers got him tested, successfully, for the school's gifted and talented program. School would become a refuge for Tomás as his home life drifted into violence.

Violence was part of Tomás Herrera's existence before he was born. His biological father severely beat his mother while she was pregnant with Tomás. Both mother and baby survived, and she immigrated from Mexico to the United States, meeting her new husband when Tomás was four. In Tomás's eyes, this man was his father. The couple had a son, and Tomás's father treated both boys equally, if anything favoring Tomás, encouraging his reading and supporting him in school. Tomás's father was a man of deep feeling, intellectually curious, an avid reader, and he saw those qualities in Tomás. He worked as a butcher and one day injured himself lifting a side of beef, thus initiating an addiction to painkillers that led to heroin. Unstable employment followed, along with a long series of moves in search of cheaper rent, and though he never hit Tomás, his father became increasingly violent at home.

It's sometimes hard to know what children see and how they protect themselves from seeing, but as Tomás explains it, "you get a little more cognizant, your area of attention broadens," and gradually he "started to take notice of the violence and drugs in our house." School and books, in or out of school, were a sanctuary, "an opposite, contrary reality" that provided some shelter from what he witnessed and the storm of conflicting emotions he felt. Such protections are partial, however, at times compromised, even fragile; we can't wall ourselves off from violence and sorrow. Tomás tells the story of his father buying sodas and books for his boys while he was en route to his dealer, then parking his car under a shady tree outside the dealer's house. The boys read—Tomás consumed the *Star Wars* books in that back seat—and his father came out regularly to check on the boys and move the car a few feet to keep them in the shade. "But every time he came out," Tomás adds, "his voice was a little more slurred. I didn't know what was going on, but I felt very, very sad about it. . . . And that's how it would happen. My educational life right alongside all that nastiness." Tomás would spend decades "trying to straighten out" the wrenching confusion of these years.

Tomás's mother was desperate, "grasping for any solution she could find," as Tomás put it, and managed to convince her husband to move the family to another state, hoping that a new environment would help him with his addiction. And for a while it did, Tomás says wistfully, for "he found religion and held onto it dearly." For Tomás, however, the change of location took its toll. His neighborhood was predominately Mexican American, but the kids spoke in a different way and had different local customs. Tomás didn't fit in, for the specifics of race and place matter, especially in youth culture. Inside school, Tomás felt little connection to the curriculum—which was laden with the history of the region's domination of Mexico—or to his teachers. His grades plummeted. His father fell back into addiction, and the family returned to their home state, to a small industrial suburb of the city where Tomás was born. More change. More dislocation.

Tomás finished middle school and entered high school, full of sorrow about home and encountering racial tensions at school "between the established White kids whose parents owned the factories and stores in town and the people who worked for them." He also encountered "a lot of White teachers who were very openly hostile, and not only to Mexican kids but, in some ways, to kids in general." Tomás tells this story: He owned two pairs of Levis. He'd wear one pair and put the other pair under his mattress to press out the wrinkles. Other poor kids did this too; you wanted to look good. His PE teacher got wind of the practice and ridiculed Tomás in front of his classmates. Tomás's science teacher made fun of the Mexican boys' pompadour hairstyles. A person can take only so much of that before reacting, so Tomás began throwing it back, challenging these teachers in class and doing the bare minimum, or worse, to get by. As we talk, he looks through the report cards he dug up for our interview. A lot of 2.0 averages over those years.

But Tomás is a fiercely literate guy. Books are his salvation. Starting in middle school when he no longer found nurturance in the classroom, he discovered the library—and got deep into comic books. And he intensified a practice he began as a child: filling out the subscription cards inside magazines he would browse at the mini-mart, subscriptions his father would pay for when those magazines started appearing in the Herrera mailbox. Tomás's out-of-school curriculum ranged from Western writer Louis L'Amour to *Sports Illustrated* and *Hot Rod* magazine to *The Silver Surfer* who was, Tomás noted, "the most tortured of the superheroes." Then he discovered *Of Mice and Men*, and a further stage in his self-education began. "Louis L'Amour was great, man, but Steinbeck was grown-up." Tomás's attention shifted to a different section of the library.

This reading sustained Tomás, provided a literary lifeline through the empty spaces in school, and kept his mind alive. And for all the disappointments, there were islands of engagement and decency in high school, and they mattered deeply to Tomás, countering the "poison at home," and slowly, if unevenly, building his knowledge and skills and his belief in his considerable ability. As he recalls these classes and teachers, his voice rises at times to the lyrical.

After flunking algebra twice—swearing at his teachers, resisting the work—Tomás landed in Mr. Connor's class. The funny thing is that Mr. Connor was "one of those guys who is off to the golf course as soon as school is over." But for some reason, not when it came to Tomás. Mr. Connor puzzled over the young man, told Tomás he knew he could do algebra, and had him come after school for tutorials—when he would typically be whacking a golf ball down the fairway! "If it wasn't for Mr. Connor," Tomás says, "I would have never known I had a knack for mathematics. He assumed I was capable, and that opens things up for a young person."

During the same time when Tomás was sitting alongside Mr. Connor mastering algebraic operations, he had a brief encounter with Advanced Placement Literature, an encounter that reveals multiple truths about students like Tomás and the schools they attend, complex, interrelated truths about self-doubt, educational opportunity, and the ways social class, race, and ethnicity play out within a student body. Tomás took a standardized test in his English class and finished it quickly. His teacher came to his desk and sternly told him to take his time. He said he did, and she turned and walked off. The next day she apologized to him, for he had gotten every answer right. That test opened the possibility for entering Advanced Placement Literature. The course was taught by a Mexican American man who was an excellent teacher, and one of the books on the syllabus was *The Winter of Our Discontent* by Tomás's favorite, John Steinbeck. But after a short while, Tomás dropped the class. Choked with shame, he tried but finally couldn't explain to his teacher, who didn't want to let him go, that he felt painfully out of place. Only one or two students looked like him, and none of the others talked to him. "I didn't believe I belonged there. I felt pretty low. I was letting my teacher down and certainly was letting myself down."

This is surely an example of one's insecurities sabotaging a fine opportunity—and the story can be read that way. But certain practices at Tomás's school—not uncommon, sadly—reinforced such insecurity. During those few days in Advanced Placement Literature, a recruiter from Stanford visited the school. A number of Tomás's classmates had passes from the school counselor to meet with the recruiter. Tomás only knew that Stanford was an important place, but wanted to learn more. When Tomás did see his counselor, he guardedly asked about Stanford, and the counselor raised vocational education as a better option. To be fair to the counselor, the young man standing before him had terrible grades and would have never been eligible for a school like Stanford. Furthermore, the counselor had a huge advising load—as do most high school counselors. But being deflected here was a young man with documented evidence of ability who expressed an interest in college—something that apparently went unseen, or was ignored. More troubling was the school's practice of sending Marine recruiters to the homes of poor kids, Mexican and White. The military, rather than higher education, was the default option for them.

Remember all those *Hot Rod* magazines Tomás was reading? Well, he checks out vocational education and finds treasure there, new things to learn, and a further boost in confidence. He took all the voc-ed courses he could and ditched other courses to go to the machine shop, his favorite. The teacher, Mr. Ladsen, "was perfect. His hair was perfect and his Levis were perfectly ironed with creases." Mr. Ladsen embodied precision, the precision he helped his students acquire as they used tools and instruments to achieve "millimetric accuracy." And there was something else. In a school with racial and social class tensions, Tomás found voc-ed to be internally egalitarian even though it was physically separated and demographically segregated from the rest of the school. "I felt a bit more comfortable," he said, "because you're there with Mexican kids like you who ain't got nothing and are wearing their second pair of Levis too. And there's the poor White kids, and all they care about is how good you are with the tools. There was a kind of leveling that took place. What mattered for all of us was, 'Can you run this lathe?' 'Do you know how to fix this carburetor?' I rediscovered my intelligence in vocational education.'"

His journey through high school was anything but smooth, and it had many moments of insult, but Tomás was developing facility with numbers and with the thinking and doing of mechanics. And fortunately, as he separated from AP Literature, he landed in a regular English class that transported him. Mr. Minervini was a small, physically unassuming man, but as he walked around the class with a book, pointing out passages, asking questions, he exuded passion and authority. "Wow," thought Tomás, "I want to do that too." Tomás started sitting in the front row.

The class read the kind of books you'd find in a traditional honors curriculum, maybe not that far from the reading list of the AP course Tomás had left behind: Hemingway, Faulkner, Steinbeck. And they watched movies—for example, one from the French New Wave director François Truffaut. "Heavy stuff," Tomás shakes his head. "I couldn't have said it this way back then, but you really love kids if you show them art.

"It felt good to run those machines," Tomás continued, "and then to read those delicate pages too." He laughs. "I felt like a Renaissance kid!" Upon graduation, Tomás worked for a year as a janitor and as a loader in warehouses. Then one day something happened that resembles what a number of other working-class students have told me. Tomás saw a commercial on television for the nearby community college, and though he lived "twenty blocks away, I had no idea it existed." It seems that his high school didn't even clue him in on this local resource. So he rode his bike to a little hill above the college and looked down at the campus for close to an hour wondering if it was okay to enter without being a student. Would he be arrested? Finally he walked his bike onto the campus, "the most nervous person you could imagine, thinking, 'they must know I don't belong here.'" Several days later he went back and enrolled. He took classes for a year, earning A's in all of them.

Tomás transferred to the state university, where so many pieces of his life came together, not always harmoniously. Some semesters he loved his classes and got A's, and some semesters he bristled, resisted, and did poorly. Sometimes he felt intellectually alive, other times his insecurities hijacked him. He changed his major five or six times. He had several serious health and legal problems. The volatile brew of love, anger, confusion, and deep sorrow from his childhood remained, though by now, he says, his father "knew that if he hit my mother again, I'm gonna rise up because at this point, I'm way bigger than him." He began to "disappear into the library," forcing himself to develop the discipline that would direct and deepen his intellectual joy, "me struggling with the book, me getting bored with the book, just training myself to sit there and try to find a way in." It took Tomás eight years to graduate. But he did. He entered a master's program in political science and did well, having found his balance. He then was accepted into a prestigious doctoral program and was far along when I met him, pen poised over Hegel. "I wish it all could have happened with the sudden force of Saint Paul's conversion," Tomás said with bemused resignation, "but it turned out to be a long, meandering journey."

———————

Tomás's journey contains examples of the ways schools crush the desire to learn. Disregard for students' backgrounds, or, worse, degrading them; class and racial bigotry institutionalized in curriculum, counseling, and teaching; the brute assertion of power. But his journey also includes various expressions of what he unabashedly calls "love": the care exhibited by his teachers in the multiracial primary grades and, in quite a different way, the care conveyed by a high school teacher exposing him to a kind of art he might not otherwise discover—or discover in such an inviting manner.

Because of the obvious connection between a teacher's introduction of a subject and a student's discovery of it, we can miss the strategy, at times artfulness, involved in initiating discovery. Consider the quite different ways the teachers we just met introduced theater, debate, the economics of gender inequality, and the making of art. To be sure, we don't always need another person to mediate our discoveries, but in many cases, it is someone more knowledgeable, from a family member to a peer to a teacher, who creates the conditions for a generative encounter with the new.

Knowledge figures powerfully in these stories. Tiffany Gamboa is on a quest to learn about the economic and social conditions that affect her community, recoiling at the thought of being "an ignorant little girl." Her teacher, Erica Garza, "[fell] in love with history" when she was exposed to women's history and the history of non-dominant racial and ethnic groups (like hers) in the United States. Mr. Johnson's classes in physics and humanities provided a cognitive lifeline to Chris Kurosawa, and it was an intellectual teaser, an esoteric reference from Greek mythology, that jolted him to "never [want] to be ignorant again." And as Tomás Herrera navigated his rocky odyssey through school, he relished his shop teacher's ethic of "millimetric accuracy" as well as his English teacher Mr. Minervini's passion and skill as a reader. We rarely see these two ways of using our minds brought together—the machine shop and literature—yet Tomás received intellectual and emotional sustenance from both. It is telling that in every story, knowledge is not only valued and used but also affects people's sense of who they are, from the young writers gaining a fuller appreciation of themselves as *writers*, to the student nurse reflecting on her teacher's judgment that "I was meant to do this," to the identity-shaping intellectual journeys of Tiffany, Chris, and Tomás.

There is another kind of knowledge at play here—the knowledge that teachers and other educators gain from observing students and listening to them. Our era is understandably concerned about surveillance and dehumanizing scrutiny, but we need to keep in mind as well the importance of being seen, of being brought into focus—especially in social and institutional settings where not being visible and not being heard results in diminishment. We're talking about a certain kind of seeing and listening attuned to ability, desire, and environment. The yield is a rich, complex knowledge that blends the diagnostic and the intuitive, the calculated judgment and the hunch. This knowledge is purposeful, combines with knowledge of subject matter to help people grow and realize who they want to be.

This richness of knowledge is matched by the rich diversity of personalities and classroom styles of the teachers who are attuned to student ability and able to foster it: the alpha male welding instructor, Mr. Ladsen; the reflective and intuitive debate coach, Ms. Rodriguez; the cerebral, distant Mr. Johnson. We will encounter an ever more varied array of teachers in subsequent chapters, but let's dwell for a moment on Tomás's algebra teacher, Mr. Connor. Mr. Connor was not known for his dedication beyond the terms of his contract. But something about Tomás caught his attention, touched him, and he saw through Tomás's anger and resistance to the ability beneath—not a common occurrence. By tutoring his student, he got Tomás to realize that ability himself. Mr. Connor's response to Tomás raises the hopeful possibility that a teacher's growth-fostering perception is not a fixed quality—you either got it or you don't—but can be called forth in the right setting, perhaps even be taught.

CHAPTER FOUR

FROM LIFE LESSONS TO THE CLASSROOM

The light went on for me and for a number of the people I interviewed in school, but that transformation can also begin beyond the borders of the campus and then lead back to the classroom. A girlfriend or boyfriend or older sibling helps you see that life has more in store for you, urges you to try something new, to take a class or enter a program, to straighten up and fly right. Or dulling routine, a dead-end job, your own gnawing boredom can lead to an epiphany, to sudden clarity about your future that leads you back to school. Occasionally the epiphany comes by chance, a lucky encounter: you see a performance or a certain kind of work and you know in your bones that this is for you. And at times the epiphany is gained at great cost, life-threatening illness or accident, family disruption, incarceration. Your past and future are refigured as change is forced upon you.

During his two years at community college, Lance O'Leary had earned a mere eight units of credit, enrolling to satisfy his parents, but, in his words, skating by, doing the bare minimum, making good money in a restaurant, partying every night. "I was living crazy," he said, "going nowhere."

One evening, Lance got into a terrible motorcycle accident on the freeway, with multiple internal injuries, broken bones, and brain trauma. He was in the hospital for three months. When he was released, he was "really shaking, stuttering, slurring my words, and using a walker." Lance had a lot of time to think. "I didn't begin immediately to get my act together, but I realized I needed to start doing things of substance. I didn't know exactly what I wanted to do, but I just knew I wanted to do it well." His recovery took years, and along the way a counselor at his old college made the improbable suggestion that Lance try a welding class. Lance enjoyed working with his hands, which unfortunately were still shaky. But that counselor was onto something, for Lance took to the challenge. The two instructors in the welding program encouraged and aided him, and he learned as well from watching the more experienced students around him. He would brace himself against the wall of his welding booth and steady his arm on his hip, producing uneven welds "that looked like snot." But with time, Lance got more control. Welding became part of his extended occupational therapy. The tremors subsided. He was really liking the work. "I'm going to get paid to melt metal and make loud noises," he laughs. "When I was arc welding, I almost felt like Zeus, the god of thunder!" Today Lance is certified in multiple welding processes and is finishing his associate of science degree. "It's been five years, and I think I get a little better every day. Welding has been my savior."

Trauma as severe as Lance's often does not end well. In addition to physical and cognitive limitations, there are strained relationships and lost jobs, anger and depression, and sometimes a downward spiral of addiction. However, a growing body of research on *post-traumatic growth* also documents the significant positive change that can follow disaster. In a remarkable moment during our interview, Lance declared that his accident "was the best thing that happened to me." A community college student I know said something similar about a spinal cord injury that left him paralyzed from the waist down. After running the streets and spending close to two years in state prison, Henry was shot in a skirmish with a rival gang. A grueling year of rehab was followed by a return to the streets, now in a wheelchair and lost—and then, finally, Henry sought sanctuary in his parents' house, where he thought about what lay in front of him. The result was enrollment in the community college where he built a new life, academically and socially—when I went with him across campus, it seemed like every third person knew him—and found his calling: working with young people who were in the kind of trouble he knew so well. As he put it, the shooting and its aftermath led him to discover someone he never knew he was.[1]

Devastating injury led Lance and Henry to a fundamental re-assessment of their lives; such reassessment can also come when someone is behind bars. One man in a community college culinary program claimed that the turning point for him came when he found out in prison that his wife was pregnant and he was going to be a father. Another student at the same college had a much longer road to travel. He was in and out of jail for decades on petty drug charges, swallowing or shooting anything he could hustle on the street. Then during his last incarceration, as he was *in his cell*, about to snort methamphetamine he had scored inside, it hit him with blunt force: What am I doing? What is going to happen to me? He flushed the drugs down the toilet and began a journey through halfway houses and to a two-year college degree. These men's realizations led them to school, where they found both structure—one class logically followed another in their trade programs—and support from other students who had also been incarcerated and teachers and tutors who took an interest in their development.

———

For as long as he can remember, Christian Tejada had a rough go of it in school, both with academics and behavior. He spent much of his time, when he attended, in special education classes, for he was so hard to control. Christian grew into a big, tough kid, a fearless fighter, a quick temper. By the time he was in his teens, he was in juvenile detention camp, then in county jail. Christian had a fractured relationship with his own parents but was close to another family in the neighborhood; both the mother and father were teachers, and they had a son who was a few years older than Christian. Christian wrote to them from jail, and they visited him. Eventually, they started talking to him about next steps, urging him to go to school. Christian held a fiery jumble of emotions—when his time was getting short, he told his buddies he'd probably be back in a few months. But something in his surrogate family's appeal got to him. They believed in him. And he had an idea of where his life was headed. So he tentatively agreed to attend the local community college, his motivation a mix of anger and pragmatism. "I figured that if I am going to play the game, then I needed to know how the game is played. . . . You know, like, 'You put me in jail. Well, I'll show you, motherfucker.'"

Christian's motivation would change and deepen over time, but upon entering community college he found that his scholastic revenge wasn't going to be easy. Anger was potent fuel, but over the long haul, he would need more than anger to sustain him. After all those years of academic turmoil, Christian had to begin with basic English and basic math. He signed up for a history course as well. "Man, it was hard. I had so much catching up to do." Christian is about 5'10", strikingly broad across the shoulders, a big voice and a big laugh—an intense presence. I can imagine the younger Christian, his raw energy spring-loaded for trouble, but redirected now toward learning to write and calculate. To his good fortune, a friend of his uncle's intervened; this fellow was an English major at the local university, and he was close in age to Christian. He would pick up Christian on the Sundays before an English composition was due and painstakingly go over the essay as Christian, grumbling and cursing but hunkering down, slowly improved his writing.

Yet it was history that turned out to be the big surprise. Spotty as his education was, Christian had been exposed to history before—the American Revolution, the Civil War—but the course he was now taking was different. It was social history, and the teacher focused on everyday lives, common folk, civil rights, labor movements, and the like. Christian had never thought of history this way, and he "ate it up," taking more courses from that instructor. "I was never any good in school," he said, "but I was getting really good at it now." He eventually transferred to the university, majoring in history.

The angry and hungry young man who came out of prison began to reshape his life with those writing and history classes and that godsend of a tutor. I met Christian six or seven years later as a graduate student in a class I taught, and over the past decade have watched him continue to grow, to tutor inmates at juvenile hall, to think about who he wants to be and the role he wants to play in society. Now he works tirelessly as a labor organizer and is considering, at his union's urging, law school to study labor law. Learning has shifted from an act of individual defiance to a means of participating in a broader social arena and cause.

———————

Physical trauma and incarceration are cataclysmic events, but awareness can come in more modest ways as life unfolds day after day. In the final scene of *Fat City*, John Huston's unsparing movie about small-time boxers in Stockton, California, Billy Tully, his best days behind him at thirty, is sitting in a diner with Ernie Munger, a younger boxer, bruised but hopeful.[2] Tully slowly turns on his stool and looks out at the tables of older men silently playing cards. The camera moves in, Tully's face filling the screen. The camera momentarily stops—and Tully's eyes register quiet terror. He sees his future stretching dully out before him, empty and without hope. This is the experience described by those I interviewed whose work and life prospects compelled them back to school.

One young woman had an entry-level job in a retail store, assisting shoppers, replenishing stock, accounting for her sales at day's end. One morning looking out over the shop, in a moment reminiscent of Billy Tully's glimpse of his future, she saw herself working there ten years later, standing behind a display of clothing, stuck, hating her life. She decided right then to quit and return to school. A former bank teller tells a similar story. She recalls one morning at her window, noticing the light coming through the door as a customer opened it, thinking about the months and years ahead of her, the sliver of light repeated and repeated, the same routine, in the same bank, at the same window.

After he graduated from high school, Manny Aguilar went to work at a large supermarket, starting as a bagger and progressing to stocking shelves on the night shift. The next step up was checker, bringing with it a raise in pay and maybe better hours. He had to take a test, a "simple" test, he explains, "just general questions." But he failed it. He had been at the market for four years, not satisfied with the work and surrounded by people who were "unhappy and complaining." Manny had never done well in school—he was diagnosed with a learning disability and placed in low-level classes—so failing this test tapped into a long history of insecurity. The humiliation of his failure and the general "negativity" of his coworkers about the job itself led Manny to decide he couldn't stay at the market any longer. This was a decision with big consequences. His brother also worked at the market and got him the job, a job with benefits and a clear career pathway. Quitting would leave him without moorings and would baffle and upset his family, working people who covet employment with security. He could study for the test and take it again. He was a responsible worker, and management wanted him to succeed. But he'd hit the wall. Should he go back to school—something he never thought he'd do? His girlfriend was in his corner. "You need to get out of there," she urged, "You can do better." His deep dissatisfaction and her support—"Her belief in me gave me the push to actually do it"—led him to walk into his manager's office and quit. "I didn't know what I was going to do, but I couldn't go on." Manny was "always good at building things," so he picked up odd jobs and entered community college in the fall, taking remedial courses to build his skills, "starting at rock bottom."

I am talking with Manny seven years after he quit the supermarket. He is now in his early thirties, soft-spoken and eloquent, polite and matter-of-fact, even when talking about the difficult aspects of his life. He doesn't have a lot to say about his education from the primary grades through high school—a long, uneventful, and unpleasant history that he'd just as soon abbreviate. What does emerge is the picture of a kid isolated by his disability, laying low in the classroom to avoid participation, left alone by some teachers, either out of sympathy or irresponsibility. He pauses and says simply, "I felt like no one." Out in the schoolyard, however, Manny lived in a different world. He was a skilled dancer, and hung out with "the cool kids," participating in hip-hop, breakdancing, anything but invisible. "I felt like I had two lives." Manny grew into an adult who was physically adroit and had a circle of friends but carried a deep reservoir of shame about all things academic.

During the time Manny was working at the market, he was getting high with his buddies and hanging out on the streets where he grew up, a tough neighborhood in Northeast Los Angeles. Like so many young men in neighborhoods like these, Manny never got into serious trouble, but he drifted dangerously close to it, could easily have ended up in the wrong place at the wrong time. So he'd work at a job that was increasingly burdensome, then blow off steam on the streets. One day he got into a fight, was arrested, and went before a judge who let him off with a warning. "I saw what was going to become of me," he said. Friends were ending up in jail. One was killed. "I saw the pattern," and it scared him to the core. All this was backdrop to him walking with finality into his manager's office. His social life and his work life had together hit the point of crisis. A dead end.

Manny didn't know much about how to be successful in school and was the first in his family to go to college. When he initially set foot on his college campus, he was pretty much traveling without a guidebook, so he "latched onto people who knew more than I did and just followed them." This is how he learned to navigate the place—selecting classes, using the tutoring center, figuring out financial aid. He also struck up relationships with tutors and other students who could help him develop his writing and mathematical skills. In turn, he built or repaired things for them. "I knew my weaknesses, and I made friends who had the strengths I lacked—I created this community." In a sense, Manny brought his social acumen from the playground and the joints on the street into the schoolhouse. Over time, he learned strategies to compensate for his reading disability. He took increasingly difficult courses in mathematics. His writing improved. He began to set his sights on architecture, a blend of his talent for construction and his growing academic achievement.

As Manny describes finding his bearings in college, he talks about being "motivated to hit this architecture thing full force." He uses the metaphor of seeing a light at the end of the tunnel and keeping a sharp focus on it. "It was running through my mind when I woke up. 'How am I going to get there? How am I going to get to that light?'" He took classes at three different community colleges in order to fulfill all the requirements he needed for architecture school, and describes the "momentum" he had as he entered that school. By the time I interview Manny, he has graduated and is studying to take his licensing exam. His portrayal of sad isolation in the classroom has been replaced with a vocabulary of force, agency, and light.

————————

Family or friends can play a powerful role in getting us to see things in a new light or in guiding us right when we most need guidance. While Christian was in jail, his surrogate family helped anchor him and eventually convinced him to try college. When Manny was struggling with his job in the supermarket, his girlfriend's encouragement to quit provided the final push he needed. Some people speak of the direction and emotional support they got from parents, grandparents, aunts, or uncles. Such testimony makes sense, for the family is central to a child's performance in school. More formally educated and economically able parents provide assistance with homework, transportation to enrichment activities, and additional resources like tutoring. Where parents have limited formal education and minimal resources, they often provide emotional support and celebrate their children's achievement. And they set an example by the way they lead their lives, "motivating me through their hard work," as one student put it. Parents across the economic spectrum can also fail to support their children, even derail them—and I heard those stories—but the majority of the people I interviewed spoke positively about the role their parents played in their development. A college senior initiated a further hour-long conversation with me to make sure I fully understood the profound influence his working-class father has had on his academic success.

People mention significant figures who come later in life. Neighbors or employers or friends and lovers pass along information about a school or program, and sometimes more specific guidance about services, and routines, and ways to behave. This imparting of knowledge is especially important for those who don't come from college-educated families and who themselves lack a history of success in school—think of the way Manny "latched onto" his more knowledgeable peers once he entered college.

Support, example, knowledge, guidance—all this matters immensely, but I think that, at heart, what most moves us toward change is the realization that someone we value believes in us. We saw the power this belief had for Christian and Manny, and for many others in this book, myself included. The affirmation of another person's ability is one of the beautiful and mysterious things we can do for each other.

Lilia Mendoza knew Martin from the clubs, fun, part of the scene, a casual friendship that turned romantic. Martin was going to the local community college, dallying with it at first, but getting more serious about school, veering toward math and science. Lilia's story was quite different, and she tells it thoughtfully, pausing with a soft *mmmm* as she looks at the ceiling, then picking up the tale, generous to all involved.

When Lilia was growing up, her family moved from city to city, and by the time she was in high school, she was repeatedly truant, staying home to care for her newborn baby sister. After several more high schools, including a continuation school, she quit going altogether. Lilia moved in with her grandmother and began a series of entry-level jobs in a supermarket and then in two retail stores, working during the day and reveling in the club scene at night. This work-party rhythm was lively and sustaining for a while, but there came a point, as Lilia put it, where her work "got really old. I felt like I wasn't using my brain. I wasn't doing anything challenging or fulfilling." Lilia had that sobering recognition: "I didn't want to end up being here for the rest of my life."

Lilia hadn't thought much about education, and when she did, it was a distant abstraction, something she might do someday—maybe.

As her relationship with Martin deepened, he began encouraging her to enroll at the community college, voicing the worry she harbored: Do you want to be doing this job forever? "I guess," Lilia mused, "he wanted better for me and saw some potential in me." But Martin's encouragement met with Lilia's doubts and insecurities. She was, after all, a high school dropout. No one in her family had done well in school or cared much about it. "I didn't think school would work out for me." Martin persisted. Finally, Lilia signed up for a class, "kinda just to shut him up."

Lilia took a French class "simply for fun." She asked a girlfriend to take it with her, someone to study with. She ended up doing well and really enjoyed herself. Martin pushed her to attend full time and guided her to a program for first-generation college students. Still insecure and nervous—"I don't belong here"—Lilia started with basic classes, then literature and the arts, then more mathematics. She reached the point where she was unhappy when she was *not* in school. She is now twenty-seven and has recently finished a class on differential equations. She tutors math, something she loves doing, and is preparing to transfer to a four-year engineering program. Her elbows on the table, she cradles her head in her hands. She nods and smiles, says she still has times when she doubts herself but cannot imagine life without being in school.

If Lilia's childhood was unstable, Maddy Mullen's was downright chaotic. Her mother and father were heavy drug users, and when her mother left Maddy's father to escape his abuse, Maddy and her three older siblings "hopped from family home to family home." Then came a long stretch living out of their car at a campground, then a homeless shelter on Skid Row that, fortunately, was close to an elementary school. Maddy started kindergarten—and thrived. As she explained it, she had nothing to go home to—didn't really have a home—so she stayed in the after-school program, which included tutoring and enrichment activities. She was above grade level in both reading and math, precocious and assertive, asking her teacher for harder math problems to solve, more difficult books to read.

Though her mother continued to use drugs, she entered a stable relationship, got a job, and qualified for subsidized housing. Secure housing was a blessing for Maddy and her brother and sisters, but there still was little structure in Maddy's young life. The kids pretty much raised themselves and each other. This lack of structure and guidance contributed to a bad turn of events when Maddy entered middle school. She "started to hang around with the wrong crowd," was going to parties in the seventh grade, ditched classes. Her grades were so bad, she was at risk of being held back. "Who cares about middle school," she thought. "None of this matters."

Maddy at nineteen is a college freshman. She is fast and eloquent and crackling smart. I can imagine her both as a little girl taking great pleasure in besting a kid two grades above her in a math game and as the seventh grader proclaiming that middle school is a drag and a big waste of time. She laughingly describes herself as "argumentative" and a lover of debate. I am awed by her ability to roll with the punches, her astounding resilience. She is a scrapper, hard-charging, and has a keen eye for injustice. She wants to be a public interest lawyer.

Given Maddy's middle school record, it was likely that she would drop out of high school. Her older sister, Dakota, three years ahead of Maddy, was also headed for trouble, but a few years into high school she began to see that her behavior was leading to a dead end. Dakota cleaned up her act and started concentrating on her studies—and she urged Maddy to do the same. "You have to start now," she warned her rebellious younger sister. "I swear you do." She told Maddy about Advanced Placement courses and encouraged her to take them. She began to look at colleges and passed along to Maddy what she was learning. She became in effect a college counselor and oriented her sister toward higher education. Maddy focused on her classes. She played sports. To support herself and contribute to the family, she went to work, at one point holding down three jobs while playing volleyball and taking AP classes. Maddy filled her life to the brim with activities that provided structure and concrete goals and that brought other adults into her orbit. But it was Dakota who reached her at that pivotal transition into high school. "My sister was my biggest inspiration," Maddy says with conviction. "She was my mom."

———————

A physician in his early sixties remembers the family doctor coming to his home when he was sick, describes the sensation of the stetho-scope on his chest, and the way that cool disc somehow made him feel better. He knew then that he wanted to be a doctor. Sometimes what we want to do with our lives is that immediate and clear. And sometimes our calling comes more slowly, incrementally. In any case, we are drawn to the activity itself, an academic subject or a kind of work or something performative. We might encounter it in school, enhanced by a teacher's passion and skill. Or the encounter can be outside of the classroom, as was the case with the doctor's house call. We have the recognition that we have found something valuable—or it found us. There is a sense of fit, a where-have-you-been-all-my-life quality that can stir strong emotion. A community college engineer-ing student remembers "getting the chills" when she visited the Jet Propulsion Lab and saw the prototypes of the rovers that were sent to Mars. Especially powerful are those occasions when people are unfulfilled or searching and find that meaningful pursuit at a critical time in their lives.

Sally Hamilton grew up in a small midwestern town, was a good girl and a good student, liked riding horses and was good at that too. Home life was caring but traditional and religious and the expectation for the girls was "to do well in school, get married, and have kids." Though Sally excelled in school, she didn't have particularly close relationships with her teachers. "School didn't open a lot of possibilities," she says. "I saw no path that seemed right for me." And, increasingly, she sought something different. She tried volleyball and cheerleading, but "had a long, gangly body and didn't know how to use it." As she puts it, life seemed "narrow."

When she was fourteen, Sally's mother took her to see *The Nutcracker*, her first ballet. Sally was "mesmerized and enchanted" by the glamour and spectacle. She especially liked "The Waltz of the Snowflakes," dancers in white tutus, snow falling, lilting music. She spent the next day looking through the phone book, pleading with her mother for lessons, but the nearest studio was a long car drive away. Sally was undeterred and eventually found a place closer to home. She stopped eating lunch at school to save money. After several false starts—one place provided little more than tape-recorded instruction—Sally found a wonderful studio with a teacher who would mentor and encourage her, recommend books, and open up a world that called to her. Sally met older girls who were more accomplished "with strong, artistic bodies. . . . I liked the way they moved and wanted to be like them," Sally says. "I never had anything I wanted to do all the time. Dance became my obsession." She would go on to study dance in college and pursue a career as a professional dancer, winning awards for choreography and participating in various arts-in-the-schools programs that had her dancing for younger versions of herself.

Though their backgrounds were very different, Deborah Frankel would have understood immediately Sally's enchantment with dance and her desire to be with and learn from other dancers. When she was in her early twenties, Deborah immigrated with her husband from Israel to the United States. She had done well in school in the subjects she liked—languages, art—and terribly in the subjects she didn't. While in Israel, she was a docent in a museum and tutored disadvantaged kids, and then, partly because she didn't know what else to do, got married and traveled widely before settling in California. She got a job making jewelry for a cousin of her husband's, and it was this cousin who drew out of Deborah her curiosity about high fashion and styling hair. The cousin knew someone at the Vidal Sassoon Academy, which had an apprenticeship program, and arranged a visit.

Deborah remembers the rows and rows of mirrors reflecting each other that made the large room seem even larger and more enveloping. The beats of European house music filled the air, redolent with shampoos and conditioners. Before the mirrors were workstations with novice stylists attending to clients, instructors moving among them, giving advice, joking, scissors in leather holsters slung across their bodies. The place exuded cool—the clothes the instructors wore, the color and cut of their hair, the ease of their interaction. Deborah was enthralled. "I just knew right away," Deborah explains, "that this is what I need to do with my life." She had liked learning languages. She appreciated art. The museum work and the tutoring were fulfilling. But nothing in her young life affected her like the activity flowing around her. "I never had this feeling before when I walked into a place or learned something new. I wanted to know what they knew, and I wanted to be what they were." Deborah would go on to learn what those master stylists knew and become one of them, at the center of a studio's training program, instructing aspiring stylists in the science and art of cutting and coloring hair.

Unlike Sally and Deborah, Maisha Curry had an increasingly rocky time in school. She got decent grades and loved sports but just couldn't put up with high school itself, was absent a lot, even got kicked off the swim team because she wouldn't go to practice. When she started dating a guy with a car, things went from bad to worse. "It was, like, 'Oh my God, I don't even want to be here.'" She had to meet with a truant officer. Her mother got hit with a fine. Her passing grades notwithstanding, she was told she might not graduate.

A friend of hers was a photographer for the school newspaper, and on one of the days Maisha showed up for school, she accompanied her friend to the journalism office to pick up an assignment. Maisha had certainly seen the newspaper on campus, but, as with most things connected to school, it barely registered. So there she was in the office, looking around, curious, admitting to the faculty advisor that she didn't know there was a *newspaper* here, also telling the advisor that she loved sports and enjoyed writing. "Well," the advisor said, "we don't have a sports editor; would you like to do that?" Maisha wondered what exactly a sports editor does, but figured "why not." She started covering all the sporting events and soon was given her own column, "Maisha's Sports." The local newspaper hired her as a stringer, writing stories on sports and other community events. Maisha went from being chronically truant to never missing a class. "I knew why I was waking up every day," she says, "why I was going to school."

Journalism provided Maisha an identity that was new to her and liberating. "It was the first time I felt like I was free . . . There are constraints, of course, space, a certain way to write . . . but there was so much freedom within that space." The anarchic freedom that came with rejecting school was replaced with freedom of written expression—expression within constraints, as Maisha notes, but expression with a purpose. And it was expression that involved others. "Are you coming to cover our game?" her readers would ask. Maisha was achieving a public presence, which affected her sense of self and her performance in school.

Before she found journalism, Maisha could at least maintain respectable grades while rebelling against the structures of high school. Not so for Billy Knott, a bright kid who attended class sporadically to kick ideas around with his teachers—but kicking ideas around was the extent of it. He spent most of his days hanging out in the band room playing piano, getting drunk at lunch, racking up absences and failing grades, and driving his mother crazy. Billy was, in his words, "just a shithead." Oh, and he decided, with no job, to propose marriage to his seventeen-year-old girlfriend. He shakes his head and speaks with an inviting self-awareness: "Talk about rebellious idiocy . . . It's like the checklist of dumb things to do as a teenager." One day his mother tells him she's taking him to lunch and instead drives him to the Air Force recruiting office in a neighboring city, "kicks me out of the car and drives away." It was in the Air Force that Billy discovered air traffic control, and it transformed his behavior.

"I was fascinated by the whole system," Billy explains, "how air traffic works, the navigation, all that. I just fell in love with it." The technical training "is notoriously hard," but Billy found that "if I just sit my butt in the chair," something he rebelled against in high school, he could learn this difficult material. He was learning that he could learn. "If I'm interested in something, work at it, my curiosity will be rewarded." Gaining new knowledge "had a really profound effect on me, made me want to continue learning." Billy's growing competence brought material reward: He could support himself. And there is a potent, verifiable outcome to his skill—it has life-and-death consequences. Finally, there are social benefits, "recognition and respect from my peers . . . the rewards of being identified with a group of high-performing individuals." This nourishing blend of intellectual challenge, structure, and kinship with like-minded peers made the light go on for Billy Knott. "I had never experienced that before," he says. And the experience took hold. Billy's hunger for knowledge stayed with him through and beyond the military, was self-sustaining. He would attend college on the GI Bill. "I loved the research, the lectures . . . listening and asking questions." He pauses. "I'm not done learning," he says simply, crisply. "I just don't want to stop."

As distinct as these activities are—dance, styling hair, journalism, air traffic control—they are all embedded in traditions, in webs of practice and codes of behavior, right and wrong ways to do things. Participating in a tradition makes you feel part of something bigger than yourself, gives direction to your life and a sense of community. The newcomer wants to be like others who are more proficient, wants to engage in the activity with them and learn from them. This attraction can provide potent entry points for people who in the past might not have seen the value of other skills or bodies of knowledge. The budding journalist has to know the conventions of written English, the novice stylist the biology and chemistry of treating hair. Subjects that might have once been thought irrelevant or forbidding become meaningful, and people will work hard to master them. Worlds open onto other worlds.

―――――――

We want our lives to matter, even if we say or do things that suggest otherwise. One of the great rewards of being a teacher is that it has allowed me to witness this pursuit of meaning, and at times participate in it. I've been exploring some of the ways people's lives have been redirected toward education by events that occurred, for the most part, outside of school. Yet even if teachers weren't initially involved, responsive teachers become crucial once the light goes on. Think of those instructors willing to work with the neurologically impaired Lance O'Leary, an unlikely candidate for a trade like welding. Consider, too, the importance of targeted educational initiatives: several of the people we met benefited from programs for first-generation college students. And the community college itself figures in many of these stories. Labeled The People's College because of its open-access mission, the community college provides opportunity for entry or reentry into education for people who have few other pathways to the classroom.

The social and educational barriers between life outside and inside school can be both forbidding and permeable. Even though I brought little of my life at home into the classroom—like my mother, I saw home and school as separate domains—what was going on at home had a profound effect on my performance in school, my ability to focus, to pursue an interest, to form friendships. And what I learned at school about math or history or about formal learning itself—I carried all that beyond the schoolyard. We certainly don't need school to acquire knowledge and skill and to create deeply meaningful and economically viable lives, but there is a synergy possible when partitions between school and life-beyond-school are breached, when we redefine and repurpose this place called school and are able to bring the spheres of our lives closer together. Then education provides structure within which our desires can be fulfilled.

————

Brody Walsh's path to a meaningful education couldn't be further from that of Mary Lopez's, but both journeys have awful twists and turns that led to lives profoundly different from where these two were when trauma hit. They glimpsed a future they desperately did not want. There were others in their lives who affected them deeply. And they were drawn to potentially transformative ways to use their minds in school or school-like settings to achieve goals that would have been unimaginable a few years before.

Brody is a medic in one of our country's Special Operations Forces, and we spoke by phone a few days before his most recent deployment. He began by telling me about his troubled history in school. Though he had a lot of fun in the elementary grades, his transition to middle school was "a real culture shock," for the "cliques and pecking order" were obvious and rigid. As a White boy whose mother was a nurse and father was a plumber, he didn't fit in with the rich White kids or with the Mexican kids from "the poorer side of town." He found some release in sports, especially surfing. And he developed into the class clown. He made friends.

It was in high school, however, where "the wheels started to come off." Brody longed for a tough contact sport but didn't make the football team, a crushing blow to his sense of self. His father encouraged him to go out for swimming, but Brody picked up the social class cues right away and saw how the other parents "looked down" on his mother and father. Reflecting back on it, Brody says he "kept looking for meaning and purpose," and he eventually found it with the Mexican kids, particularly those in gang life. As so many young people who join gangs explain, the affiliation, at least initially, gives them a sense of community: older guys pull their cars over to talk to them, they're welcome in people's houses, they hang out together, getting high. Brody's physical skills were channeled into fighting; by his sophomore year he was expelled from school and in juvenile hall. Through all this, Brody's parents were beside themselves, doing everything they could think of to get him to straighten out. Nothing worked. He was building "heavy street cred," was "an up-and-comer," felt himself to be, as so many street kids do, "invincible."

The novelist Pete Dexter once said something to the effect that violence never unfolds as you think it will and, in the midst of it, is unlike what you might have imagined.[3] Brody was on the fast track to either an early grave or a long time in prison, then the event occurred that interrupted that future. He and his crew challenged guys from another gang, and before he knew it, they were "getting our asses kicked" and sprinting madly to safety. Suddenly blood splattered alongside Brody, and his buddy lurched forward, his femoral artery cut. The others braked and turned—what to do?—as Brody dropped to his knees and thrust his hand into the wound, putting pressure on the artery. The boys hauled their injured friend to their car and got him to an emergency room. Shaken, Brody went in search of his girlfriend, a young Mexican American woman he met in his adopted neighborhood. He loved her deeply and would marry her. "She was with me through thick and thin," he says. "She saw potential in me even when I lost my way." Standing before her, his friend's blood all over him, he realized all he could lose. He felt a lot less invincible.

Brody began to pull his life together. He went to adult school and got his GED. He worked for his father. He rented a "crappy little shack in the hills" and moved in with his girlfriend. He saw clearly the need for a reliable and challenging career and decent pay, and revived a childhood dream—"it came screaming back to me"—to be a medic in Special Forces. "The fight, the whole thing scared the shit out of me," Brody says, his voice dropping, "but it also showed me I could be calm in the middle of a horrible event." He counts that lifesaving experience as a life-changing moment for him.

When Brody was a child, his mother would explain and demonstrate things related to medicine—like how to remove stitches—and by the time he was nine, she had him in CPR classes. He has a vivid memory of his younger cousin having a seizure and how his mother "remained calm and knew exactly what to do." Her grace under pressure made a deep impression on him. Thinking about his mother and about his own response to his wounded friend, Brody at twenty-nine muses, "I never wanted to feel helpless or not be able to help someone. I wanted to be the person who can bring calm to chaos and be the one people look to for help." When he turned eighteen, Brody enlisted and headed off to basic training.

Much of Brody's schooling was so disrupted that he lacked the academic skills needed for advanced medic training, an intense, yearlong program. But he "really, really wanted this"—a phrase he uses several times—so he dedicated himself to his studies in a way he never had before. His instructors must have perceived his desire, for they tutored him after class. They also taught him how to study and how to take notes, providing, in effect, an academic boot camp. Brody tells me with regret about a math teacher he had in middle school who "really tried to reach me." He remembers saying to her, "When am I ever going to use algebra in real life?" There is no doubt whatsoever about the usefulness of the math he struggled to learn during medic training; he would be making quick judgments about drug dosages in the most dangerous situations imaginable. His education was now contributing directly to Brody Walsh becoming the person he longed to be.

————————

At sixteen and having her first child, Mary Lopez didn't know what to expect. Her labor was long and difficult, and when she finally gave birth to her son, the activity in the delivery room changed dramatically, "like an alarm went off." Exhausted and scared, Mary asked a nurse what happened, and the nurse told her that they thought things were going to be okay because her son was moving his legs. His legs? Mary realized something was terribly wrong with her baby. She didn't know the term they used—spina bifida—but within hours her son was taken to a major hospital nearby to close up his spine.

Mary was transferred to a recovery room frightened and disoriented. Another woman was there, and the staff would bring her healthy baby in every few hours to nurse. A social worker came to talk to Mary, and all Mary heard was that her son would never walk. Never sit up. Mary went home without her baby and broke down. "You have all these dreams and hopes about your child," she tells me, thinking back on that day, "but I didn't even know if he was going to live."

Mary had dropped out of high school after the first week of her freshman year. It made a lot more sense to work. Her three older siblings had quit as well, and all had jobs. Her parents didn't have high school degrees, worked hard, created a loving family, raised good kids. "I never realized what school was all about," Mary says. "I kinda thought it was a place you go because your parents worked during the day."

When she was fifteen, Mary fell in love, and against her parents' wishes got married. Both she and her husband worked for minimum wage at fast-food restaurants and couldn't afford proper prenatal care, so Mary had no clue about the severity of her son's disability. During the first year of his life, he underwent close to a dozen operations, bringing Mary into sustained contact with pediatric surgeons, neurologists, urologists, social workers, physical therapists—bewildering to anyone, especially a working-class adolescent mother. Mary began to think that if she was going to be a good parent and do right by her child, she needed to get educated, to get back into school, for she "didn't know the difference between a neurologist and a urologist, and I didn't understand what they were saying to me."

Once her son, Johnny, stabilized, Mary signed up for a class at the local community college, a speech class. To her surprise, she really liked it. She enjoyed listening to her peers give their speeches and got a kick out of speaking herself—it reminded her of drama in junior high. Next term she took psychology, which she also liked, then, semester by semester, she completed basic skills courses in math and English to make up for all she had missed in school. She could only take one course per semester, for she had to work full time and care for Johnny and for the other children she would have. Her husband became increasingly resistant to her going to school, so she had to deal with that tension in her household as well. But Mary was hooked. "School gave me a little time away from work, family, and taking care of children," she writes in an email. "Being a student made me feel like I was smart and that I had the potential to learn and grow out of poverty. Getting good grades and encouragement from my teachers reinforced my hopes and dreams." A few years before, school had seemed like a giant waste of time; now it was vibrant with possibility.

It took Mary ten years to complete her courses at the community college. She transferred to a university on the other side of town—"How could I ask my children to go to college if I didn't?"—and by then was able to attend full time. Mary would go on over the years to get a master's degree in social work and a doctorate in education, working in some clinical or administrative capacity with battered women, abused children, and incarcerated youth. "And I still don't have a high school diploma!" she laughs.

Mary begins reflecting on how her long career evolved since those first classes at the community college. She increasingly found that she "loved learning," and the more she learned, the more she wanted to learn—the cognitive momentum we've seen with other people in this book. Several times as we talk, she uses with emphasis the word *exposure*—exposure to ideas and bodies of knowledge, but also exposure to kinds of work, ways to make a living that helped others, women in trouble or children in need. She met people doing this work or training to do it, saw how they prepared for it, what courses they took, the opportunities they pursued. "I was exposed to whole new worlds that I didn't know existed."

And of course, another world she was exposed to, suddenly and harshly, was the world of disability. She had to learn to care and advocate for Johnny—and school emerged as a vehicle to develop her advocacy. She did indeed become a strong advocate. Johnny would go on to graduate from high school and, with a care provider, live independently. But, she says, what she finally came to realize—and her own training in social work solidified this realization—was that her difficulty in understanding Johnny's medical professionals was not just a function of her own level of education but more so the result of professionals' inability to communicate with laypeople. Her education wouldn't change that, but it did provide a career that allowed her to support Johnny. And it provided a level of competence and fluency, a bearing, that enabled her to engage those professionals and, if need be, challenge them. When Mary Lopez signed up for that speech class, she hoped that it would be the first step toward helping her better comprehend what the doctors and social workers were telling her. What she got as well, through her long educational journey, was a change in the way she perceives and acts in the world.

CHAPTER FIVE

EXPECTING MORE
OF YOURSELF

While a number of the people I interviewed had an uneven path to success in school, some did well all the way along. "I created a sense of achievement for myself," a college student told me, "a real sense of satisfaction." At the least, these people had learned how to "do school," finding a routine of adequate performance, moving systematically forward from assignment to assignment, grade to grade. Several were at the top of their class. When the light went on for them, it transformed their understanding of subject matter they thought they knew. Or they deepened their proficiency at intellectual work, exerting more focused effort, operating at a new level of performance. Or they used their education to further develop personal characteristics or social and political commitments that mattered to them.

Several people had a class that changed the way they read literature, including literature they had read just a few years before. As one put it, the teacher "opened up a new way to see these books." For another person, a single book, Toni Morrison's *Beloved*, was the catalyst. No novel or play had affected her that way before, leading her to think differently about what literature could do. And yet another woman took several humanities courses in college that integrated separate areas of study from high school, demonstrating the inter-connection of the literature and painting and music of an era. "My brain came alive," she said, for she now had a more comprehensive way to understand what used to seem like isolated works of art.

For Emma Joyce, a big conceptual shift came with writing itself. Writing in high school, even in her Advanced Placement English class, seemed to Emma to be like "an extended test format" where the student's job is to figure out the "right answer" and present it in a formulaic way: have a clearly stated topic and make a certain number of points with evidence. She thought she might be able to test out of her freshman composition course when she got to college, but her professor told her that though her writing was fundamen-tally sound, it could be improved, and she, the professor, would help her. What followed would have a powerful effect on Emma's understanding of writing and her execution of it. On an essay she wrote on Martin Luther King Jr. and Malcolm X, for example, the professor wrote comments like "This is interesting. What makes you think this?" or "Tell me more about this claim." The professor wasn't looking for a "right answer" but, Emma realized, "wants to know more about what I think," was taking her writing seriously as the expression of someone who has something to say. This response led Emma to want to think harder, write more, to interact with the woman reading her papers. Writing was becoming for Emma a rhetorical act, an activity involving communication and persuasion, vital and interactional, leading to "a fundamental change in the way I thought about education and learning and what it meant to write."

A bit further along in her college career, Katrina LeClair also had a profound shift in her understanding of a subject: mathemat-ics. Though she had her bumpy times with math—she dropped Advanced Placement Calculus in high school—Katrina became a math major in college and was doing well. But it was in linear alge-bra where "for the first time, I saw math for what it really is," not simply as memorizing formulas and executing procedures, but as a way of thinking. Katrina always got satisfaction from her technical proficiency in a field dominated by men, but her new awareness took math beyond the technical. "It was exciting to know you could use your mind this way." She began to see the creativity in mathematics, that you could bring to bear on a problem all the things you've learned to do. "Here's a problem. What do you think about it? What's going on here? How might you approach it?" This new understanding affected her engagement with and commitment to mathematics. Math became more than just a major; Katrina "found something to be passionate about."

This development in understanding can occur more than once as one masters a subject and can happen far along in one's education. Richard Symington was in the midst of medical school when he encountered a new professor of surgical pathology who had begun his career in internal medicine and therefore thought both as a physician and a pathologist. Richard was "captivated" by this man's ability to get to the heart of the research on a topic and focus it on a particular case, "making a really useful decision about a patient." Up to that point in Richard's training, many of the faculty lectures had been narrowly focused on a professor's area of research alone, but this exemplary pathologist was "comfortable with the complexity of a wide range of research" and knew how to bring it to bear on patient care. Watching and listening to his new mentor crystallized for Richard what surgical pathology could be. "I wanted to do what he was doing."

These shifts in understanding represent an advance from what we might call a textbook or procedural grasp of a subject to a more dynamic and processual mastery of it. Emma, Katrina, and Richard are now *thinking* with what they know, and with this advance comes a significant change in their commitment to what they are learning.

Sometimes what people experienced involved a change in their understanding of a subject but more so marked an intensification of intellectual effort and a transformation in the very way they approached academic work itself. This shift in the magnitude of effort is deeply familiar to me, beginning with my experience in Mr. McFarland's class. For Marcus Williams, the transformation in the way he approached his studies came much earlier, at the hands of his fifth-grade teacher, Ms. Adams.

Josephine Adams was no joke. An African American woman in her late fifties, Ms. Adams was about 5'3" tall, moved slowly, and, knitting her brow, looked out at the class over the top of her eyeglasses. Marcus remembers her always carrying thick bags full of books and papers and materials for history or science lessons. If you were having trouble with long division, then you skipped recess to work on it with her. If you needed to stay after school to have Ms. Adams tutor you on your writing, she'd call your parents to explain you would be getting home late. "She was so hard," Marcus says, "so demanding, and she never let up. Her whole philosophy was that you could always improve." It will come as no surprise that Ms. Adams was not big on smiles and hugs; a measured nod of approval was her preferred mode of affirmation. Marcus and his buddies "did not like her at all."

But as the school year progressed, Marcus noticed that some of his classmates who had been struggling in earlier grades were beginning to catch up. And though he had always been a good student, Marcus realized that Ms. Adams "was helping me do things I didn't know I could do." He learned how to take notes and how to effectively study from them. To this day he uses some public speaking techniques Ms. Adams introduced to his fifth-grade class. He might not have been able to express it this way at the time, but Marcus was being guided to work more diligently and try harder— and he was seeing the benefits of his efforts. He and his classmates were also seeing that Ms. Adams "didn't ask anything more of us than she asked of herself." She gave her students detailed feedback on their work; she was in her room before class and after to tutor them. Stern, no-nonsense, she "poured herself into her teaching."

As unrelenting as Ms. Adams was on academic excellence, she also was in the business of developing her young charges into full human beings. "When you walk out of this classroom," she would say, "you represent yourselves, you represent your families, you represent this class." You can imagine a group of fifth graders rolling their eyes at such life lessons, but—and this is the point Marcus makes—in a classroom rich in meaningful activities with a teacher who students were coming to see had their best interests at heart, who "believed in us more than we believed in ourselves," in such a classroom, Josephine Adams's life lessons had weight and soul to them. Marcus would continue to visit his teacher who he once thought was so mean well after he left elementary school, for she helped shape his young life. The last time was when he was home from college. She was "proud as all get-out. Then," he laughs, "she starts in about getting another degree after I graduate! She always pushed us to be a little better."

Brad Bowman was an A student, a multi-sport athlete, and in line to be the valedictorian of his high school class. He had it made. And because of his reputation, his teachers assumed he would perennially excel. "Once you got labeled as successful, everything became easy," he says in retrospect. His past achievements influenced teachers' perception of his current performance. "I knew I could get A's without really trying." Who wouldn't want to be in that sweet spot? Brad put maximum effort into sports and shifted down to three-quarter throttle in his academic work. He bought into the narrative of his own success and, in his words, "got lazy."

Then came Physics II.

Mr. Curry was an enthusiastic and creative teacher who made physics come alive with demonstrations and experiments. Brad called him "Mr. Wizard." Brad had Mr. Curry for physics I, worked hard, did well. But by Physics II, Brad had lessened his effort. And it began to show on his tests. When he asked Mr. Curry what his grade for the course would be, his teacher told him he had a B. Brad was gliding through his senior year, but he did want to be valedictorian, and a B could jeopardize that honor. "This was a wake-up call," says Brad, shaking his head and smiling at the panic that gripped his eighteen-year-old heart. He pulled himself together and asked his teacher if there was anything he could do. Mr. Curry thought about it and finally said that yes, there was one thing Brad could do. He went to his desk and pulled out a packet of physics problems. One hundred of them. College level. This happened on a Friday. Mr. Curry gave Brad until Monday. If Brad could get 70 percent correct on the entire packet, he would earn an A.

Brad swears that "they were the most difficult physics problems I'd ever seen," including in college—and he was an engineering major. He threw himself into physics over the weekend, pushing himself harder than he can remember doing before. It was arduous, all-consuming. "It was as if time stopped. It was just me and the problems." Brad went into the weekend with the goal of "getting that A," but working so intensely right at the edge of his ability led to a shift in his understanding, not only of physics but also of the responsibility that came with his gifts and about what a difficult problem demands of us. "This was the best work I had ever done," he said, "I honestly wasn't thinking about my grade. I learned so much about physics."

On Monday, he brought the set back to his teacher. His score: 68 percent, missing the mark by two points. But Brad Bowman's good fortune was still with him, though this time he earned it.

Mr. Curry could see the effort Brad put into the problem set, and, more important, his level of intellectual engagement. "I've never seen anyone work so hard on these problems," he told Brad, and granted his student the two points he needed to get that A. Looking back on it, Brad, who is now a career officer in the military, thinks his weekend ordeal showed him that he can face a truly difficult problem and learn from it—and "if I sit down and shut everything else out and work as hard as I can, I at least have a shot at solving it." Brad was fortunate to have a number of good teachers, going all the way back to first grade, but he credits Mr. Curry as one of the teachers who "made a huge impact on me . . . made me who I am today."

———————

Brad Bowman's fevered weekend with physics illustrates the way subjects learned in school can have not only an occupational pay-off—acquiring knowledge and skill to become an engineer—but can also affect our responsibility to our abilities and sense of who we are.

Years ago I was among the late-night stragglers at my neighborhood bar. The bartender had already announced last call, and three or four of us regulars were shooting the breeze with each other and the two remaining servers as they were closing out, doing side work, counting tips. Craig, the bartender, was talking about something he had heard on the radio concerning exercise and heart disease, and when he was done, Ashley Butler, one of the servers who was enrolled in the local community college's nursing program, picked up what Craig said and modified it, correcting in her typically easygoing way a misconception about the remedies for arterial disease.

Ashley was a favorite at this place. A longtime employee, she had developed strong friendships with some of the other servers, and new hires would go to her when a customer got under their skin. Regulars asked to sit in her station.

Ashley had been a professional snowboarder. She always did well in school without exerting a lot of effort, and by the time she graduated from high school, she was on the competitive snowboarding circuit, working in clothing stores and restaurants and doing some sportswear modeling. A concussion brought her athletic career to an end, and she moved to Los Angeles and to the restaurant-bar where I met her. Ashley really liked her high school anatomy and physiology elective. She had thought off and on about becoming a nurse, took a few community college classes here and there, but snowboarding and all its demands and seductions interfered. After the concussion, Ashley settled into restaurant life with its flexible hours and quick money. Before long, though, she found herself thinking about getting older and wanting a career with more stability and one in line with her desire "to be of service," a value manifest in the restaurant but that would be much more substantial in nursing. When two other women at the restaurant decided to go back to school, Ashley took the plunge and enrolled.

So there we were closing down the bar, and Ashley Butler, former champion snowboarder, current restaurant server, was emerging real time, out in the world as the nurse she wanted to be, redirecting and deepening a need to be of service from the hospitality industry to the helping professions. I talked to her about this moment a few days later, and she told me that she had been copying material from textbooks for the other servers who were on birth control and sections on child development for her friends with kids. "I like knowing things that everyone might not know," she said. "I never really had that." As she was getting ready to start her shift, she mentioned a seemingly small thing: She always sells her textbooks at the end of the term, but not the ones from her nursing classes. "It's important that I'm accurate in what I'm telling people." Talk about doing things with books! Knowledge from those textbooks made its way into the restaurant as the barriers between classroom and the world beyond it dissolved and Ashley began establishing a new identity with all she was learning.

It was not uncommon for the people I spoke with to talk about the way their education led to profound and extended reflection on their identities—involving race, gender, sexuality, class, and other social markers. One college student found in a course on LGBTQ individuals and the criminal justice system a new direction for study and career: "that course changed everything about my life." A young woman praises a community college program for African American students that helped her understand "what it means to be Black." And a woman expresses gratitude for her high school history teacher who "was insistent that we think about what we're going to do with our lives. He got me to thinking, 'What do I have inside me?'"

Lauren Nummi's professor of comparative literature, Mariana Popescu, was exceedingly knowledgeable in the literature of several languages, and Lauren was impressed by her professor's breadth of knowledge. But there was something else going on in her class—a class Lauren discovered by chance and took as an elective. She was captivated by the way her teacher "carried herself," and the way she presented the literature, a mix of quiet confidence and an inviting stance that made Lauren feel part of a larger experience. Literature was integral to Mariana Popescu's being, organic, and it became a medium of interaction—a means of fostering the growth of her students. In Lauren's mind it was as if Professor Popescu was saying, "Come along with me and together we'll learn something bigger than what we started out to learn." Lauren had not encountered anything quite like this before. Her teacher "really held the room" with her command of the literature and her passion for it—and her offer of intellectual partnership with her class. "She was strong and feminine and I saw something in her that I wanted to be," said Lauren. "I wanted to be that interesting. I wanted to be like her as a woman. She was so curious and adventurous and ready to connect."

It would be hard to divide the brain from the heart in Lauren's story, the intellectual content of her professor's class from the social and emotional benefits she describes. Yet there is these days a tendency in education and psychology to treat separately the cognitive and the social dimensions of schooling. We create programs to foster social and emotional growth or the development of qualities of character like grit, or flexibility, or empathy, yet many of these ventures make no substantial connection to the humanities, the sciences, or the arts. Equally troubling, we conceive of academic achievement in insular ways, measuring it—and thus for all practical purposes defining it—through reductive indicators, like scores on standardized tests that miss so much, from insight and intellectual excitement to social awareness and ethical engagement. This approach leaves us with a segmented model of humanity. When the light goes on for some of the people we've been meeting, the motives that drive their learning, the subject matter they pursue and their feelings about it, the qualities of their character, and the identities they shape are all of a piece—and from their development emerges not only a defining self but social and political commitments as well.

For as long as she can remember, Marlee Wood lived in both White and Native American worlds, her house halfway between the city where she went to school and the Reservation where her father grew up. Both her White mother and Native father encouraged her involvement in her tribe's culture and ceremonial practices, which "reached my heart" in a way that her participation in Catholic ritual, even as an altar server, did not. Marlee excelled in her predominantly White schools, but the achievements that increasingly brought her the most recognition were athletic, "the highlights of my youth." She was a standout in track, soccer, and basketball and would go on to build a career through college and beyond as an athlete. All the while, she maintained a deep personal connection to her Indian relatives and their Reservation community, to those people and that place that meant so much to her.

As Marlee's athletic career advanced, it provided opportunities to speak about Native issues, opportunities Marlee welcomed but that eventually led to a weighty recognition: she needed to know more than she did about Native Americans. Yes, she knew the ceremonies of her people and learned a lot about their history from her father and his kin. She carries all that deep within her; it's who she is. But she lacked knowledge of other Indian Nations and of the more general history of Indigenous cultures. When she was in college, "I didn't think to pursue connection to other Native people outside of my own," but now that need was clear. She had to get more education.

Marlee enrolled in a graduate program in American Indian studies and found an abundance of scholarship on everything from tribal sovereignty, public health, and economic development to American Indian language and literature. All this was both exciting and intimidating. "It was an extremely steep learning curve," she says and laughs. "I was blasted with an overwhelming amount of information," and with reading and writing demands unlike any she had encountered before. More unsettling than the sheer volume of work were those readings about the violations inflicted on Native people, violations Marlee certainly knew from her own family and tribal network, but that now were presented in more historical and sociological detail across a wide sweep of Indigenous societies. The accounts she read were a blow to the heart. But as painful as this knowledge was, it was also enlightening, enabling Marlee to understand in a broader context the conditions she saw on her father's Reservation and the resilience of the people she's known since childhood.

Over her time in the program—not without self-doubt and mis-steps, and with the aid of mentors and peers—Marlee acquired the skills to synthesize and connect what she was learning. And she worked hard to incorporate the frequently opaque language of academic disciplines into a speaking and writing style that felt right to her, that non-academics could understand. After all, her purpose for entering the program was to be able to communicate more knowledgeably about Native America to a wider audience. I thought about the way Marlee had characterized herself early in the interview as a "bridge between both worlds," Native and White, and also remembered something she said about her passion for team rather than individual sports: "I am not the best version of myself alone." Through her graduate program, Marlee advanced her abil-ity to bridge and communicate, to advocate with more authority for Native people. "It's been the most valuable thing I could have done," she says, reflecting on her studies—a journey that took her from deeply meaningful personal experience to public expression.

———————

Leigh Masson chooses words carefully. As we talk about the shifts and changes in her academic pursuits, Leigh wants to make clear that they were not ruptures or abandonments but rather "a retooling of what I've studied in the past, retooling for some future thing." She speaks of "reimagining" and "reinvigoration," an affirmation of continuity over loss.

Leigh had a rocky time through elementary and middle school. Diagnosed with ADHD, she had trouble focusing and manifested motor and verbal tics. "It was pretty rough," she says simply. She received individual assistance through special education, and that was helpful, but it was medication, begun late in the fifth grade, that changed things dramatically. "Before I would get caught up in details and get derailed, but now I could do the work. It was very

powerful to be able to sit down and do the work I needed to do."
She laughs. "All of a sudden, I was the smart kid." Leigh gravitated
to the sciences and developed friendships with other students who
liked the sciences as well. Over time, the medication would lose
its potency, and Leigh's high school record was mixed, but the experience of academic success had a lasting effect: It demonstrated
beyond doubt that "academics can be for me . . . can be very much
for me."

Leigh is both methodical and forgiving as she talks about the
twists and turns of her life, injecting a mild laugh after a challenging
event as if to say *wasn't that something*? It was during high school
that Leigh, as she puts it, turned her analytical bent on herself, on
thoughts and feelings that had been in some fashion present from
a young age. "There was something that separated me from other
people in ways I didn't understand." She was drawn to the LGBTQ
community and to school-based clubs like the Gay–Straight Alli-
ance. What followed was a period of exploration and reflection
and a somewhat haphazard transition from high school to a nearby
community college. Leigh's sense of difference intensified, leading
at times to a bleak sadness. She couldn't imagine a life beyond her
immediate confusion. But she continued to take courses, now in
the arts and social sciences, and "then I found anthropology, and
that seemed exactly what I wanted to study—people and behavior."
Through reading, through campus LGBTQ groups, Leigh "finally
figured out that I was transgender." This recognition brought clarity—a tremendous exhalation of breath—and over time a sense of
the future. Leigh squeezes the top of her left hand with her right
and tells me that during the period when she was trying to figure
out what made her different, she set a consequential deadline: If she
couldn't resolve her jumble of feelings by the age of twenty-three,
she might take her life. To have her "identity question answered
in a way that felt very satisfactory opened up the possibility of a

future . . . you know, a road I couldn't see down, but at least it wasn't a dead end." She "doubled down" on anthropology, feeling again an "investment in school" that was "exciting and invigorating."

Leigh's story continues, for she sees herself as a work in progress. She transferred to a university, majored in anthropology, and got involved in a number of campus activities related to LGBTQ issues, which provided the occasion both for further growth and for an on-the-ground education in leadership and organizational behavior. "I feel very fortunate that I'm at a place where I have many streets I could take that are not dead ends." She has recently arrived at another of her "reinvigorations" as a career goal is shaping itself: to become a therapist working with transgender youth. As she reflects back, her study of anthropology provided a framework and set of analytical tools to think about gender and identity. And the involvement with LGBTQ campus groups at the community college and university had boundless social benefit as well as providing a way for Leigh to move beyond herself, to have an effect on the world she inhabits. And as she was participating in those groups, she began to do volunteer work with trans kids in a hospital support group and a summer camp. It was this work with children that finally grabbed her heart. "I understand now that my career can be about being the person I needed when I was younger." This is the ultimate reimagining of a life, a career that offers both a homecoming and a future helping others thrive.

Carl Hawkins was a college sophomore when he took Professor Jackson's Modern Black American Culture course, which included literature, history, and social theory. It was the hardest course Carl had yet taken, and over the semester, it changed the way he thought about education, shifting him from what he called "regurgitation" to "really, really thinking critically." Rather than overwhelming Carl, the considerable demands of the course "allowed me the space to think." School became a forum for contemplation.

There aren't a lot of people with Carl Hawkins's background who end up in college. Homeless for part of his youth, moving from apartment to apartment, to one relative's house then another, spending time in foster care, attending multiple schools. Carl tells his story without embellishment, sitting alongside me, elaborating when I ask for it, matter-of-fact, but pain and uprooting run through the details of what, in his words, became normalized childhood life—simply the way things are. By the time he was in the fourth grade, Carl was diagnosed with a reading disability and had problems with speaking so severe that "my teachers couldn't understand anything I was saying." He received speech therapy and some limited assistance with his learning disability, though in all the moves, his records were lost. He entered high school reading way below grade level.

Carl was a terrific athlete, and sports provided him a circle of friends and a connection to school. Carl believed in school. Deeply. Though his mother and father did not go beyond high school, he had an aunt who was a college graduate and was doing well in corporate America—she was one of the relatives who provided shelter when Carl was young. Carl saw that "college was a way to get out of poverty," and had his sights set on a better life. That goal came within reach when he was selected for a program through which he boarded in an affluent community several hundred miles from home and attended its local, well-resourced high school. Carl was dropped into an alien world that he worked fiercely to navigate, staying up most of the night to finish assigned reading, getting what tutoring he could from volunteering college students. Eventually he developed strategies to help him compensate for his reading problems. He got decent grades and was accepted at a good private college.

The elite high school Carl attended provided him a strong academic education—and he is grateful for it—but socially, culturally, his was one odd experience . . . and not only because there were few African American students on campus. One well-intentioned activity was to have students in the special program eat dinner once a week with the family of a regularly admitted student, typically White and upper-middle class. As Carl describes it, the dinner was an awkward mismatch worthy of a Michael Che skit—though for the adolescent Carl, there wasn't a lot of comedy in the moment. When he got to college, also an overwhelmingly White place, Carl pledged a Black fraternity, giving him a comfortable social network and the collective institutional wisdom of older Black students. Carl began what would be a long and rich involvement with campus projects aimed at improving the academic success of Black undergraduates. This was the era when Barack Obama won the Democratic nomination to run for president of the United States—a time of possibility. It was in the flow of these events that Carl found Professor Jackson's classroom.

History was Carl's favorite subject in high school, but Professor Jackson's course was "the first time I looked at history from a Black perspective." And one of the books in the course, Ralph Ellison's *Invisible Man*, "changed the way I thought about what it means to be Black and to have social consciousness." Carl pauses here and refers back to his high school: "I got a better education . . . but I came out of it really broken." To be immersed in Black literature and history, to be urged and guided to think critically and creatively about it, to be, in fact, participating in this tradition yourself—well, this is intellectually and existentially liberating and broadens your understanding of what education can do. "I realized I can actually use what I'm learning to make things change."

———

There is no doubt that Marlee, Leigh, Carl, and all the others spurred by new expectations—everyone we've met so far—have benefited from their studies in the ways the standard narrative about academic success predicts. When the light goes on, people get better grades, move up the scholastic ladder, gain certificates and diplomas that typically lead to economic benefit and to increased security and status in the social order. These benefits have become the focus of and rationale for schooling. There's nothing wrong with attending to, even celebrating, such outcomes, especially for people who start out behind the economic eight ball.

What gets scant notice, however, are all the other things that happen when the light goes on. Perhaps the economic rationale for education is so strong that it keeps us from seeing them. Or we lose sight of the fact that education can have co-occurring effects: We're gaining economic advantage but also learning about the world and about ourselves. It's as though we can't raise our eyes from the ledger sheet. But when we do, we see a much richer story of education unfolding: from the affirmation of a skill and advice on how to improve it; to the discovery of a body of knowledge or an activity; to a consideration of who one is and wants to be; to a social or political commitment and the development of a public self. Elements of our humanity. If we don't acknowledge these multiple benefits of schooling, there is the danger that we won't advance them, leaving us with attenuated definitions of education and achievement, thin on imagination about the good life and the good society.

CHAPTER SIX

BECOMING SMART

People's abilities can be stifled, hidden even to themselves, by debilitating family circumstances, or societal biases, or a learning disability, or physical or emotional trauma. Ability can also be constrained by a lack of knowledge about school, from how to study to how the system works. All these barriers, formidable as they are, are susceptible to intervention. Ability can be realized. People become smarter as one skill learned lays the groundwork for another, as they begin to rethink their ability, as new pathways to achievement open up before them.

Several of those I interviewed grew up in families wracked by addiction and violence; they cycled in and out of foster care; they lacked the basic domestic structures that prepare children to make their way in the world. I once took a twenty-four-year-old community college student—a bright, affable guy—through a supermarket, wheeling a cart slowly down each aisle, teaching him how to shop for groceries, for he had never learned that basic task in the tumultuous churn of his childhood and adolescence.

Other young people have a more or less stable home, but one that is frigid and distant, bereft of everyday gestures of affection and guidance. School can be a source of sustenance for them, but when it's not, when they feel alone and unrecognized both at home and in the classroom, they have few places of refuge to gain a sense of worth, to be challenged in a healthy way, to simply believe that they matter. Their spirit is worn away by one disappointment after another. A woman described a middle-class home that was emotionally barren and a school life where she felt increasingly frustrated and embarrassed by what she didn't know how to do. When she went to her father for help, she was met with a short temper and exasperation. The pattern of lonely frustration and rejection continued, leaving her feeling "invisible and misunderstood" until "all I wanted was for high school to be over—and to get the hell out."

Patsy Messerling would have understood exactly what this woman was describing. Little wonder, then, that it took a lot of convincing to get Patsy back into a classroom to finish high school—in her thirties. A lot of convincing. "I never had self-confidence," she says flatly. "I mean, I didn't fail at everything in school, but it was always harder on me." She remembers "like it was yesterday" the first few weeks of middle school art class. The students were outside drawing trees and landscape. When the teacher got to Patsy, she held up her paper, looked down at Patsy, and said she "drew like a kindergartener." Patsy lets out a long breath. "Since then, I've never drawn." When she began having trouble with mathematics, she was placed in "a special math class" that turned out to be little more than a study period. She fell further behind, and by the time she entered high school, she was "pretty lost."

Things weren't much better at home. Patsy's father was a heavy drinker, and that contributed to her parents separating. Her mother was given custody of Patsy and her older sister but "started going out a lot. . . . She wasn't around too much in those years," says Patsy. The kids would be on their own until their grandmother found out "that our mom had left, and she'd come over and take care of us." Patsy speaks with a tone of regret and resignation—"You can't change the past"—but is pretty clear about the effect of it all. "After a while, it just kind of felt like, well, we're not really worth taking care of or being around for."

Patsy wasn't in high school for long before she began "realizing how far behind I was . . . and it made me not want to go at all . . . you know, kind of like, what's the point?" She quit, got married, and had children, picking up jobs as a babysitter and, once her kids were older, working in truck stop convenience stores. But Patsy's marriage was increasingly unhappy, for her husband treated her badly, contributing to her sense of inadequacy. Eventually she came to a realization. "People are always saying how they don't leave because of the kids . . . you know, 'I'm going to make this family work' . . . and then in the long run, you find out it's worse for the kids too. So . . ." So Patsy took her kids and left. And this is where the path toward reentering school began.

Patsy cannot say enough good things about Terry, the fellow she met after leaving her husband and who she has been with ever since. It was Terry who started pushing her toward the GED. "It'll make you feel better," he would say, "knowing that you finished high school, knowing you can do it." When Patsy deflected Terry, pointing to the needs of her children, Terry said he'd help out, take them to school before work, pick them up, all that. "Anything I would say," Patsy says and chuckles, "he had an answer for it . . . It's just that having someone believing in me and being willing to help me . . ." Her voice trails off. She enrolled in GED classes at a satellite campus of the local community college. After some testing, she ended up in Melanie Wilson's math class.

Melanie remembers Patsy as quiet, serious. She sat toward the back of the room. She didn't talk much to the other students, or ask questions during class, especially at the beginning, though she eventually asked questions of Melanie after class was over. Patsy's account matches Melanie's, though Melanie couldn't know how "out of place" and "really nervous and self-conscious" Patsy felt at first.

This was *math*, "my worst subject." And there's Melanie, blonde and outdoorsy and upbeat and comfortable in her own skin.

It didn't take long, however, for Patsy to see that "the way Melanie taught and walked around the room didn't . . . didn't make you feel stupid. It didn't matter if she had to show you something two or three times . . . It was, you know, she just taught you like you were one of her."

Patsy settled in, and though "it was still a struggle"—she failed her first attempt at the GED exam—she gradually began to build her skill and her confidence. Some of the math Patsy was doing was a repeat of material from elementary and middle school and "it came back to me and made me feel like I'm not that stupid." But a real breakthrough came when she "started doing stuff that was new, that I didn't know—and I caught on." This was empirical proof, observable to Patsy herself, that she wasn't stupid.

Passing the GED test, having that certification, provided a psychological boost to Patsy, as Terry predicted it would. And it enabled her to move into a more secure and gratifying job in the local school district's food service—regular hours, benefits, and interactions with kids, which she loves. "This is what I wanted to do," she says simply and finally, "and I'm able to do it now."

Patsy's story illustrates the power of someone close to us affirming our ability, particularly when we doubt it ourselves. Terry played such a role in Patsy's life; his affirmation primed her for another shot at school. But given her history of diminishment, something else needed to happen for Patsy to succeed in Melanie's classroom, and Melanie provided it: a sense of mutual regard, of common humanity. Though Melanie was clearly the teacher and knew way more about mathematics than Patsy, Melanie treated her students like they were "one of her" and used knowledge as a resource to be shared. As another student of Melanie's put it, "she thrived off of seeing a person move forward."

Terry's encouragement and Melanie's skill and support enabled Patsy to take on the cognitive challenge of mathematics, a challenge fraught with a long history of failure. She got to witness herself thinking, to experience her ability to work with numbers. Good teaching creates the conditions for students to observe their own intelligence in action.

———————

We get identified early within our families and sometimes within the institutions closest to us, church or school, as a certain kind of person, possessing certain characteristics or inclinations, and these identities can be hard to shake off. The child labeled as clumsy can become a juggler and ballroom dancer but still be remembered and spoken of as a stumblebum. Sometimes we find it hard to reject the labels ourselves.

Isabel Terry describes herself as having been a "daydreamy, fairy child," so her parents, fearful of what might happen to her in a regular school, budgeted tightly to send her to a private school with a curriculum rich in crafts, drawing, music, reading, and storytelling. Isabel found it "magical" and describes the woman who taught her for multiple grades as "saintly." When Isabel moved on to public school, however, she was "hugely unprepared" and was made to repeat fifth grade. Middle school was "horrible," a curriculum heavy with computer-scored testing that bedeviled her. By the ninth grade, she had fallen so far behind in math and science that she was placed in special education. Her mother and father quickly transferred her to a performing arts high school where she threw herself into dance and theater. Both she and her parents "came to believe that I wasn't an academically intelligent person, and I should just focus on the arts." She pauses. "It was like a lot of switches got flipped off in middle school . . . You know, you're not good at this, but you're not good at that either."

This was the way Isabel saw herself, but she also did things that pushed against her self-definition. After graduating from high school, needing work and being drawn to the physical and tactile, she enrolled in a program for massage therapy, which involved courses in anatomy, physiology, and kinesiology. Her parents worried that the science would be beyond her, but she graduated and passed her licensing exam, "showing me I might not be the total idiot that I always imagined I was." The other thing she did involved motor-cycles, a passion she shared with her father. Isabel wanted to work on her own bike, so she talked a guy who owned a repair shop into teaching her about maintenance and repair—mechanics, applied mathematics, technology.

Despite these accomplishments, Isabel wanted most of all to get a college education: "I really, really wanted to have a degree." While working as a massage therapist, she enrolled in college and ended up taking a course in literary analysis from Phil Metzger, a poet and critic of high expectation and strong opinion. For one of his early assignments the class read Conrad's *Heart of Darkness*, and Isabel "absolutely hated it," thought the main characters were "rep-rehensible" and the African natives were "undeveloped figures." She was "really heated" in her dislike, and Phil worked closely with her to "base those feelings on solid facts," to turn her reaction into an argument. This took time, and Isabel was struck by Phil's investment in her thinking, "the way he proficiently guided me toward critical thought." Isabel was producing the kind of hard-core analysis that represented to her a rigorous use of her mind, a kind of writing she thought was beyond her. "I felt like my brain was waking up."

Isabel took another literature class from Phil and a creative writ-ing course as well. Phil remembers Isabel as smart and determined, reading philosophy and literary theory on her own and "boring into the material, asking those commonsense but rare questions, working to really understand it." An essay she wrote on navigating the gender minefields of the motorcycle shop was keenly observed, funny, and stylistically sophisticated. Phil thought she had real talent. As for Isabel, her work with Phil was "rewarding in a way I had never felt before. Phil Metzger changed my life." In a follow-up letter, Isabel wrote something that could have described what happened to me under Mr. McFarland's guidance: "All through my early educational years, I'd been a person who existed in feeling and fancy. Phil helped me plant all that firmly in the ground."

"I wish I had a dog muzzle I could put on her," wrote Courtney Smith's third-grade teacher on her report card. That period in Court-ney's life was, she admits, "tumultuous," for her parents were going through a divorce, so she probably was voluble and needy. But a dog muzzle? Courtney holds your gaze when she talks, acknowledging your questions with a nod and a murmur, her voice melodious, punc-tuated with intonation and gesture, a laugh running through some of her sentences. There's no laughter, though, when she recalls her early memories of schooling—mostly punitive. "Oh you're a talker— that's bad." Or "You're a . . . whatever it was. That's not a good thing either. I started to really dislike the classroom." In the fourth grade, Courtney's parents enrolled her in a private nontraditional school. She had freer reign to write stories, draw, read, and talk about books. It was a "heavenly place." But she had significant problems with spelling and syntax and mathematics that were not addressed and would intensify when she entered the town's public high school. She was placed in remedial math and relied on a girlfriend to help her with her writing. "I got by with dismal grades, just kinda slid by, sneaked by." She figured that, purely and simply, she "wasn't smart."

What Courtney did have was a flair for the arts—encouraged by her earlier schooling—so she got involved in the theater program, where she flourished. She reflects back on her seventeen-year-old self sizing up her prospects. "I'm not that bright and I'm not that funny. I'm semi-pretty . . . I'll be an actress!" And in fact, Courtney Smith would go on to work successfully in film and television, though she remained troubled by the sense that she "wasn't good enough, wasn't smart enough."

Courtney longed for a "rigorous academic experience," wanted "to have an intellectual conversation about an article I read in the *New York Times* or something I heard on NPR." So during those times when she wasn't filming, she'd take a class at the local community college, and the classes were "a struggle." Her husband had been encouraging her for some time to get tested for a learning disability, and when her English composition teacher also recommended testing, she did it. The results devastated her. She did have language processing problems and ADHD, and according to one assessment, she was reading at a fifth-grade level. Courtney was a "voracious" reader, read Shakespeare, for God's sake. She threw the results of the test in a drawer and "refused to even talk about it."

After one year, however, Courtney gave all this a second thought and sought treatment that over six demanding months enabled her to understand how she processed language and what she could do to compensate. "I learned how I learned. I could sense when I was getting distracted and get myself back on track." It might take her twice as long as her husband to read that *New York Times* article, but she knew she "would get the same thing out of it in the end." She experienced a profound change not only in her reading and writing but also "in how I perceived my ability." She signed up for more classes. "I could be good at school."

Courtney tells the story of being on location in Alaska and writing papers for biology, which she emailed to her professor. Being able to write papers. On science. In college. She was giddy with the breakthrough. "This is *it*. I love this." She laughs and mimics a heavenly choir: *"This is the mean-ning of life!"*

She transferred to the university and before long started an organization for older community college transfer students that would lead, upon her graduation, to her being hired by the institution to run the office for transfer students. The curtain had been pulled back on so much that mystified her, and Courtney was able to see for herself the way her brain functioned and make whatever adjustments and work-arounds she needed. She had a level of control over her learning that she never had before, and that control not only made a world of difference to her personally, but also helped her figure out how a complex institution like a university functioned and how to navigate and work within it to help others in need create their own path to achievement.

————

One tragic fact about the path to academic achievement in the United States is that it is littered with barriers that have nothing to do with individual ability and effort or with the dynamics within one's family. As is the case with all our major institutions, the school absorbs the larger society's biases and inequities. Remember Tomás Herrera, the fellow I met in a university's student lounge reading Hegel who is pursuing a doctorate in political science? His account of high school contains both incidents of bias and person-to-person racism (such as his teachers ridiculing the clothing and hairstyles of the Mexican kids) as well as racist and classist structural norms and practices—for example, providing college counseling to students on the academic track while sending military recruiters to the homes of the other primarily working-class students. Other people of color I interviewed had similar stories to tell. Several spoke about not being guided to take honors or Advanced Placement classes, even though they had good academic records. One Latina explains that she succeeded by sticking close to her White girlfriend and taking the same courses she did. Assumptions were made by teachers and counselors about who would go on to college. "How do you give a kid an A in math," another woman asks rhetorically, "and not talk to him about college?" And sometimes bigotry is direct and nasty. A young Black man describes being ridiculed by his AP teacher for enrolling in the advanced class. "Man," he says in exasperation, "it was all over by tenth grade."

A widely held belief in our country is that once evident barriers to opportunity are removed—from segregationist restrictions to discriminatory hiring practices—then the playing field is leveled, and merit can triumph. To be sure, as social and state-sanctioned barriers are cleared—by social movements, by law, by evolving attitudes—opportunity widens. But bias and inequity die hard, are so embedded in our daily lives and institutions that they persist in many guises. Two further stories illustrate the shape-shifting persistence of social class and racial inequality—and possible ways counselors and teachers can respond.

Kateri Allen was a model student. Her father was in the construction trades and her mother was a homemaker and volunteered at Kateri's school. Of the five children in their family, Kateri was the scholar. "I wanted to make my parents happy," and her achievement did just that. By the time she began her senior year in high school, she was an athlete and a member of the National Honor Society. She took Advanced Placement classes and was a straight-A student. Kateri was compiling exactly the kind of record that would open doors to college, to lots of colleges, and she was Native American, a group notably underrepresented in higher education.

The high school's college counselor, Mr. Torres, was also Kateri's Advanced Placement Government teacher, so fortunately, he knew her as a standout student. They meet at the beginning of the year in his small, cramped office for a mandatory check-in. What are your plans after high school, he asks? Kateri shifts in her chair, says she doesn't know, but guesses that she'll get married to her boyfriend, have kids, and settle down there in town. This is not the answer Mr. Torres was expecting. As he's formulating a response, let's leave his office for a moment—Kateri earnest in her answer to her counselor's question, Mr. Torres strategizing—to fill in the backdrop to this routine, if surprising, encounter. Kateri certainly knew about this place called college—from the culture at large, from AP classes, from her peers. This general knowledge is one thing, but imagining yourself *in* that place is quite another . . . that you can afford it, that you belong, that there are particular goals important to you that you can fulfill there. Put another way, given your family's background, you might not have a specific sense of what your achievement in school—even notable achievement like Kateri's—can make available to you, what interests and occupations you might pursue beyond high school. Is Kateri's choice to get married and raise a family truly a choice if she is only marginally aware of the other options she has created for herself over the years?

Back now to Mr. Torres's office. He is explaining to Kateri the significance of her achievements and that she would have "a very strong application" to the university. He lays out next steps and the possibilities beyond. Then he removes financial barriers to a gatekeeping test and to vital information for Kateri and her family. He arranges for her to take the Scholastic Aptitude Test and gets her a fee waiver. He signs her up for workshops she and her parents can attend to prepare her for the college application process and secures fee waivers for those as well.

Students with a record like Kateri's typically have a keen eye on higher education, but, Kateri explains, "it was never my plan to go to college." None of her siblings did well in school, so the joy Kateri's achievements gave her parents was her primary motivation. Her mother and father supported and took pride in Kateri's accomplishments, though they "barely made it through high school" themselves. They didn't have the institutional know-how, or, for that fact, the money to help Kateri prepare for college. Sociologist Roberta Espinoza has documented the crucial role teachers and counselors with Mr. Torres's resources and sensibilities play in the lives of such students.[1] He certainly changed the direction of Kateri's life. From where she stands now, Kateri is exceedingly grateful and considers Mr. Torres "a great man." But she also realizes that her high school didn't provide her with early and consistent guidance on college preparation. "When I reflect back on it," Kateri says, "I don't think anyone ever told us what you needed to do to go to college. Not until the very end." Kateri is unusual in the magnitude of her achievements but otherwise represents a sizable number of high school students who are hidden in plain sight, who have the grades and accomplishments to participate in higher education but lack the resources and guidance—including guidance to an imagined future—to make college a tangible possibility.

———————

One of the many troubling outcomes of the insults and assaults involving social characteristics like race, class, and gender is that we can internalize them. They come to define us, limiting the expression of our ability. Tyree Payton, a young Black man, describes himself as the guy who would get to class early to claim a seat in the rear corner of the room. "That way," he says with a clipped laugh, "nobody looks at me, and I don't have to look at anybody or talk to anybody." It was his freshman year in high school, an awkward time for anyone, and on top of it, Tyree came from a Black and Latin American public middle school, a young man of modest means who was admitted to this wealthy and White private high school. And he played football. No way was he going to risk saying something in class only to have the others think, "Oh, that's dumb. He plays sports. That's why he's here." Tyree pauses—he's a deliberate speaker—and says, "I wasn't going to be their entertainment."

So there he is, in the back row, corner seat, a few weeks into ninth-grade English—and a fight breaks out! Tyree jumps up and stops it. So much for being invisible. His teacher, Ms. Jorgensen, is immensely grateful, as you can imagine, and begins talking to Tyree after class, discovering that he is a classic underachiever, repeatedly told by past teachers some variation of "We know you can do the work, why aren't you doing it?" Ms. Jorgensen acknowledges that Tyree likes to keep to himself but asks him if he'd be okay with her calling on him in class. Her reading list was substantial: *The Odyssey*, *The Inferno*, *The Great Gatsby*, *Animal Farm*, *The Catcher in the Rye*, *One Flew Over the Cuckoo's Nest*. Tyree found that these were books he "actually liked to read," and he had things to say about them. And Ms. Jorgensen's invitation encouraged him to say what was on his mind.

In addition to essays on the readings, Ms. Jorgensen had her class write narratives and poetry. She would ask Tyree and a few other students for their feedback on these assignments, and her interest in Tyree's opinion gave him a further "boost of confidence." Ms. Jorgensen valued what Tyree had to say, both in class and privately, and Tyree believes "the relationship definitely helped me be more vocal in class because I got the sense of trust and respect from her."

Tyree knew from day one in this high school that he "didn't fit in," that the whole scene was "very strange." He complained to his father who pleaded with him to stay, for it was such a good school: "You can't pass this up." Tyree struck a deal. He'd give it a year, then he and his father would revisit the issue. His father agreed that "we can sit down and have this talk again." Then came freshman English, his intervention in that classroom fight, and the emerging connection with Ms. Jorgensen, who, fortunately, also taught sophomore English. Tyree stayed. And the developments that began in Ms. Jorgensen's class carried over to others. "Even though I was in the advanced math class," he explains, "I believed these other kids were smarter than me. But over time I saw that I could keep up with them and was at their level."

There is a heavily studied concept in social psychology known as stereotype threat—essentially that people who belong to stigmatized social groups can perform beneath their ability on certain tasks because of their worry about conforming to stereotypes about them.[2] We don't know if Tyree would have done less well on assignments for Ms. Jorgensen because of his beliefs about the way his schoolmates saw him—the lower-class Black kid, the jock—but those beliefs certainly did keep him quiet and in the corner, limiting his involvement in class and the revelation of his talents. He kept his smarts under wraps. His teacher's invitation to participate and her ongoing support overrode Tyree's concerns, leading to the public display of his intelligence. Ms. Jorgensen would leave the school when Tyree was a junior, but she kept in touch with him and, as he moved into his senior year, was instrumental in guiding him to a well-known university close to her, where she and her husband continued to mentor him through the potentially perilous transition to college. Tyree "loved" his time at the university, got his degree in psychology, and now does challenging work that really matters to him as a counselor in a residential center for traumatized or abused children. "Some are really young," he explains in his even-keeled, serious way. "It's mind-blowing to think that they could be only six years old and have gone through so much—things that somebody who lived a whole lifetime could never imagine."

This young man nurturing these kids . . . I think of him sitting silently in the back of the class ten years before. As we're finishing up our telephone conversation—he's in another part of the state—I thank him for his time and candor. "Thanks," he says in turn, "for the chance to talk."

———

Colleen Murphy sat spellbound in the darkened classroom as pulsating stars, supernovas, and distant swirling galaxies glided by on the screen before her. She had never seen anything like these images from the world's most powerful telescopes, narrated by the enthusiastic instructor of this introductory course in astronomy. Colleen had entered community college to complete her high school degree, which she did, and was now taking general education requirements to try to make up for time, a lot of time, lost. Colleen's childhood was tumultuous and assaultive, her father on the run from other drug dealers and the law, Colleen yanked from school after school, finally dropping out at sixteen. She eventually stabilized her life and, seeking a modicum of normalcy, enrolled at twenty-one in her local community college. When she was younger and able to go to school, she had liked it, for it provided a structure her life didn't have, and she was in the midst of adults who wanted to help rather than violate her. No surprise then that she loved being at the college. And here were these captivating celestial images and an instructor who "made the universe come alive."

Colleen's education was a shambles. She had no science or technical background to speak of and was currently enrolled in basic algebra. But sitting there, listening to the story of astronomy being spun by her instructor, the beguiling light of the cosmos shimmering a few feet in front of her, Colleen envisioned herself at a future point in time high up on the walkway of a huge telescope, talking in a specialized technical language with other astronomers about some remarkable object they had discovered. "I knew," she said, "that this is exactly what I wanted to do with my life."

Colleen speaks in a soft, cadenced voice, hesitation and chuckling self-effacement oscillating with steely resolve. She methodically ticks off all the courses in mathematics and physics she had to take, all the catching up, step by step, waiting tables, then managing a restaurant, long days in the library and late, late nights at work. But the courses were systematic, orderly, the knowledge and skills learned in one course establishing a level of competence, a platform from which she could build to the next. And she was bringing this knowledge to bear on the astronomical phenomena that beguiled her, for majestic as they are, they are rule-governed, explainable. It was a long hard slog, but Colleen would transfer to a four-year school, and from there go on to complete a graduate degree in astrophysics. Through an extraordinary fusion of imagination and will, Colleen Murphy labored her way from algebra into a scientific community.

Over all the years I've been in education—teaching, running programs, studying how people learn—I've come to expect the unexpected, the surprise that, according to Dictionary.com, can yield "a sudden feeling of wonder."[3] I interviewed people who lived through years of disruptive chaos or debilitating anguish—and then begin to find their way out, find purpose and meaning that had long eluded them. They discover or develop—with painstaking effort—abilities that had not been revealed before. They begin to understand their past in new ways, begin to compensate for it and redirect it, and are motivated powerfully toward a defining future.

––––––––

When you first meet Hector Rodriguez, you wouldn't guess the hell he has been through. With warm brown eyes, a full smile, Hector is an expressive, engaging conversationalist. He has a nine-year-old son who is his spitting image: round face, soulful eyes, polite and well-spoken. He leans into Hector's side, Hector's hand cupping his shoulder, the connection palpable between father and son.

Hector is about to begin the final calculus class in the mathematics curriculum of his community college. He is preparing to transfer to the university with the goal of becoming either an engineer or a teacher of mathematics. This is an improbable goal for a guy who started in remedial math; who "barely scraped by" in high school;

who was, in his words, "rebellious" and "a menace"; who had to swallow his pride and beg his hard-nosed government teacher to change his F to a D so he could graduate and join the Marine Corps.

Once in the Marines, Hector trained as a machine-gunner, mastering both the technique and the applied mathematics and physics of the weapon. He ended up teaching new Marines and was proud of his ability to convey what he had learned. Upon his release, Hector worked in retail for several years but could only go so far with a high school education. Then he was recalled to service, right around the time of the surge in Iraq, just after the bloody operation in Fallujah. "Being in combat," he says, "absolutely and fundamentally changed everything about me." Hector is a big man—he was a linebacker in high school—whose arms are covered with tattoos. He crosses them across his chest, lowers his head, and looks at the table between us. "During training you get to see machine guns do awesome things. In real life, you get to see them do horrendous things."

Friends died beside him. He entered houses where people were hanging upside down, mutilated. He was knocked unconscious by bomb blasts multiple times. As we talk, he occasionally loses the thread of conversation. "I had a really difficult time readjusting when I came back." His family was scared of him. "You would just sit in the corner for hours," they tell him now. "I would talk to you," his sister says, "and I could tell that you were looking at me, but you weren't there." For years, Hector drank, took prescribed medications and unprescribed ones. He worked in construction, gulping painkillers to mask a spinal injury sustained in Iraq.

Hector fathered his son during this madness and later married another woman he knew from high school. She was the one who began urging him to go back to school, to stop hurting himself, to please just take one class. Please. So reluctantly, with hesitation, remembering how much he hated high school, he started, in the preparatory math program for which he now tutors. He went regularly, using the college's computers and getting assistance with his homework. Mathematics, which was once so mystifying, "now made complete sense to me." He formed strong relationships with the head of the program and one of the staff, himself a Marine veteran. Hector was on the road. But fate had one more circle of hell for him to travel. His spinal injury and depression from PTSD landed him in the hospital for an extended stay, and everything slid out from under him. He was hooked on pills. He separated from his wife. He lost custody of his son. He was sleeping in his car. "I was completely lost."

But the two men at the program stuck by him, as did his family. His brother encouraged him to go on what he calls a "spiritual retreat," which he at first pushed against. "How do you believe in a god," he said to his brother, "that lets us do the things we do to each other?" Hector credits a lot of people for his recovery: friends, family, therapists, and "my desire to be a good father. My son drives me. He absolutely drives me." Hector straightened out and regained custody of his boy, "my beautiful, young little man." He speaks about his ordeal to other veterans, trying to assist them as they reenter civilian life. He calls the program "a sanctuary" and his "second family. . . . They accepted me back with open arms. . . . They continue to see something in me that I . . . well . . . I, I'm just doing what I can."

————————

Stories like Hector's are testaments to human resilience. They are, indeed, wondrous and result from so many factors: the love of others, spiritual insight, the emergence of purpose, medical and psychological intervention, and more that, frankly, we can't explain. But something we can say with certainty is that once this awakening happens, a lot needs to be in place to guide and nurture it: attuned and caring teachers and counselors, substantial courses and curriculum, and social services. A resource that figured prominently in Hector's story is the tutoring or learning center, sometimes available to all students on a campus and sometimes targeted to vulnerable groups—first-generation college students, for example, or disabled students.

Particularly for people who have had a hard time in school, these centers and programs, simple and spare as they often are—a few posters on the walls, mismatched couches—become infused with feeling. Mathematics or writing or difficult academic reading that had been bewildering and distant are embodied in a flesh-and-blood encounter. Even the casual give-and-take of greetings and chitchat about the events of the day become, so to speak, part of the intervention. "This is why I run a center," an administrator of a community college tutoring and guidance program explains. "I want there to be many ways for people to make connections." These connections amid books and computer screens and handouts scribbled on and highlighted are especially important if your school history is permeated with failure, for one of the awful things about failure is how lonely and isolating it is. "It's okay for me to not know something," one woman said. "I can see other people doing what I'm doing. I'm not alone." It is telling how often people use the word *family* to describe these places.

It was during her sophomore year in high school when Carla Bennett, an outgoing, standout soccer player, began to turn inward and away from her many friends. Carla never cared much for school, was "rebellious" and "a wild child," the center of attention among her tight circle of girlfriends. Then, seemingly overnight, without an obvious cause, "I forgot how to talk to people. I used to be confident and now I wasn't comfortable in my own skin." Her parents hired tutors, took Carla to therapists, tried antidepressant medication. Carla was deeply unhappy and "gravitated toward the rougher kids" at school. She began smoking marijuana, which made her feel better. Though her grades were awful, Carla graduated from high school—she's convinced that her mother intervened—and went to another part of the state to attend a community college. Though she never enjoyed school and barely scraped by academically, there was a part of her that wished she could be more studious like her sister, who was a top scholar and a source of pleasure and pride for Carla's parents.

Unfortunately, Carla's attempt to live away from home and attend college was a disaster. She drank and discovered cocaine, which lifted her momentarily out of her depression. "Thank God. I felt like talking to people again." She was away from home for almost two years and never completed a class. Thus began a sadly familiar pattern of going into rehab, followed by a period of sobriety, then a relapse, then rehab and sobriety. Carla supported herself waiting tables and went to school to become a makeup artist, building a successful resume in the movie and music industries. And during her sober periods, she would attend community college "because I wanted to make more of myself and have a better life."

The bottom fell out when Carla began using methamphetamine and descended into the grisly world of meth addicts. "I started living a life that was only for people in horrible C-rated movies. I got detached from the life I had known." Carla's family cut ties with her. She drifted from one cheap motel to another. The man she was with fractured her skull. "Meth took over everything." Carla describes a depth of misery that is hard to imagine—"I became a shell . . . just a walking, empty human being with no soul"—and that only the next rush of methamphetamine could relieve. She got pregnant, yet continued to use.

One night in yet another bleak motel room, her partner nodding off on heroin, Carla had "a moment of clarity," one, she admits, she had many times before, but this time "I really believed it in my heart: *Oh my God. Leave. Get out.*" She threw some clothes in a suitcase, snuck out, and went to a shelter she knew. There, Carla Bennett began to turn her life around.

The great, humbling gift of this period was that Carla's daughter was born healthy, "a blessing I can't forget." Carla stops, looks away, and composes herself. "When they handed me my daughter, it was like everything I had been running from my whole life disappeared."

Carla was able to move into a long-term halfway house close to a community college. She lived with other women who were in the same boat, pulling their lives together, supporting each other. At the college, Carla got her daughter into daycare and registered with the Office for Students with Disabilities, and that office and its services developed into "one big family." She went to math tutorials and became a fixture in the Writing Center. She visited her professors during office hours. She got help from wherever she could. And she stayed sober. She showed me a photograph of the little table she set up in a bathroom at the group home. That's where she would study. She got good grades. And for the first time she was "gaining confidence from school." Good grades led to more good grades and a sense of all that school could mean to her. "I've been a fuck-up for so long. School allows me to be the person I want to be." Carla transferred to the local university and thrived. She is close to graduating.

We finish the interview, an intense ninety minutes, and I walk Carla out to her car. It is a warm summer afternoon, a soft breeze coming in off the coast. I thank her and ask what the rest of her day has in store. She looks at her watch and a gentle smile comes over her face, suffuses it. She has time, she says, to go to a coffee shop and read a book. She explains, a little self-consciously, but bright with anticipation, that reading a book that way is something she's seen other people do and always wanted to do herself.

As she drives away, I think of something Carla said about her first month or so at the community college, taking classes, meeting new people, discovering intellectual sustenance in the tutoring center. "I had been in such a dark and ugly place, and now I was just so happy to be alive." School helped Carla create a new life and reclaim what she nearly lost of her old one—her relationship with her parents, her infant daughter. A meaningful future and career lay before her. These are the kinds of capital-O opportunities education is making possible for Carla Bennett. But her story also brings to the fore the many small-o opportunities that can emerge when the light goes on, the ways education affects the daily texture of our lives—what we notice, conversations that become possible, questions sparked by something we see, hear, or read, more territory for our mind to wander. When Carla settles into that coffee shop and opens her book, it will be a simple pleasure and a small wonder.

CHAPTER SEVEN

FINDING EDUCATIONAL OPPORTUNITY

P resent in the stories we've been reading, sometimes high in volume, sometimes as background melody, is the issue of opportunity, which by one definition is "a set of circumstances that makes it possible to do something" and by another is "a good chance to advance oneself." Whenever I return to my old neighborhood or neighborhoods like it, I think about what our society makes possible for the people who live there. Who has teachers like those we've been meeting? What academic and enrichment programs are available? Is there a library close by—and what is its condition and when is it open? What are the legacies of discrimination that impede young people trying to find their way in school? And since educational opportunity is embedded in economic opportunity—parental income is the most potent indicator of educational achievement—we need also to consider the stability of the surrounding economy, housing and food security, transportation, the safety of the streets. All this affects education: a school's resources, the place it holds in its community, the sense of hope or despair students carry into its classrooms. The light doesn't go on in a vacuum.

About thirty of the people I interviewed grew up in neighborhoods like mine. Of that number, I was able to conduct long follow-up interviews with seven of them while we walked and drove through their neighborhoods, the terrain of their childhood: their parental homes, elementary schools, the car or bus routes to high schools, landmarks (burger joints and mini-marts, parks, churches, the homes of relatives or friends) associated with happiness, or sorrow, or, occasionally, violence. Interviewing people in the very places you're discussing with them often results in more vivid recollections. And you get to see the houses and schoolyards that shaped them, move with them across the landscapes they once inhabited, get a sense of the experiences of opportunity as people lived them. Educational opportunity is typically analyzed in structural terms of funding and access. Is the distribution of resources equitable? Are there barriers to access? This broad scrutiny gives us measures of opportunity at the institutional and societal levels used for monitoring and possible legal remedy. The stories here take us closer to day-to-day practices and routines, to the way teachers' and counselors' beliefs about education play out in words and actions, to family dynamics and neighborhood culture. We get a more intimate view of opportunity, see how it is generated in the moment.

All seven people I spoke with were successful in school—not an outcome associated in the minds of many with urban public education—and in all cases there are teachers, counselors, coaches, or parents who are central to their achievement. Each of their stories, however, offers a different portrait of educational opportunity and the meaning school had in their lives.

––––––––––

Traveling with Danny Oliveros through his community in Central Los Angeles, a few miles northeast of where I grew up, is like browsing through a thick photograph album. In his amiable, soft-spoken way, he directs my attention to one story-laden site after another— like the courtyard apartments where his parents lived when they first came to the United States. His mother holds fond memories of the place, for "she raised a lotta kids in the neighborhood." At the end of the block a right turn takes us to a busy street with a new shopping center. Danny remembers the center as a metal recycling yard that "was huge and really ugly." Then we go to the park where he started playing soccer, a growing passion that consumed him all the way through high school. We pass his church, parishioners gathered around tables of food by the entrance, festive Sunday suits and dresses. That's where Danny took his First Communion. Turn here and we pull up to his middle school where two eighth graders bullied him and took his Pokémon cards. Down one block, then another, and here's his uncle's house, hibiscus and roses, where the families still spend Thanksgiving and Christmas. Danny expresses an affection for, even a commitment to, this place where he came of age. As we drive, he reflects on all these points of connection, a moderate increase in the volume of his voice for emphasis, a little rise at the end of a sentence for a question. There are big problems on these streets, for sure, and Danny is well aware of them. But this, finally, is home.

Danny has warm memories of elementary school; his teachers were "supportive and caring" and he "really connected to them." He talks about Ms. Grunwald who, with her own money and contacts, had equipped her classroom with computers. He remembers being in a production of *Peter Pan* in the school's auditorium, seemingly massive at the time. The transition to middle school, however, was difficult, as it is for lots of children. Though the school was close to his home, few of his friends were there, and none in his same class. He remembers being afraid and "feeling out of place . . . disconnected from everyone." An astute counselor placed one of Danny's best friends in his class, and that helped. Then something else happened, more complicated, that also had an effect on Danny's sense of isolation and vulnerability.

We are standing on the spot where those older kids took his Pokémon cards. Flushed with shame and anger, Danny ran home crying and found his brother Marco mowing the lawn. Marco, who was four years older and had been entering into gang life, took Danny back to school, found the kids, got Danny's cards back, and told them what would happen to them if they messed with Danny again. Marco then spread the word to his friends to look out for his younger brother. As a sixth grader, Danny was aware of "what was happening in my neighborhood with gangs and drugs," but didn't comprehend the full meaning of it all. What he did know was that he felt protected; "if I needed help with anything I knew who to talk to." At his age, feeling vulnerable, having that security was all that mattered.

Danny would eventually settle into middle school, throwing himself into sports, which yielded huge social benefits. He fondly remembers his science teacher, Mr. Yamamoto, who kept his room open at lunch; students would hang out, talking, seeking advice, working on their science projects. We pull up alongside the school's grassy playground and Danny begins talking about a yearly football game in which the eighth graders would split into two teams, with the teachers playing alongside the students. Danny, skilled at soccer and basketball by the eighth grade, loved this annual event for the rapport it built between teachers and students. A little further down the block is the school's large auditorium where Danny graduated, much more assured and confident than a few years before. He now comes to this auditorium to vote, his adult civic life connected to his middle school campus.

Whereas his elementary and especially his middle school were close by his house, Danny's high school was a long walk away, about twenty blocks. He tells me with admiration about a girl he knew in the elementary grades who was moved into a magnet program at their middle school and then was bused to a high school in a more affluent area of the city. From there she was admitted to Yale. "She was always bright and talented," Danny says, and he is now better able to articulate what he sensed then. "By going to different schools, she had a whole different environment, different resources" from those available in the schools around him. We pull up to a street corner where Danny asks me to stop. He tells me about one of the boys who looked out for him after that middle school incident with the Pokémon cards, a guy who became a good friend. One afternoon the boy was pedaling home on his bicycle and was shot to death right at this spot. Danny saw his body covered with a blanket. "Every time I drive here, I think of him." Danny turns and looks at me, then looks back out to the street. We wait a few minutes before continuing south to his former high school.

When we arrive, we find the place has been refurbished and relandscaped—a fresh face, new beginnings. We drive around the expansive perimeter, and Danny tells me about two events that would change his life. As is the case in a lot of communities like Central Los Angeles, a long walk to school can take you through rival gang territory. One day Danny and a bunch of friends from his neighborhood—people he grew up with, male and female, some gang-affiliated, some not—are heading home along a busy thoroughfare; "everything seems normal, we're laughing, making jokes" when a car speeds down a side street, angles into the curb, and out rush three older guys with knives and baseball bats. Danny and his friends start running, but the older guys are fierce and gain on them, causing some of them to run in terror out into traffic, cars swerving, screeching to a halt. Danny trips and two of the assailants are on him, holding him by his backpack, one swinging at him, Danny throwing up his hands to protect his face, then squirming loose from the backpack and running furiously down the street, ducking into an auto repair shop to hide behind the cars. The gangsters are still in pursuit, firing shots into the shop before dispersing. Danny, heart pounding, scared beyond words, looks down at his hands to find them bleeding. When that guy was swinging at Danny, he was holding a knife or razor, cutting deep into Danny's palms and right shoulder, close to the collarbone. The mechanics wrap some bandages around Danny's hands and call an ambulance.

Danny and I park in front of the shop—it's still there—and he holds his hands out for me to see the scars across the fleshy side of his palms. The shop is one of many along this street, shabby with handwritten signs and a stack of old tires and scrap metal by a narrow, dark entrance that likely saved Danny's life.

Danny was traumatized by the attack, was afraid to walk to school, and had trouble finding an adult to talk to about it. Finally, he connected with two teachers who provided solace and counsel. But the attack would have a longer-term effect on Danny's understanding of where he lived. "I never thought this would happen to me." He began to rethink some of his friendships. Before the assault, he saw the presence of gangs and the entry of some of his neighborhood friends into gang life as "normal . . . something you see every day." But the attack "made me realize that this is not normal at all." There were lots of young people in Danny's life: neighbors, schoolmates, cousins, kids his mother watched over when she first came to this country. They saw each other on the street, at the park, at church, played together, walked to school together. They were, by turns, familiar, funny, brash, needy, kind, courageous, petty, sad, jealous, close—the young fabric of the community. Looking back, Danny can see how they began taking different paths, sometimes making choices, sometimes the choices made for them, incrementally, going to this place or doing this thing rather than another, moving toward particular social networks, small steps that over time would have monumental consequences—and consequences for others around them. His community, he realized, "could be a warm and loving place"—he had so many deep connections to it—"but also a place of a lot of pain—sometimes unexpected."

The second thing that happened that year, much later in his junior year, couldn't have been more different, a small, spontaneous event, barely causing a stir for anyone but Danny. Danny was playing varsity soccer and soccer was his life; school provided the vehicle to play. He kept above a C average to maintain eligibility. He started a few applications to local colleges but never completed them. He was "focused only on soccer."

His Spanish teacher, Mr. Garcia, knew about the attack. He had his eye on Danny, was aware of his passion for soccer but also saw how he handled himself with his peers, how well-liked he was. Mr. Garcia thought Danny had some special qualities, and he wanted to give him an option beyond soccer. A path after high school. So one day in class, he takes Danny aside and starts talking to him about college. Danny tells him about the incomplete applications, the uncertainty, and, *snap*, right there, his teacher pulls out his cell phone and calls a counselor at a local college's program for low-income students and sets up an interview for Danny. "He saw some potential in me," says Danny, "that I didn't see in myself." A year later, Danny would enter the college as a probationary student, beginning a new and unexpected phase of his education that would require he work harder than he ever had before.

There are so many young people like Danny in our schools; I was one of them. He did well enough to not raise any flags; he didn't get into big trouble. Fortunately for Danny, he had sports and supportive, mentoring coaches, which gave school added meaning and kept him compliant, borderline studious, but by no means getting what he could out of the academic side of things. Once soccer was over, what would remain? It seems that Danny's teacher, Mr. Garcia, was asking the same question—and did ask it, quickly, briefly, of Danny.

Then he made the spur-of-the-moment phone call that opened a door. Would Danny walk through it?

When Danny told me this story, I asked him if Mr. Garcia knew of Danny's success—after completing a bachelor's degree, he would go on to graduate school. I urged Danny to find Mr. Garcia and tell him. Thanks to social media, Danny did track down his former teacher, who was really happy for Danny and wanted to get together to have lunch. But, in a telling postscript to this story, Mr. Garcia did not remember taking out his phone and making that call. Danny tells me that Mr. Garcia was a popular and respected teacher; Danny calls him "genuine." My guess is that pulling a student aside, having that college pep talk, even making a connection between a student and an institution was part of what Mr. Garcia did routinely. He was on the lookout, tuned in, alert. Years later he might not remember that particular talk on that particular day, but for Danny Oliveros, "it only took one teacher who was willing to take the initiative" to change the direction of his life.

———

Beatriz Valdez and I meet outside the apartment building where she has lived since childhood and drive the short distance to her elementary school, passing older folks working in their yards who wave to Beatriz. "They watched me grow up," she says affectionately as she waves back. A left turn, then a right—there's her cousin's house—and within minutes we pull up alongside her elementary school and park. Spanish was Beatriz's first language. She looks at the window of an old classroom and begins talking about how she struggled "getting the hang of English." We get out and walk along the border of the schoolyard. She remembers "going over vowels and consonants and how to pronounce words." She was "so scared that I couldn't think about what sounded like what." Beatriz's mother had limited schooling in rural Mexico, but, realizing that her daughter and younger son would need to learn English, she enrolled in language courses at the local community college and tried to teach her children what she was learning. Still, Beatriz has strong memories of being reprimanded for her accent and feeling terribly self-conscious. She shut down and was getting poor grades. Beatriz explains that her mother did garment work at home to give her some control over her time, and "though she didn't feel comfortable with English, she would volunteer in the classroom, go on field trips, never miss a parent conference." All the while, Mrs. Valdez stressed the importance of school and of avoiding the path toward trouble some other neighborhood kids were already traveling.

In a few minutes we're at Beatriz's middle school. The transition to middle school is often a bumpy one, but for Beatriz it set in motion some powerful recognitions. Beatriz's voice is fluid and expressive, melodic really, but under the lilt runs a deep sensibility and fierce determination. Sometime during her first year of middle school, Beatriz began to realize just how hard her mother had been working to keep the family afloat and to assist her in school. By then her mother had remarried, and she saw her stepfather getting up at four o'clock in the morning to bicycle many miles to work. "It really clicked for me. I began to understand my parents' sacrifices." She thought back over her own difficult times in the earlier grades and things she heard teachers say about "kids from immigrant parents . . . that they're not going to go anywhere." She saw peers who she knew were easily her academic equals get into big trouble in school and then with the law. Beatriz pauses and taps the dashboard for emphasis: "In middle school, things became very real to me." She vowed that she was going to do the best she could to both honor her parents and to prove the naysayers wrong. A complex epiphany and a heavy burden for a child to carry.

Since those demeaning days in elementary school, Beatriz had become more fluent in English—and with that fluency came the confidence to speak up and answer questions, revealing her ability. She remembers two math teachers particularly who told her she was smart and encouraged her—one of them urging her toward the high school she would eventually attend. Along with her commitment to her parents, this affirmation was powerfully motivating, a counterweight to the negative judgments she heard in the earlier grades. She was also making friends with other students who were serious about their education, giving her daily, intimate support for her developing interests. Beatriz took off academically and ended up being the school's valedictorian. She gained admission to the prestigious high school her math teacher had recommended, the only student in her graduating class to do so.

Off we go, then, to the high school that represented such a remarkable achievement. By car, the drive takes about twenty minutes, but by bus, it took Beatriz anywhere between one to one and a half hours. Three buses. That's the route I follow as I turn out onto the heavily trafficked boulevard that will take us to the first of Beatriz's bus stops. There is lots of small commerce along this street—from fast food to auto repair—and weathered apartment buildings, and vacant lots, thick with weeds behind chain-link fences. Much of the route, except for stretches of industry and warehouses, looks like this. Beatriz points out a market where she worked during high school and then another place, another job, in the administration building at the community college her mother attended. But much of our conversation is about the bus ride itself and all the anxious thoughts and feelings associated with it. Beatriz describes standing with a bulging backpack, watching the time, anticipating bus stops in front of a McDonald's or Carl's Jr. With three buses to catch, there were multiple possibilities for trouble—traffic jams or breakdowns. Beatriz talks about the relief she felt when the bus sped up along those long corridors of industrial landscape. But then there was the inevitable sprint from the last stop to her first class. Beatriz laughs without amusement. "I was always running."

High school was demanding beyond belief. There were nights when Beatriz got about a half hour's sleep. I ask her how she could stay awake, let alone concentrate. "I was just so invested in doing well," she says straightforwardly. "I didn't want anybody questioning my intelligence, and my family was depending on me." And it's not only family. "There are so many kids who could have come to this school, and I'm the only one who got chosen. I can't screw this up for people after me." Beatriz's mother would meet her at the last bus stop and walk her home. When, as a senior, Beatriz took a night class at a college affiliated with the high school, her mother rode the buses halfway to meet her daughter en route. Love weaves through this tale of fatigue and determination. Never during our drive together—nor in subsequent conversations—do I pick up a trace of self-pity or complaint. Rather, I sense an anxious urgency, a deep, driving responsibility to parents who work so hard and to a community that is stigmatized. Beatriz would graduate with excellent grades and attend one of California's major universities.

School becomes a complicated place in Beatriz's story, a site of both degradation and opportunity. It was in school where teachers, at the least, were ill-equipped to foster her developing English and, in some cases, were thoughtless or downright bigoted. But it was also in school where teachers saw her ability, encouraged it, and guided her toward a high school that would make possible her emerging desire to honor her parents and open doors for more kids like her. However, opportunity for Beatriz was not without its barbs. "I lived in two worlds," she says, as we approach the third and final bus stop, close to landscaped town houses and thick palm trees that represent an academic and economic path out of a community Beatriz does not want to abandon. "I could blindly do my work and pretend nothing was wrong," and yet return to a neighborhood where people "were not provided with the resources to develop their talents." As the crow flies, Beatriz's high school is about six miles from her home, twice that far by bus, and a thousand miles in social distance—a distance Beatriz won't let herself forget.

———————

"People tried to ditch class, right in here." Brian points to a storage area along the wall of the walkway leading to the grassy schoolyard. "Or come to make out," Francisco slips in. "The girls with these tall guys. You'd be awkwardly walking by, trying not to look . . ." he drops his voice, "but *looking*!" We walk slowly, fanning out onto the brown grass. Brian Zamoro and Francisco Estrella have been best friends since they met at this middle school ten years ago. I've come to know them through their former high school English teacher, Jonathan Meyers, who has mentored and befriended them and set up this meeting of the four of us to travel through their old and current neighborhoods, see where they went to elementary school, visit their middle and high school, and talk with some of the teachers who mattered to them.

We are now at the tables and benches on the edge of the school-yard. Francisco sweeps his hand outward: "The punk rock kids were here . . ." "No," Brian interjects softly—these two easily pick up each other's threads of conversation—"they were at *that* table, remember?" "Oh, yeah," Francisco says and nods. Brian continues, "The Emo kids were *there*. The Black kids, they were here." Mr. Meyers says it sounds like the students were pretty segregated. Brian, who has a thoughtful way about him, ponders his teacher's observation and explains that there were a lot of students here, packed into a relatively small school, so, yes, "there were all these little pockets, but everybody kinda coexisted." Francisco is looking out across the grass and suddenly turns to us with a rise in his voice: "But remember when there was that race fight here on the field?

The whole PE class, like, separated and everybody just jumped in and started whaling on each other." Black guys versus Latinos. I ask Francisco what he did. He laughs. "I was a spectator, man. I wasn't about to get my ass whipped by anybody." Fights like this, as is usually the case, reflect larger tensions. In many of the low-income communities in the sprawling Los Angeles Basin, the last three or four decades have seen major shifts in population that yield some cross-racial friendships and alliances, but that also create conflict in local politics, the street, and the schoolyard. A few more steps and the topic shifts again as Brian gestures toward a beige box of a building. "And this is the cafeteria," whereupon he and Francisco recall with glee a food fight that they thought happened only in the movies. But there it was, fish sticks flying through the air.

It is close to noon, the sun right over us, no breeze, the heat rising off the asphalt. The loud, high-pitched horn signaling lunch comes on with no one but us and two custodians on the other side of campus to hear it. We'd better get to our next stop, the high school, to meet up with another of Brian's and Francisco's former teachers. We start walking out to our car when Francisco offhand-edly brings up an essay he wrote in the eighth grade, an argument that film directors are underappreciated, that actors take the spot-light directors deserve. I stop in my tracks when he then explains how he made his argument: by examining the styles of directors like Alejandro González Iñárritu, Guillermo del Toro, and Martin Scorsese. Iñárritu?! In the eighth grade? Earlier in the year, I had spoken at length with Francisco about his education, and this paper never came up. Walking and talking with people in the places where they grew up yields these surprises.

———————

Both Brian's and Francisco's parents came to the United States from Mexico. Brian's father was studying to become a veterinarian, but when his father died, he had to quit to help support his family. That obligation led him to pig farms in Nevada, then to textile factories in Los Angeles, where he met his future wife, a woman who likewise had come north from Mexico. Francisco's parents also came to Los Angeles to create a better life, living in a small room attached to their relative's house. That was when Francisco was born.

The two families would move to different parts of Los Angeles where they could afford to rent. Initially, Brian didn't care much for school, getting C's and D's in the first grade, but by third grade he got a series of teachers he liked, read *Treasure Island*, did science experiments, got his first exposure to history, a field that he would later pursue. Still, he was fiercely independent and selective about where he put his energies, playing music rather than doing homework. He began middle school in a magnet program where "the teachers were very passionate" and where he "started to really focus on school." He was beginning to thrive. But his neighborhood was a violent one where "every weekend SWAT teams were in the alley, and people were getting shot up." His parents worked late, so he and his brother had to walk home alone from school, risking threats from the streets. "It was very dangerous to be a kid." So his parents decided to move to another part of LA County, to another low-income community where Brian entered the middle school where he would meet Francisco.

Francisco's grandmother played an important role in his early education; she read to him in Spanish and eventually had him read to her. By the time he entered kindergarten he was a proficient reader of Spanish, and he caught up quickly in English, given his overall familiarity with the conventions of literacy. For second grade, he had five teachers, a chaotic mess. His grandmother died when he was in third grade, a loss he deeply felt. Francisco was placed in a gifted and talented program, and he did well through the rest of elementary school, making friends who remain with him to this day.

The transition to middle school was difficult, but Francisco eventually found his way. Two eighth-grade classes stand out. A history course taught by an acclaimed teacher—one Brian also took—convinced him that he wanted to study history. And the course for which he wrote that essay on the film directors required lots of writing that students had to revise and proofread for a class newspaper the teacher distributed to the entire school.

During one of our conversations, Brian noted that during middle school, Francisco was the class clown. "By the time I met him, he already had a reputation." I can believe it. Both young men have an ironic take on things and a finely tuned bullshit detector. But while Brian expresses himself in an eloquent baritone, Francisco plays with intonation and timbre and is a dead-on mimic. As we were driving out of the middle school parking lot, Francisco mused, "I was really obnoxious. I got on people's nerves . . . Man, I got on *my own nerves* later on. I thought, 'God, was that *me*?!'"

Off then to the high school, where Brian and Francisco met their influential teachers, one of whom was driving us there, and whose voice and bearing, by the way, Francisco can imitate perfectly.

————

Teachers, counselors, and other staff are at the high school for orientation, so the center of campus presents a vibrant contrast to the empty yard we just left. People cluster in groups of three or four, talking, laughing, hailing others in nearby groups, catching up after summer break. Some of the older teachers are dressed in professional blues, grays, and browns, but most of the faculty are in denim and sportswear. Jonathan spots old friends. After years of being laid off and then rehired at the last minute—a pattern common with young urban teachers—Jonathan decided to go to graduate school to study schools like this. He sees Matthew—Mr. Adams to Brian and Francisco—who has been waiting for us. We will spend part of the afternoon with him. Mr. Adams looks to be in his mid-thirties, slim, a boyish face, and clean-cut as the milkman on a retro postcard. He has been teaching for twelve years. Among other humanities courses, he is responsible for Advanced Placement Art History, which Brian and Francisco took with him. They told me that he used to be in his classroom by six or six thirty in the morning and sometimes not leave until six at night. Students would come early, visit at lunch, be there late to study, take practice tests, or simply talk about all that was crowding their minds, from the features of a painting to romance to crises of faith. Jonathan kept similar hours, as did a history teacher named Mr. Wittaker, the third person Brian and Francisco credit as preparing them for college.

"They challenged the way we thought," Francisco said as we were driving over. "Because of that, a lot of us changed in high school . . . a change most people would experience in college or later life." Both young men dwelled on the nature of that challenge, the way it was executed. "They would actually listen," Brian observed, "and would then help guide you—'Well, what do *you* think about this or that?'" The bottom line for Francisco was that their influential teachers "just wouldn't talk down to us." I didn't have to wait long to see what they meant.

Jonathan had split off to shake hands with another old friend, pulling me momentarily into the greeting. When I turn back to Mr. Adams, he and my two traveling companions are in deep discussion about *Straight Outta Compton*, the biopic of the West Coast gangsta rap group N.W.A. Mr. Adams is wondering if you can have a reliable narrator when the people who are the subjects of the narrative are also centrally involved in creating the narrative. (Former N.W.A. members Ice Cube and Dr. Dre are co-producers of the film, and the film omits some of the more unflattering details of the group's history.) Mr. Adams is bringing to bear on popular culture an important question from narrative theory, and Brian and Francisco engage it and serve it right back to their teacher, wondering if any narrative is trustworthy, in that there will always be omissions, embellishments, and such. I think about the kinds of discussions I used to have with Mr. McFarland once I graduated, hungry to talk about everything new. The young men and their former teacher go back and forth, probing, respectful, until that ubiquitous horn sounds again, and Mr. Adams suggests that we find a classroom so that he can duck a few of those orientation speeches.

———————

Matthew Adams doesn't remember reading a book until he was sixteen. His life was baseball, before school, after school, on weekends. He'd fall asleep picturing a perfect throw from second base or the ball cracking off the tip of his bat. Then toward the end of tenth grade, his grand obsession began to fade—and to this day, he's not sure why. A girl broke his heart. He failed exams that would have gotten him into eleventh-grade Advanced Placement classes. His parents had to move, so he started a new school. Were these the cause? He quit baseball, drifted from his buddies, and began to read. Big books. Tolstoy. He ditched school to go to art films and museums. He became the kid alone on a bench lost in his paperback.

At his new school, Matthew's mother urged him to take another shot at Advanced Placement and to tell the counselor about all the books he had been reading. The counselor placed him in AP Art History and English, courses he now teaches. Though Matthew had sought admission, once in AP he wasn't sure he belonged. A year before he'd felt the physical assurance of the ball and glove, the swinging weight of the bat. He was part of a team, the close coordination of movement, the hard-won camaraderie. All that was gone and in its place were isolation and insecurity—despite his yearning to read and see what he had not read or seen before. One day fairly early in the semester, he was by himself at lunch reading Walt Whitman's *Leaves of Grass* when his English teacher, Mrs. Howard, walked by and spotted the book. He remembers the look on her face, her head turning, quizzical. She started calling on him in class—and he tentatively began to participate. She would talk to him after class about movies they had both seen. Her public recognition of him and his interests was an affirmation that began to affect the way other students and faculty perceived him. "I was a strange kid," Matthew would later tell me, "but not to Mrs. Howard. She saw me. She saw me the way I wanted to be seen. It changed my life. Every day I work to see kids the way they want to be seen."

Mr. Adams takes us to a classroom that was occupied several years ago by Jonathan Meyers. The room is freshly painted an institutional cream and the walls are bare. Mr. Meyers walks slowly between the tables. "This was my last room," he says with mock wistfulness, "the end of my career." Mr. Adams sits at the front desk and unpacks his lunch while Brian and Francisco reminisce about tenth-grade English where they first met Jonathan Meyers. Francisco was at the height of his wisecracking career. "He loved to get a rise out of people," Brian explains, "especially teachers—get them irate." But Mr. Meyers didn't get irate. Rather, he caught the young man completely off guard. When Francisco directed a personal barb at a classmate, Mr. Meyers, as Francisco tells it, "wouldn't hold back. He'd approach me with that deep, intimidating voice and ask, 'Why would you say that?' And he'd repeat it with this sharp gaze. It cut right through me. He didn't just say, 'Don't say that,' but made me reflect on what I said. Not everyone sees a joke the way I do. I realized I could really hurt someone."

As is the case with many of the teachers we've met, Jonathan Meyers and Matthew Adams not only try to respond to the problems that emerge before them—like Francisco's unwitting cruelty to his classmates—but also are alert to problems or needs that might not be clearly defined. "Hey, Mr. Adams," Brian asks as he and Francisco take seats by the desk where their former teacher is eating. "Do you still bring kids to the mountains?" Mr. Adams noticed early in his time at the school that many of his students had a limited exposure to the natural world beyond their communities. Transportation isn't available or is too costly. The adults in children's lives are consumed with work and childcare and themselves might not know about nearby resources. And then there is a history of exclusion from certain beaches and natural attractions and a sense among some young people that, as a Black travel writer I know puts it, "this is not something people like us do." Francisco, mocking his earlier self, put it bluntly: "I could give a shit about hiking, man. I live in the city." Mr. Adams's solution was to start the Environmental Club, a means to take his students to wetlands and tide pools, to Mount Wilson and the hiking trails in the Santa Monica Mountains.

One of Brian's main diversions growing up was playing in an abandoned furniture factory that, along with other industrial sites—a wooden pallet distributor, a junkyard—was mixed in with housing, a common residential pattern in the inner city. The factory is huge, a block long at least, and Brian and his brother would explore the dark interior or skateboard on the loading docks. Over time, the place deteriorated, rust and rot, broken glass, graffiti upon graffiti, crack addicts and drug deals, accumulating human waste and debris. About one year before Brian's family moved to the neighborhood we're in now, a fire ravaged the factory. The city announced it would clear everything and build a public park. Years later, that has yet to happen. Thinking back on the empty factory as his playground, Brian raises his eyebrows and cocks his head. "When you don't have much, you make do with what you have." Thus the need for Matthew Adams's Environmental Club, which, in answer to Brian's initial question, still exists.

———

Matthew Adams has been teaching longer than Jonathan Meyers, but both had a lot to learn when they first came to work at the high school. White men who grew up in middle-class suburban homes, they had to learn about the community surrounding their school, about the lives of the students in their classrooms. Jonathan is more politically oriented than Matthew, more knowledgeable about the history of social movements, but still both men had to find their way in *this* school with *these* students. "We tended to not put a lot of trust in White teachers," Brian told me. "We kind of learn that there's this program where if you teach at an inner-city school, your student debt will be covered, and then you'll move on to a better district. You won't stay here."

Mr. Adams and Mr. Meyers gained that trust by doing the work. They created challenging courses, made themselves available, intervened when students needed intervention, responded to students with respect and expectation. "I treated them like they were smart," Jonathan said, "and could do important things in their lives and the lives of those around them."

From the outside, it would seem that Brian and Francisco were sure bets to go to college; they're bright, intellectually curious, and had a number of positive experiences in school. But overall, both had uneven academic records and both marched to their own drums. Francisco was more invested in his developing identity as the funny guy than in becoming a scholar. Mr. Adams had many conversations with him, trying to convince him of his ability. As for Brian, from a young age he saw no purpose in homework or in putting effort into classes that didn't engage him. Mr. Adams told me that he soon found out that grades weren't an incentive for Brian; they simply didn't matter to him.

At first, Brian resisted higher education. Except for a few teachers, he hated high school and "didn't want to think about college." He halfheartedly applied to a local college but botched the application.

When Mr. Adams and Brian's history teacher, Mr. Wittaker, found out—perhaps from Francisco—they went after Brian. "What the hell are you doing? You belong in school." Brian replied that he didn't want "four more years of the same crap," but after continued late-afternoon pleading and probing, he also admitted that he was worried that he might not live up to what people expected of him. What Brian calls the turning point occurred when his teachers—as serious as he had ever seen them—said that being scared was normal, but that "you have to take risks like this. You will thrive. You will. You were made for college." Looking back on it, Matthew Adams has an astute take on this crucial encounter. "It's hard to understand someone like Brian's reluctance from an adult perspective," he said. "We think, 'This kid has it all.'" But we, all of us, can easily forget the churn of desire and doubt that most young people experience—and how paralyzing it can be.

Francisco felt that churn as well but had an additional conflict. His parents always supported education but saw no purpose in the direction of his studies. His father works in construction, which has gone through countless booms and busts in Southern California. Money is a constant worry. So he keeps urging Francisco to, yes, continue with school, but learn something practical and quicker, the electrician's trade, or welding. Francisco applied to colleges in and beyond California, including several prestigious ones. He got accepted to all, but his father insisted he stay at home. In contrast to his irreverence toward so much else, Francisco is deeply attached to his family, so he obeyed his father and enrolled in a nearby college. The tensions in his family sadden Francisco, and he has spoken to Mr. Adams over the years about them. "You're kind of chained to your life by the ones you love," Francisco told me later that afternoon. "Sometimes it's the ones you care about the most who keep you there."

Both Brian and Francisco are majoring in history, and both very much want to return to this community, this school if possible, to teach. Several of their classmates who also had Jonathan Meyers, Mr. Adams, and Mr. Wittaker want to do the same. Mr. Adams had Brian give a guest lecture in his art history class, and Brian loved it. And both Mr. Meyers and Mr. Adams have been having ongoing conversations with the two young men about a career in teaching. That conversation continues today during the last few minutes of our time with Mr. Adams as he tells Brian and Francisco that they have the benefit of knowing both what it's like to be a student here as well as insight into the challenges faced by their teachers. And, he continues excitedly, imagine what might happen if "three or four of you come back and start teaming up with other teachers. That's what really changes a school." As Mr. Meyers puts it to Brian and Francisco, "when you're from here and you really understand the way your students grow up and the way they live, that is a great thing and is irreplaceable." Francisco picks up the thread. "We want kids to see what they can do and that it's not just people coming from the outside who are helping us. We can help ourselves." Brian nods and touches Francisco's arm. "We talk about this a lot. But I wouldn't want to see the day when there are no more White teachers here. Kids need positive White faces—not just police officers harassing them or the guy not hiring them because they're Black. They need to hear a White face saying, 'I'm gonna treat you with respect.' 'I'm gonna be there for you.'"

Commenting on the bond between Brian and Francisco, Matthew Adams uses the word *love* and adds admiringly how they accept each other yet "hold each other to account." Much of what was said today in the midst of the banter and casual reminiscences has been about being seen and heard, authentic talk, and respect. Brian and Francisco's friendship began in middle school and might well have developed elsewhere, but I can't help but wonder if the teachers who meant so much to them helped create the conditions for their friendship to deepen and mature—while maintaining its mordant edge.

In the courtyard outside the windows, teachers are milling about, another break in the day's activities. Matthew Adams has to slip back into orientation, and we need to be on our way to the next leg of our journey, getting Brian and Francisco home and seeing the neighborhoods where they now live. As we're picking up lunch bags and putting chairs in place, Francisco looks around the room and says, "They introduced us to this world, opened it up to us. I've always wanted to come back, to do something, feeling that what I did might change someone's life."

———————

Roberto Alfaro and I are walking down a long flight of narrow stairs that cuts through a lush wooded hillside in the middle of the city— overgrown flowering bushes, thick trees pierced with sunlight. Until recently, Roberto lived in an apartment with his mother, siblings, and other relatives a few blocks from the top of these stairs. He now rents a small place in another part of the city, but his mother and the rest of his family still live in that apartment, a concern for Roberto because much of the broad stretch of Northeast Los Angeles where Roberto and I will spend our day is rapidly being gentrified. He worries about how long they, and all the neighbors around them, will be able to stay as rents continue to go up and older buildings are renovated and priced out of reach, or torn down.

Along the hill on one side of the stairs, in some of the leafy alcoves under the trees, there are empty bottles, clumps of clothing, a shopping cart, a collapsed pup tent. Roberto explains that when he was in high school, local gangsters rather than homeless people hung out on the hillside, hassling the kids on their way to school, roughing them up, robbing them. After a few run-ins, Roberto started walking with some guys who were from the same block as the troublemakers, so he was given relatively safe passage. Turf dynamics are unstable for small-time gangsters, so, over time, the guys on the stairs dwindled, replaced by the homeless. As Roberto and I near the busy thoroughfare at the bottom of the stairs—a few quick steps out of nature into the rush of traffic—a skinny, disheveled man comes walking up the stairs unsteadily toward us and tilts into the woods.

Roberto was fifteen when he came to the United States from a small town in El Salvador. His house held two beds, a table, a few chairs. He remembers when his family got electricity and running water. Roberto was placed in an English as a second language program in his Los Angeles high school, mostly among kids from Mexico, whose Spanish was different from his rural Salvadorian Spanish. The town he came from had a population of four to five hundred people; his high school, one of the largest in California, held five thousand. "There were so many students in the hallways that you couldn't make it to class on time." Roberto was shy, an outsider, but was a good soccer player, which helped him make friends and become a member of the school's team. He had developed in El Salvador a fierce work ethic, which he channeled into learning English and doing well in his classes. There were few opportunities in his crowded apartment to do homework, so he would study in the bathroom or outside on the steps with a flashlight. His mother worked an early shift as a housekeeper at a convalescent hospital a half hour away by foot through a rough part of the city. His grandfather was out the door before dawn for a factory job on the other side of Los Angeles County. This was what Roberto knew, from El Salvador, from his new country: life is hard and demands much of you. He had no long-term goal for his studies other than to get the best grades he could. He held a number of part-time jobs, but school was his full-time occupation. School provided a soccer team and teammates. And there was free breakfast and lunch, a huge benefit, for hard as his family worked, there were days when there wasn't enough food to go around.

Roberto and I drive the path he walked to school and then drive and walk through the ethnically diverse, densely populated street commerce—a Vietnamese ninety-nine cent store, a Chinese acupuncturist, a *lavandería* or laundromat, little shops to buy Salvadorian food, and a host of sidewalk vendors—where Roberto and his family would go on weekends for food and services.

Roberto talks about his soccer coach and the park where he practiced. And a boy who was picking lemons in a neighbor's yard and was mistakenly targeted in a drive-by shooting. And exceptional events at school, such as the time his English teacher walked the entire class through the city to visit the renovated Central Library in downtown Los Angeles. Standing at the entrance, Roberto was awestruck, for he had never been in a building that size, and he "was fascinated to see so many books in one place." His teacher had all the students get library cards, which opened up for Roberto the resources of his local branch.

Walking in his old neighborhood, Roberto slides from the past into the present, the situation with this street corner, or apartment building, or stretch of small commerce—a present he enhances with the past, with his experience or the knowledge of old-timers or a continual probing of the internet. "I studied history as an undergrad," he shrugs and smiles, "so I guess it's the historian in me." Roberto tells me about walking the long distance with his grandmother to pay her bills, send money to El Salvador, and buy tamales and pupusas. His reminiscence is laced with analysis of the changing demographics, the homeless encampments nearby, and the dreaded internationalized gangs that control different sectors of the area. And repeatedly, time and again, he brings up the gentrification visible in the renovation of an apartment building, the beautification of a park or tennis court, the opening of a gym or coffee shop, the appearance of Audis and BMWs in driveways.

Roberto tells me about a bar close to his neighborhood that used to be the hangout of the local gangsters. It was a tough place. Over time other businesses on the street began to change; an old shop would close down and something more trendy opened up. The owner sold the bar and it started stocking craft beers. White twenty-somethings now occupy the bar, but the aging gangsters "refuse to give it up, so [they] sit at tables in the corner drinking their Modelos and Coronas." An uneasy, potentially volatile coexistence.

Roberto has a keen eye for everyday scenes that tell a complex sociological story. It is good to have public spaces made cleaner and safer; he thinks of the threat present in his mother's walk to work, his sister's walk to school. But what angers him and others in his and similar communities is that the locals, the longtime residents, primarily working class and Latin American, have been complaining to the city for years, to no avail. "Students in my English class would write papers about the condition of the parks, but no one ever paid attention to us. But the moment that some folks with money started to come in here, the parks got fixed up, the whole community got fixed up." And these improvements lure further development, which contributes to further displacement. One bitter upshot is that Roberto would very much like to move back to his neighborhood to be closer to his family, but the rents are out of reach for him and many like him.

Roberto works for a college outreach program at a major Southern California university, serving many of the low-income neighborhoods we are visiting. The schools he's involved with are like the one he attended; some of the students he assists bear resemblance to him.

Roberto's grandmother and uncle came to the United States to escape the civil war in El Salvador. Once they became citizens, they petitioned to bring Roberto's mother and her children here as well, for their home country was by then in the grip of gang violence.

So Roberto lands in Los Angeles, in a high school with ten times the population of his hometown, in a city overwhelming orders of magnitude larger than anything he knew. Many young immigrants with Roberto's background get lost—lost at their schools, lost to the streets, or lost in dead-end jobs, if they can find those jobs at all. Soccer saved Roberto from anonymity, then his academic achievement distinguished him to his teachers. Spending time with Roberto on the cityscape of his first few years in the United States I can begin to imagine his mix of innocence and growing experience, of reserve and determination, working as hard as he can, but within a narrow silo of achievement—"a little world," in his words. He studies for the next test, goes to the library for the next paper, gets a good grade. Roberto had few resources available to help him think beyond his high school and the areas of the city that he and his mother could reach by foot. Then in the fall of his senior year, the early incarnation of the program for which he now works presented itself to him.

It was during second-period English when a student worker entered the room with a slip summoning Roberto to the counselor's office. Someone was there who wanted to meet him. Though he hadn't done anything wrong, never had, Roberto assumed trouble. Who was this person? His mind rushed to a terrible possibility: What if social services had come for him? What if they found out his family didn't have enough to eat? "Somebody finally caught on," he thought, "and they're coming to take me away."

It didn't help when he entered the office and saw a professional-looking, middle-aged White man sitting at the desk. The guy was a social worker for sure. But as the man talked, a very different story began to unfold. He was a university professor and had established a mentoring program to help promising students like Roberto prepare for college. College? Roberto was ranked third in his class, but he "didn't know much about college at all," didn't know, for example, that there were several community colleges fairly close to his high school. After learning that this man was a professor, he went on the internet to find out what exactly a professor does.

Over the next few months, the professor, Daniel, continued to work with Roberto, remembering him as initially nervous, generally shy but engaging—and willing to do whatever was asked of him. Roberto learned about college, and, more importantly, saw reasons to go, intellectual and social reasons and economic opportunities, kinds of work he had not imagined for himself. His understanding of education—what it is and what it would enable him to do—changed substantially. It was as if Roberto had opened a thick and intimidating book to find, as he put it, "all the things that are possible after high school." Now Roberto's job has him traveling across Los Angeles fostering that opportunity for others.

————

Mariam Wright's parents owned their trim stucco and wood house close to Vermont Avenue, and she walked to the junior high school right around the corner and down the street from where I lived. Mariam's house had a covered porch, brick-enclosed flower beds with roses and irises, and floral ornamentation over the windows. Her father kept the lawn green and manicured. The other houses on her block, with some small variation in style and color, looked pretty much the same.

Mariam is ten years younger than I am, and to our knowledge, our paths never crossed when we were growing up. But we've both been teaching in Los Angeles for much of our lives and became friends decades ago. We start at her old house and retrace her short journey to her elementary, middle, and high schools, all of which she walked to and all of which, she says, gave her a strong education. The story of Mariam's block, from her birth to her graduation, is a representative story of opportunity and the loss of it in South Central Los Angeles.

Mariam starts naming with affection the families and their children who lived in the houses close to hers. Sarah and Karen who came from Texas lived right in this corner house. And the Carters—they were teachers—lived across the street. And, Jackie, oh Jackie, Mariam's best friend, she lived right *there*. One day, Mariam laughs, she and Jackie are walking to school when a large duck comes waddling out of a yard—a duck in the middle of the city!—and starts chasing the girls. Mariam wrote a story about it for her classmates.

As we go around the block and out to the main thoroughfare of Vermont, Mariam sees the Baptist church where she played piano for the children's choir, and she remembers an auto shop where the White mechanics saw some stranger in a car talking to Mariam and her little sister and ran out to protect the girls. The young people on this block walked everywhere; parents looked after neighbors' children; merchants knew the families and their kids. As Mariam put it simply, "I never felt afraid."

We don't see anyone on the street or in their yards on this Sunday morning. The church is still there, but the auto shop is now a community garden. The houses on her block are weathered, with some badly in need of a fresh coat of paint. There are bars on most windows. The yards vary from green and flowered to brown and spare. But overall Mariam's block is intact and has fared better than mine.

Most of these houses, Mariam explains, were owned by the people who lived in them—a few teachers, but everyone else had non-professional jobs: a butcher, a letter carrier, a processor of bank checks, a truck driver, and assemblers working in the many factories located in surrounding communities. Two of these families were White; the rest African American, a number of whom, like her parents, had migrated from the South during and after World War II in search of work. They encountered what other African Americans found in Los Angeles. Certain jobs, typically lower-level jobs, were more open to them than others, and where they could live was restricted as well. Mariam and her three siblings were always begging her father to take them to the beach. He claimed fatigue, dodged the request, flat-out said no until one day he relented. The kids were joyous. Into the car and down the long haul of Manchester Boulevard, he drove as close to the shore as he could and slowed down. *There's the beach*, he announced. Then he accelerated, turned around, and headed home. The kids were crestfallen and puzzled. It was some time later that Mariam realized the lesson in her father's stunt. Large sections of the beach were off-limits to Black folks, one of the many barriers they faced in mid-twentieth-century Los Angeles. But within these residential and employment constraints, ugly as they were, families like Mariam's were able to buy a house, participate in community life, and send their kids to school.

Mariam thrived in school. "I had perfect attendance," she laughs as we head west toward her elementary school. There is a pleasure in Mariam's reminiscence that makes me think in contrast of Beatriz Valdez's account of her daily bus ride to high school—long, lonely, physically and emotionally taxing. Mariam walked to her neighborhood schools with friends and sat in classrooms with a solid percentage of students and teachers who looked like her, and overall those teachers provided her with what she characterizes as "a wonderful education." Her story has its harsh moments. The walk to junior high took her by several apartment buildings where the kids would throw eggs or threaten her, but she soon figured out how to navigate that leg of the journey.

As we head to Mariam's elementary school, she talks about how rich the curriculum was in reading and writing. The school even had a newspaper, for which she wrote. This emphasis on literacy culminated in the sixth grade, where the English, history, and art teachers created an interdisciplinary curriculum, showing their students how the subjects connected. The children read historical fiction and did art projects related to the literature and history they studied. And all the teachers incorporated writing in their lessons. "Much later when I started teaching," Mariam says proudly, "everyone was excited about interdisciplinary instruction, but I thought, 'This isn't new. I've been doing this for a long time!'"

Mariam has me turn right onto the street where her elementary school was located, but we don't see it . . . at first. Then in a flash she realizes that her school is surrounded by tall iron rods that bend at the top to secure the school grounds. Once she reorients herself, Mariam points to an area of the yard we can see through the rods. "We had square dances on that blacktop and meetings every month where the class officers would give reports to the student body." We get out of the car for a better look. "During the weekend and during the summer, they'd open up the campus. We had a place to go. I loved this school. We had fabulous teachers." Her voice drops. "I didn't recognize it at first. It looks like a fortress."

We drive back to her house to take a sharp turn in the other direction to her junior high school. Driving there we see more signs of decline and neglect than we've seen so far: razor wire on fences, graffiti, furniture in the street. "It looks poor," Mariam says. "It's not the South Central I remember." Along the front of a large church, men and women are lined up for a warm meal. When we pull alongside her junior high school, Mariam is surprised by a newer building added onto the classic red brick structure she and I remember. The landscaping is neat and basic, and the grounds are clean. Mariam reminisces about field trips to museums and to plays—her seventh-grade English teacher loved the theater. The school put on book fairs. Mariam praises two Black women who taught her math, and her African American history teacher, and the man responsible for social studies who prepared a unit on the stock market suitable for middle schoolers. Mariam's essays were regularly among those posted on the bulletin board outside the principal's office.

Mariam was clearly a model student, it seems from day one. Though all her siblings graduated from high school and had successful lives, she was the scholar in the family. As we begin our drive to her high school, she watches the houses pass by and drifts into reflection about her father, how, despite a third-grade education, he could buy a house, and how her parents could build a middle-class life. It was the same story for most of the people on her block. They were not the professional Black middle and upper-middle class that lived in wealthier African American communities to the northwest like Baldwin Hills or Ladera Heights, but blue-collar folks who labored and economized their way into a propertied, secure existence. They created a platform of opportunity for their children.

Mariam brought her yearbook, and as we pull up to the front of her large high school, festooned with banners, she shows me pictures of her girlfriends, poised young women who would go on to college, some becoming doctors and lawyers. Mariam is one of those fortunate students for whom school was an extended source of pleasure and stimulation. From geometry and chemistry to her beloved literature classes, Mariam was in her element. She took creative writing classes. She read Du Bois's *The Souls of Black Folk*, Camus's *The Stranger*, Beckett's *Waiting for Godot*, Ellison's *Invisible Man*.

Mariam Wright's life was one of the many lives possible in South Central Los Angeles, a fortunate one, academically and socially. She remembers, though, when she could start to see the changes on her block that reflected the broader changes already occurring in the area. Thanks to the stability of her household, the employment of her mother and father, the location of her immediate neighborhood, Mariam was partially isolated from the housing projects and concentrated poverty to the east of her and the threats from both the street and the police that other residents of South Central experienced with demoralizing regularity, though both her father and, once they could drive, her older brothers were routinely pulled over by the police. Mariam also benefited from her early identification as a model student and all the reinforcement and support that status brings, enabling her to draw on the best her schools had to offer.

But economic and social forces way beyond Mariam's block were in play that would affect its residents and her family. In 1965 when Mariam was finishing elementary school, Watts, a community one mile to the east of Mariam, would erupt, one of the many American cities to burn during the mid-to-late 1960s. Mariam remembers sitting on her porch with her family anxiously watching the smoke rising in the east. Over the next few years, one of the White families on her block would move, as would several White business owners on Vermont, including the mechanics who protected Mariam and her sister. As she progressed through junior high then high school, she saw fewer White students. Though she was only partly aware of it at the time, experienced it indirectly and in isolated events, Mariam was also living through a gradual intensifying of gang activity and the proliferation of guns and, soon after, drugs. By the time she was a senior, she says, her hands palms down on her yearbook, there were fewer football games on Friday nights or dances at her high school. Her sister, only a few years behind her, would have a high school experience quite different from Mariam's, more limited and regulated.

The real blow to her neighborhood, Mariam says, was the loss of work. The many manufacturing plants that provided solid employment for people like Mariam's father began to shut down—automotive, steel, and a wide range of manufacturing and other industries—and with plant closings came the loss of all the ancillary work that supported those industries, from transportation to food service. After twenty-five years driving a truck for one company,

Mariam's father lost his job and his retirement. Younger men and women had far fewer employment opportunities to even get close to the life Mariam's father could build. When Mariam graduated from college in the mid-1970s, her minister told her that she should leave, that "things are happening" in the community that would affect her future chances to make something of herself. He didn't say more than that. Over the next two decades, some Black families would move into Los Angeles suburbs or to adjoining counties, or, in a reversal of the World War II–era westward migration, move back to Texas and the South. Immigrants from Mexico and Central America would move into many of the areas these Black families left. We just met the children of several of those migrants, living, a generation later, in communities similar to where Mariam and I grew up.

————

Though the largest numbers of people migrating into Central and South Central Los Angeles since Mariam and I lived there have been Latin Americans from Mexico and Central America, there have also been Black immigrants from Africa, the Caribbean, and the eastern coast of Central America, particularly Belize and Honduras. Edward Barrow's mother came as a teenager from the Caribbean, met his father, an African American man from the Midwest, and had Edward, their only child—that was thirty-two years ago. Edward and I are driving south on Vermont Avenue, passing my old house and approaching Mariam's as we head toward the former home of his grandparents—a modest two-bedroom house of quiet happiness.

Edward's mother worked as a police dispatcher and her shifts began early in the morning, way before school started. So she would bring Edward in his pajamas to his grandparents' house where he would have breakfast and prepare for school, "all that morning ritual of getting ready." Then he'd be off to school on the expansive front seat of his grandfather's "huge tank" of a Buick. Edward chokes up recalling those rides, for "that was our time together," telling jokes, talking about the television shows they watched once his grandfather came back for him later in the day: *Magnum P.I.*, *CHiPs*, and Edward's favorite, *Knight Rider*, the adventures of a high-tech crime fighter driving a computer-controlled Firebird Trans Am. After work, his mother would pick him up, they would have dinner, talk about school, and Edward would settle in for the night with his homework.

It takes about fifteen minutes to drive from Edward's grandparents' house to the Christian elementary school he attended. The school occupies half of a small city block in its entirety, parking lot and all. Edward and I walk slowly around the school's perimeter—a tall fence of blue iron bars—and stop in front of the playground, which is separated from a main South Central thoroughfare by that fence and a narrow sidewalk. Edward scans the empty schoolyard as though it were a memory theater: the basketball court, the chapel, benches, a wall for handball, the side of a primary-grade classroom thick with morning glories. He pauses at each landmark and comments both on things that happened there and the feelings they stir. His voice has a pleasing, tempered quality to it, and his observations come gently, enunciated, searching for the right word. He got a solid education at this school. His teachers were all Black Christian women who saw their goal as developing the character of their young students as well as building their academic skills. As Edward talks, he'll do things to assure his connection to you and to add a layer of commentary to what he's saying—a slight chuckle, a soft *yeah*, a glance sideways to catch your eye. He thinks about what he says, so there will be pauses in conversation, but they are not uncomfortable. He is taking you seriously as a listener.

Edward points to his old classrooms, to where he hung out, where he played. He remembers going to chapel on Thursday mornings.

He talks at length and with great warmth about his second-grade teacher, Mrs. Longwood, who treated him with affection, bestowing a nickname on him, talking easily with him before and after class. "She was someone who knew me, cared about me . . . there was a way she was there for me as a human being." Edward stayed in touch with her long after he left her classroom.

Edward and I are standing about a foot in front of the fence, the busy main street at our backs. Even on a Sunday morning, the traffic is heavy and loud. On the other side of the street, maybe thirty or forty yards behind us, is a huge South Central public high school, similar to the one Mariam Wright attended a generation earlier. To our right, ten yards to the corner, is a bus stop where kids from the high school would gather, loud and rambunctious, young Edward watching them from the other side of the iron bars.

"There was a lot of stability here," Edward says. "And the educational foundation I got set me up to be academically pretty strong." He pauses. "I don't know if I would have had the words for it then, though I think I had the feeling"—here he wraps his arms around himself—"I felt sort of sheltered, closed off." He laughs, dropping his arms to his side and looking at me. "Can you believe I never set foot on this sidewalk?"

As a police dispatcher, Edward's mother listened daily as people called in distress, urgent, afraid, sometimes directly facing danger. Edward was her only child. She would protect him in any way she could from the threat of the street. Though their family was Catholic, she chose this Evangelical Protestant school because of its reputation for safety. In the mornings and after class, the staff would open the gate and people would drive in single file, Edward's grandfather among them, to drop off or pick up their children within the schoolyard. Then they would drive out through another gate by where we are standing. Edward wasn't joking—he never had to stand on the sidewalk.

Edward's transition to middle school would thrust him onto these streets, right into the rough-and-tumble world surrounding the bus stop, which we walk toward—no one is there now—and round the corner back to my car. We head east to his middle school, deeper in South Central LA. Edward's mother, always the strategist, chose it because it had a magnet program that was a potential pipeline into a nearby well-ranked public high school. But the middle school had many more students than the Christian school, and from a broader socioeconomic mix, including a fair number from the community's housing projects, which we pass as Edward describes the magnet program. A few more blocks, a right turn, and there is the expanse of mowed lawn and diagonal walkways in front of his middle school. We park and head to the entrance, camellias on either side of the gate. Hanging above and across the main building is a long row of beaming faces, large portraits of students on the honor roll.

Edward smiles and shakes his head. "Everything I imagined about that school across the street from my elementary school—that's what I found here." There were others like him for sure, earlier incarnations of the students on the honor roll, but a lot of tough kids too. Edward watched in amazement and fear as they got into fights—and school had barely started! He tried to keep a cool exterior but inside fretted about his safety. He had neither the physical prowess nor the temperament to fight these guys. Gradually he learned how to live in the presence of threat, "keep my head down, make as few waves as possible." He takes a deep breath. "Most of my memories are of lying low." But while lying low he pursued his studies, "did what I already knew how to do, make this place as familiar as possible." And he had some teachers who enabled him to do just that. Evelyn Donaldson in eighth-grade language arts, for example.

I had met Ms. Donaldson years before. She grew up in the nearby projects and graduated from this school—and has taught here since obtaining her credentials. There wasn't much she didn't know about this community and the young people in it. "Children can tell right off," she once told me, "those people who believe in them and those who patronize them . . . it's as if there's a smell in the air." Her curriculum was abundant in reading and writing, emphasizing autobiography and autobiographical novels, mature books, consequential, Maya Angelou to Elie Wiesel. "Her class was all about intellectual pursuit," Edward says appreciatively. "She would ask questions and expected us to participate. She took us seriously and expected us to take her seriously." Her no-nonsense warmth created a forum for thought and expression.

Classrooms like Ms. Donaldson's became safe zones for Edward, enabling him, as he put it, to do what he already knew how to do. He also found the local public library a few blocks away, and it became a "home base" where he would do homework and "browse through the books," a casual pleasure. When she got off work, his mother would pick him up. He laughs self-consciously and points over his shoulder toward the street. "Walking to the library was my little taste of the sidewalk."

The high school that was the end goal of his middle school's magnet program lived up to its reputation. Edward had a number of good teachers there, particularly in Spanish, which he learned to speak and read, and calculus. His calculus teacher was masterful at explaining the why of mathematical operations, the logic underlying them. His Spanish teacher explored culture along with language and made multiple connections to Southern California art and history, important in a community that was increasingly Latin American. But much of our conversation at his high school was about the contrast he began to recognize back behind that fence at his elementary school and that he would dramatically experience in middle school: protected academic opportunity versus the unfettered and less secure life of the streets. Edward was grateful for the benefits and safety he was afforded, for he certainly wasn't equipped to thrive on the streets. Yet couldn't, *shouldn't*, there be ways to bring these worlds closer together? In a way, his Spanish teacher demonstrated the kind of unifying activity he envisioned by having young African Americans and Latin Americans—groups sometimes in conflict in this community—jointly study language and culture.

Edward grew up astride multiple worlds. He is the offspring of an immigrant mother and a native-born father. He was a Catholic in an Evangelical Protestant school. And he benefited from his parents' hard-earned and quite modest social class advantage in a community suffering from job loss and increased violence. Edward tells me how once he got to college, his thinking about the questions that vexed him for so long continued to evolve. The choice that seemed available to Edward as a youngster—and that would seem likely to many of us—was to toughen up and do battle with aggressors or sequester oneself away from them. But might there be other ways to engage the tumult of the streets, or other conflicts, for that matter? After all, those kids who once alarmed Edward were in the grip of their own injuries and fears. This new thinking influenced his education, its purpose, the courses he took. It also led him to get involved in campus activities and organizations dedicated to community building and intergroup dialogue, finding ways "to bridge communities that are in conflict with each other."

Edward began to "develop a language" for his early experiences and for the kind of work he wanted to do. Communities like the one he grew up in live through multiple conflicts, shaped and stoked by larger forces beyond them, from the dynamics of race and class to policy decisions concerning criminal justice, economic development, and more. There is much work to be done, and Edward had found his entry point. He devoted himself after college to creating and facilitating programs in schools, community forums, police departments, and religious organizations to help people who live in conflict with each other—often pitted against each other—imagine other ways to be, and to use that reimagining to change the world around us.

————————

Traveling back and forth across the long corridors of inequality that run through Los Angeles, I was struck by the strong emotional connection my companions had to their neighborhoods. South Central Los Angeles is deep in me and has shaped the way I see the world, and though I certainly felt my parents' love and had good times there, the primary emotions associated with my house and my block are worry and isolated longing. Most of the men and women I accompanied had extended family in their communities, neighbors who watched them grow up, and, generally, people who looked and spoke like them. Several had long histories with sports and coaches who mentored them. Though all of them knew the danger in their communities—everyone had some kind of direct exposure to violence—they had a warm affiliation to place, a warmth I didn't know.

The seven people I interviewed in a car and on foot are success stories. Several were top scholars from the day they walked into a classroom and several had to find their way. All graduated from high school and went on to college. As I listened to the stories my traveling companions told me about their time in school, I thought about the different ways educational opportunity presented itself to them. Did opportunity emerge organically out of the events and interactions of their daily lives, or was it unexpected, a surprise, perhaps unknown and unnamed until they experienced it? Who or what represented opportunity? And once manifest, what sustained or threatened it?

For Danny Oliveros, the soccer player who had the violent run-in on his way home from school, opportunity came suddenly and unexpectedly. His Spanish teacher noticed Danny's skill in navigating the complex social world of high school, his ability to get along with a variety of young people. This social finesse revealed something out of the ordinary about Danny, whose grades were average and whose horizons at seventeen didn't extend beyond the soccer field. Danny's teacher converted his hunch into opportunity through a simple but hugely consequential act: He pulled out his cell phone and initiated an educational future for Danny right on the spot.

For Roberto Alfaro, the immigrant from El Salvador, opportunity also came unexpectedly through a college professor who had established a program that took him into the schools, close to the daily lives of the kinds of students he wanted to reach, creating opportunity for this young woman sitting before him or that young man waiting at the door. Roberto had a strong academic record but little knowledge about higher education, and the size of his high school and an outlandish student-to-counselor ratio worked against him getting the guidance he would need to prepare for college admission. It is unlikely that an understanding of what college could mean for him and a subsequent pathway to college would have emerged for Roberto without some kind of intervention from outside his school and family.

Opportunity emerged more gradually and incrementally for Brian Zamoro and Francisco Estrella. Bright, brimming with potential, iconoclastic, these two had the kind of uneven academic record we often see, doing well in the classes they liked and much less well in the ones they didn't. If students like these don't come from families of college graduates, they aren't primed for higher education and can easily slip through the cracks, perhaps drop in and out of college, get an entry-level job with few prospects. I saw myself in them. Brian and Francisco credit three of their high school teachers with making their education meaningful and for guiding them toward college. These teachers saw their ability and both honored and challenged it—and directly confronted them when they didn't honor it themselves. These two, in turn, want to return to their community, to their own high school, and teach others the way they were taught—educational opportunity now generated from within the community itself.

And let us not forget Matthew Adams, the two young men's art history and English teacher, one of the three teachers who had such a profound effect on the direction of their lives. Mr. Adams himself was the beneficiary of a perceptive teacher, someone who noticed him alone with a book and invited him into a world of books, and, in his words, saw him as he wanted to be seen. Other people we've met have expressed a similar phenomenon: this remarkable act of seeing someone in a way that fosters development. Now Mr. Adams brings this way of seeing to a new generation.

Educational opportunity was present throughout much of Edward Barrow's time in school, but it would take many years for his educational success to yield a truly meaningful vocation. From the safety of his Christian elementary school through the prestigious public high school he attended, Edward Barrow was guided toward academic achievement; even in his rough-and-tumble middle school, he found sanctuary in some of his classes where the work was demanding and the expectations high. He was an astute and dutiful student, benefiting from the opportunities afforded him. But his education gained full relevance through college courses and activities that helped him to resolve a long-standing tension between a cloistered opportunity and the raw, sometimes dangerous life of the street, leading to his life's work helping people and communities in conflict imagine productive ways to live with each other.

For Beatriz Valdez, educational opportunity was hard-won. As is the case with so many students who are non-native speakers of English, Beatriz had some teachers in the early grades who were ill-prepared to work with children like her. Beatriz's mother played a key role in creating opportunity for the young Beatriz, both by attending school herself to better assist Beatriz and by her involvement in Beatriz's education. Observing the sacrifices her parents made motivated Beatriz to devote herself to her studies; she advanced to the top of her middle school class and onward to a prestigious and demanding high school—a golden opportunity, but one that exacted a price. Beatriz pushed herself past the point of exhaustion and was increasingly troubled by the fact that others in her neighborhood did not share in the education opened up to her. For Beatriz, opportunity brought a complex mix of advancement, moral conflict, and the weight of obligation.

And the story of Mariam Wright, the woman who lived down the street from me, reminds us if we need reminding of the broader social and economic contexts of educational opportunity. One has to start with the stability of Mariam's home, her parents' employment, the safety of her neighborhood where both residents and merchants looked after the children on the block. She walked to all her schools with friends and had friends in her classes, some of whom, like her, were thriving in school. Her teachers had been in their schools for years, solid, established, and they did well by her. Mariam uses the word *love* several times to describe how she felt about her education—think of that, to feel so strongly about what and how you were taught. Mariam's love for what she was learning was reflected in her achievement, an ongoing and cumulative record of excellence with the public recognition that comes with it—her essays were posted outside the principal's office. Mariam was increasingly defined by her performance in school, which affected the way she was treated and the activities opened to her. Opportunity begets opportunity.

All opportunity is dependent on the economics and politics of a time and place, but in poorer communities, it is especially vulnerable to changes in the economy or in public policy—a factory closing or the defunding of a social program can erode opportunity. We saw this happen in my neighborhood and Mariam's. There are also fewer resources available to young people, both within schools that are underfunded with staff stretched thin and within families that can't afford tutoring, enrichment activities, and other private educational services, like college counseling. And when opportunity, at times wonderful opportunity, presents itself because a student has worked hard and played by the rules or possesses some unusual quality that gets noticed—when this good fortune comes to pass, a student's housing and finances and family obligations can require an extraordinary level of solitary effort and commitment: Roberto reading by flashlight on his front steps, Beatriz studying through the blur of fatigue. In circumstances like these, the vigilant teacher or counselor, the special program, the extra layer of support from within or outside the student's community are essential to sustain opportunity—to make the light go on and keep it on.

All seven people pointed to particular teachers and other school personnel who made a big difference in their lives, in some cases made *the* difference, but they also credit their families for providing food and shelter, for supporting them, for discipline. They had conflicts, for sure—what family is without conflict?—but in some cases especially, mothers or fathers emerge as foundational figures in achievement. Brian Zamoro, one of the duo visiting his high school teachers, emphasized that "my dad taught me how to think, seriously think, and my mother taught me how to be strong—she's the strongest person I know." Over my years of teaching, I have witnessed family members disparaging, even sabotaging, young people's efforts in school. With one exception, there was little of that here.

My traveling companions also spoke with regret about others in their neighborhoods and schools who weren't as fortunate as they were. They knew the ability of the kid next door, of their cousin, of the child in the desk alongside them, knew that ability better than most, for they had an immediate, close-up view of it. But those young people didn't have a connection to school or the school wasn't responsive to them; or their family life was disrupted by chronic unemployment or by illness, deportation, addiction, or incarceration; or they experienced some awful trauma; or they succumbed to the seduction of the streets; or they just drifted haplessly, without guidance, in a direction that in one ill-advised step after another led to a bad end.

Every time I'm in South Central LA, I think of the human ability squandered, but I think, too, of the promise inherent in every block of every street. If you travel the main arteries of this area—Western or Vermont or Figueroa or Central—you'll see some of the more visible evidence of LA's widespread informal economy: People trying to make a go of it on street corners, tending to metal racks crammed with secondhand coats and sweaters, blouses and shirts. Along boarded-up lots, vendors hang long lines of clothes, one shirt or coat after another, facing out to passersby. Women sit at rectangular folding tables—the kind you'd find in a school cafeteria—selling everything from kitchenware to hair products. Other women have pots of hot food, bottles of soda, bags of chips. Depending on the neighborhood, sometimes within just a few blocks, you see pockets of redevelopment: a big box store, a supermarket, a bank, a movie theater, a Starbucks. More often there's a proliferation of fast-food franchises, mini-markets, liquor stores, and various kinds of automotive shops. Small independent businesses are everywhere: a beauty salon, appliance repair, used clothing, secondhand furniture, plumbing, laundromat, lots of family-owned taco or burger stands, pupuserias, botánicas. The Happy Fish Market declares *You buy, we fry*. Some stretches of Western, Vermont, or Central are vibrant with these places, with fresh storefronts opening as new arrivals, often immigrants, get enough cash together to set up shop and announce *We're here* with a fresh coat of paint: bright blue or orange or yellow.

You see the same variation in housing as you go up and down the side streets. Within a half dozen blocks there are bungalows with mowed lawns and trimmed shrubbery and decorative expressions of impatiens and petunias, nasturtiums and calla lilies. Here's a sylvan statue and a birdbath; there's the Virgin of Guadalupe amid red and yellow roses. Not far away, sometimes on the same block, there's a place that's boarded up, another that's inhabited but choked with weeds and rotted wood, and another with a dirt yard and a car up on bricks. Pick a Sunday morning. A father holds his daughter's hand as they walk into a mini-mart. Families with three generations are heading to church. A young couple, a bandana around the woman's hair, are mowing their lawn and trimming a flowering tree. A guy in torn clothes sits at a bus stop, legs splayed, lighting a crack pipe; another man, thin, eyes glazed, stands unsteadily in the middle of the street. Churches are everywhere, from large established de-nominations—St. Agnes Catholic, African Methodist—to bountiful storefront Evangelical and Pentecostal affairs: Iglesia de Dios, Min-isterio Christiano Roca de Salvación. A hand-painted sign above a doorway reads, "God's Helping Hand Holy Deliverance Church." Faith is spread across this uneven terrain.

Many of the influential teachers we've been meeting are able to perceive, often through tumult, a student's ability. As several people put it, these teachers could "see something in me that I didn't see in myself." This kind of keen perception is the very foundation of opportunity, a discerning and generous perception that invites a person to grow, to stretch beyond the present. In a sense, policy makers—and all of us—need to perceive communities like the ones we're traveling through in the same way, with the same eye for the possible. But we're not primed to see that way. So much of what is delivered to us about these communities is pretty grim: blight, murder, despair. To be sure, there is violence and hopelessness, but there are also stories like those we just read, more than we think.

We need a *binocular vision* when considering communities like South Central to be able to see at one and the same time the ram-shackle houses, the people who have lost hope, the drugs and violence *and* see simultaneously the people getting up before dawn for work, the storefront business with a fresh coat of paint, the children in the library and the teacher staying late in the classroom, the mowed lawns and flower beds, the many small civic and religious organizations and activist groups daily working to create a better life.[1] For things to change, much has to accompany this way of seeing, from economic development to enhanced social services. But as the troubled history of urban renewal and school reform has shown us, these efforts will fail if they are not driven by a comprehensive understanding of a community's strengths as well as its liabilities, perceiving simultaneously the damage poverty wreaks and the capacity ready to be released.

———————

It is a singular and revelatory honor to have people take you physically through their lives, to walk with them the streets they walked as children. Danny, Beatriz, and the rest shared with me their everyday pleasures and tactics of survival, their struggles in school as well as their breakthroughs—and all within the material intimacy of the front porch, the aunt's garden, the asphalt playground, the classroom doorway. As we talked and lingered, things we saw or memories they shared would trigger my own memories. One is of me sitting at the desk my mother bought at Sears, one of the modest things within her grasp to enhance her son's opportunity, crammed between two beds before a locked window that faced our small backyard. The wallpaper is beige with fading vines and flowers; there is a bulb in the center of the ceiling covered with a frosted canopy. The one other light in the room is from a desk lamp, also bought with my mother's tips, casting a bright circle on the book from Mr. McFarland's class folded open in front of me. The memory brings with it both a sad claustrophobia and a kind of release, a momentary deliverance. Maybe that was what hope felt like at the time.

For Mr. McFarland, the vehicle for educational opportunity was the mid-century Columbia Western Civ book list, but the vehicle could be any substantial body of knowledge, chemistry to fashion design, that is thought to be out of reach for some group of people. Unattainable. Too difficult or too rare. A while back, I was studying a remarkable bilingual third-grade classroom, rich in reading and writing, science and art. Two teachers from a neighboring district with a similar student population were also visiting. I overheard one say to the other, "This is too much stimulation. Our students couldn't handle it." The door slammed shut.

The reading list for Mr. McFarland's senior English came from a place in the social landscape very different from my own—and from that of most of my classmates. It is true that Mr. McFarland assigned this upper-crust curriculum because he was fresh out of school himself and gave us what he knew, but it didn't seem to cross his mind that it might be beyond us, that we couldn't handle it. There was no implication that these books were not for people like us—or that reading them would make us better human beings. He didn't lay on us any messages of cultural uplift. Here are the books, he seemed to say. They're important. And hard. And full of ideas for us to discuss. You'll need to know these books for college. So let's get at it. And we did, even if some of us were just tuning into college, a wispy aspiration nurtured by this teacher who believed in what he was doing and believed in us.

CHAPTER EIGHT

HOW THE LIGHT GOES ON

This book results from a professional lifetime in classrooms and from a particular classroom in my life long ago where the routine of schooling became decidedly unroutine, changed the way I thought about education, and initiated a future much different from the one likely for me. Though deeply personal, *When the Light Goes On* trades in broad questions about human development and education—about motivation, ability, and achievement—and the social and economic landscape on which development occurs. The individual human level and the level of public policy. I hope the journey we've taken helps us see why these two spheres of modern life should not be as separate as they typically are.

For me and a number of people I interviewed, education provided a way out of a bad situation, out of economic hardship, restrictive social roles, an occupational dead end, or a history of destructive behavior. New possibilities, a new life. People spoke about the importance of using their minds, the need for intellectual stimulation, the satisfaction of being challenged. There was pleasure in the activity itself, the pleasure of writing, or science, or one of the arts or trades. People had fun. Some reflected on the power of having their identities confirmed, their sense of who they are and what they like to do, or they were led to an identity, to a skill or disposition they hadn't considered before—an existential discovery. Some people experienced a political awakening or the commitment to a kind of work or a cause. And some found community as they deepened their connection to school, the bonds formed with like-minded souls who shared interests and goals.

What is remarkable is that except for its connection to economic mobility, we rarely hear education discussed in this way. For more than a generation, most American students have gone through schools operating within philosophically narrow educational policy—which has a significant effect on how they are defined and evaluated and what and how they are taught. The stories here give us another way to think about education. And the first thing to learn is what these transformational experiences reveal about the basic activity at the core of education: learning itself.

The most common way we talk about learning in school is in terms of test scores: an individual student's scores, or the cumulative scores of a school or district, or comparative scores—one district compared to another, one state to another, one nation to another. We also rely on broader indicators of learning: courses completed, certificates, diplomas. We are a credentialing society, so we seek documentation that a body of knowledge or a set of skills has been learned.

We certainly can apply such criteria to the people in this book. Once the light goes on for them, their test scores do go up, and their grades improve. They earn certificates and degrees, credentials that have a measurable effect on their economic lives and social mobility. What also comes through in their stories—and we hear much less about this—is the experience of learning and the effects learning has on the quality of their lives. We get reports on the psychometrics and economics of learning but not what could be called the biography of learning—how learning is lived.

One of the striking things about the accounts of learning we've been reading is their emotional quality. Learning new things, from physics to styling hair, generates feeling in the people we met, ranging from puzzlement and challenge, to a quiet confirmation of competence, to animation and excitement. And the positive feelings can be more than an in-the-moment spark; there can also be an eager anticipation of what's to come. What is learned leads to something beyond the present, from the possibilities opened up by mastery of a new tool to entrée to an unexplored field of knowledge. We heard this anticipation from a seventeen-year-old reading about the gender wage gap and from a medical student exposed to a new way to think about surgical pathology. Learning generates desire for more learning, the surge of cognitive momentum.

There can also be an emotional connection to the origin of what we learn—from learning to cook in our mother's kitchen to learning a method of inquiry from an academic mentor. People from carpenters to sociologists say something like, "This is the way so-and-so used to do it." Knowledge carries with it the memory and feeling of its acquisition.

Learning has a rich variety of social consequences. The activity of learning has the potential to bring people together, forming social bonds as they work jointly on projects or simply share a space where they learn. People meet each other and have common goals in classes, workshops, tutoring centers, and study groups. Learning becomes a public endeavor. Sometimes, as happened with me and several of my peers in Mr. McFarland's English class, solid and supportive friendships form, the social glue being the subject you and others are learning and sharing. School also provides one of the few places outside of family where young people have the possibility of forming growth-fostering relationships with older adults. And learning new things—from the economics of inequality to breakthroughs in cosmology—leads to new ways of thinking that possibly revise or supplant old beliefs and worldviews, and these new outlooks establish the conditions for expanding one's acquaintances and affiliations. Some of the people I interviewed—and this certainly holds true for me—spoke about their immediate world being small and limited, and the opening up and out onto the world that education afforded them. And some people, through what they were learning, resisted and rethought social categories that defined them—race and ethnicity, gender and sexuality, socioeconomic class—as they explored their identities and began to redefine themselves. Knowledge becomes infused with hope.

Education is typically connected to economic mobility, and the people I met improved their occupational prospects, at times considerably, as a result of their engagement with school. In addition, what some people learned opened up to them entire categories of work—for example, in human services—that they didn't know existed. Education led not only to a move up the economic ladder but also to an expansion of occupational imagination. What is curious is that the economic rationale as typically expressed does not do justice to the *economic* dimension of our lives. Consider the people we met who are preparing for the GED exam or are learning a trade. They certainly are motivated to improve their financial lot in life, yet their economic advancement is interconnected with the anticipation of mental stimulation and in some cases participation in a desired social setting. They are thinking about the place of work in their lives and what it might make possible for them and their families. As economics is lived, it is not sealed off from psychological and social issues, from philosophy, from politics, yet you will be hard-pressed to find in policy documents dealing with occupational preparation mention of any curricular content beyond the specifics of the occupation itself. Learning is strictly functional, monetized, focused on job skills alone. We can educate people for work without stripping them of the full meaning of making a living.

These many dimensions of learning affect our sense of who we are and what is possible for us. People change the way they think about themselves, how they comprehend their past and their abilities—and thus the way they see their place in society and what the future might hold for them. Engagement with a subject can affect not only what we learn about biology or literature or the culinary arts, but also more generally can affect our understanding of our dispositions and capabilities. Drawing on the legal and philosophical literature on human rights, education scholars Manuel Espinoza and Shirin Vossoughi tightly connect learning to the foundational concept of dignity, viewing learning as a civic and moral as well as cognitive activity, necessary to achieve the full development of our personhood.[1]

The kinds of educational transformation we've been witnessing can be a solitary affair, but family and friends, counselors, athletic coaches, and especially teachers are typically involved, if not at first spark, then once the person begins to find their way in school. The teachers who have been described to us and who in some cases we've met are a varied lot: young and not so young, from different racial and ethnic backgrounds, with differences in social class, religious affiliation, and sexual orientation. They exhibit a range of teaching styles and ways of presenting themselves in a classroom—their bearing and persona. There are, however, a number of qualities that most of them share, qualities similar to those identified by research as the qualities of good teachers.[2]

Good teachers know subject matter and how to teach it, how to explain things, how to ask questions that lead students to discovery. They are skillful at reading a room, knowing when they're getting through to students and when they need to change course. Good teachers have high expectations of their students but also provide assistance to reach those expectations. They affirm their students' cultural and linguistic backgrounds and draw on them as educational resources. They have a sense of the threats and worries their students experience and are knowledgeable about their students' communities, the assets and challenges. Teaching is a value-laden activity, and teachers express different core values that drive them—political, humanistic, spiritual—but what is common is a commitment to helping people grow and learn. As one student in a GED prep course put it, his teacher "thrived off of seeing a person move forward." Students of valued teachers talk about the sense they have that their teachers care about them, have their best interests at heart.

These qualities are interrelated and interact in practice. How teachers ask a question, for example, is intimately related to what they know about a topic and the resources they have in their intellectual repertoire to explain what they know. Questioning is affected by the way teachers define their work, by their assumptions about the children or adults they teach, and, more generally, by their beliefs about ability—how the mind functions and how to nurture it. These beliefs might not be elaborately articulated, might be more tacit than explicit, but they are powerful determinants of behavior. We might, as part of teacher education, isolate the activity of asking a question in order to help someone pose a question more clearly and strategically. But these refinements in technique will get us only so far if, let's say, the teacher is not well versed in the subject or has a narrow concept of student ability. We live in a time that tends to treat complex human activity as a phenomenon that can be understood technologically—which often means breaking the complex activity down to its constituent parts and mastering them. But with teaching, all its qualities work in a tight interweave. Most of the teachers who have made a difference in the lives of the people we've met come across as multidimensional and fully present. They care about their work and are intellectually curious about their subjects and their students.

The interviews help us appreciate teaching as a deeply human and humane activity. Teaching becomes a special kind of interpersonal intellectual work whereby certain people are educated and certified by our society to use their knowledge to help other people grow and acquire knowledge on their own. The teachers people respected were knowledgeable about their fields—welding and hairstyling to literature and science—and believed these fields were worth knowing and wanted to pass them along, share them, open them up for students. Some teachers could present their subject with more verve than others, but students picked up and commented on their teachers' attachment and commitment to what they taught, sometimes using words like *enthusiasm* or even *passion*. These words make sense: we respond positively to signs that people are invested in their work. Furthermore, to share something that matters to you is a sign of care and trust. (I think of Tomás Herrera's observation that "you have to love kids to show them art.") A teacher takes a risk sharing something she or he cherishes, and the people I spoke with valued the generosity in that sharing.

Both in teacher education and public discussion about education, we tend to separate subject matter, the cognitive and intellectual, from the emotional, affective dimensions of human experience. That distinction fades in the stories I heard. There are cases, particularly with younger students, where good old-fashioned kindness and affection are remembered fondly—especially for children who are having a hard time at home or feel out of place at school. But it is notable how frequently in people's early recollections that emotional well-being and a sense of self-worth are connected to an activity with significant cognitive content: helping other children with math or reading, or translating for new arrivals, or receiving public acknowledgment for work on a difficult task. An early childhood teacher tells me about the importance of children witnessing their own emerging competence as they take on a challenging activity—realizing that, as she puts it, "I'm doing something big in my world."

As we move into the middle grades and beyond, caring and concern are often experienced integrally with subject matter. What seems to be especially important is the teacher's skill in conveying that knowledge, the ability to judge when an explanation or illustration works or doesn't, and the facility to shift gears to spark student understanding. Some of the people I interviewed experience such teaching as a sign that a teacher cares about them. To be sure, many teachers are demanding—Mr. McFarland certainly was—but as one person emphasized, her teacher "wasn't tough just for the sake of being tough," but because she believed her students could do the work and wanted them to succeed.

Teachers' knowledge about their field, the way they teach it, the way they establish relationships with their students through it—all this carries emotional weight and contributes to students' sense that they matter. The notion of *respect* is relevant here. People refer to the way teachers speak to them and interact with them, even when they are being reprimanded. But I'm also struck by the respect, the caring regard that is communicated by the way a teacher handles subject matter expertise. For some teachers, their subject becomes a medium of connection with students, a vehicle for intellectual partnership. A principal I know offers yet another perspective. "Even the curriculum," he insists, "has to be challenging enough that it's respectful." Respect becomes a vital force that runs through the teacher–student relationship, contributing to trust and to a student's willingness to work hard and, if necessary, to reveal need or hardship.

Perhaps the most memorable quality of the teachers we've met is the degree to which they are observant, perceptive, attuned. There is a long tradition in education that emphasizes the importance of refining teachers' powers of observation, from eighteenth-century theorists like Pestalozzi and Froebel (the founder of the kindergarten movement) down to contemporary research on what teachers notice as they do their work.[3] The teachers in this book are keen observers of their students, noticing their behaviors, their interactions, what they say, what they're reading. But there's something else going on, and it is a remarkable quality. It is the ability to pick up on those needs or states of mind that might not be readily observable but that suggest an educational opening. These teachers have an eye for the possible.

They sense burgeoning talent: a teacher writes a comment on a student's paper that encourages her to write more. They are tuned in to longing, searching, hunger, unfulfilled need. Youth development experts Beth Bernstein-Yamashiro and Gil G..Noam put it succinctly and well: "adolescents' expression of their needs are subtle or even imperceptible."[4] "I could see it in his eyes," a middle school teacher says of a boy she recruits onto a nascent debate team. Perhaps they notice inconsistencies in behavior: the drifting student who gets caught up in a novel and writes an impassioned paper; the kid in perennial trouble who is captivated by mechanics. Or they see through sullenness or anger or other emotional static and deflections. This sensitivity requires knowledge of students' backgrounds and circumstances. Are there social and historical factors that influence what we see and what students are willing to show us? Where one teacher sees a rebellious middle school girl as a troublemaker in need of discipline, another teacher is struck by the girl's moxie and by her verbal ability. The second teacher wonders how she can help this girl find her way in school without losing her spark.

These teachers observe what someone can't do or can't do well but also seek alternatives, are curious about what someone *can* do. Think here of actor Emily Blunt's teacher noticing that she doesn't stutter when imitating someone or speaking in a silly voice. There is a forward-looking quality to this perception; the teachers imagine what someone can become and project a future. "When she looks at you," one person said of her automotive technology instructor, "she sees the finished product."

––––––––––

We've been exploring the qualities that enable teachers to see potential, but what contributes to a student's openness to be seen? What leads a person to be receptive to the rich educational encounters that make the light go on? There are many profiles and many points of entry; I'll sketch out those that are evident or can be inferred from the stories we read. Though treated separately for the sake of clarity, in reality they often blend and are affected by people's environments and life circumstances.

In my case, I came into senior English with a complex mix of emotional and intellectual needs that weren't fully clear to me: an unfulfilled intellectual curiosity, a desire for recognition, the ache of a lost father, and the vague anxiety of a future without prospects. Much of this personal history and interior life was, of course, not known to Mr. McFarland, but he could see my early, fumbling efforts in class discussion and assignments and, it seems, could sense the yearning behind these efforts. Several other teachers we've met spoke about a "hunger" they perceived in their students; that word fits here. My story illustrates a crucial point: what a teacher initially responds to might be just a glimmer of all a student carries, but a positive response opens the possibility of deeper connection to that teacher and to school.

Sometimes students' needs and interests are clear-cut: A student likes to draw, or write stories, or is captivated by history or psychology or computer coding. The teacher's response might range from a few words of feedback and encouragement to providing substantial resources for further development. Getting more books or art materials for students or connecting them to enrichment programs can be life-changing, but we've seen the generative effects of small gestures as well: the targeted feedback that refines skill or the aptly timed comment that deepens one's investment in a subject. A sixth-grade teacher jots "When are *you* going to write your first novel?" on the top of a budding writer's essay on her favorite novel. Feedback and encouragement make a person's interests and accomplishments public and can contribute to the way one is defined in the classroom, which for many students is the primary public space of their childhood. A young person is becoming an artist, a writer, a scientist. And finally, we see how an interest in a subject—anthropology to physics—can be intensified, even transformed, to such a degree that it has an effect on one's character and is used in the service of creating an identity.

We get to witness people discovering a subject or activity, the blossoming of an interest. In some cases, there were precursors, related pursuits—the ballet dancer who was unsuccessfully participating in cheerleading and volleyball. And in some cases, life events, at times traumatic events, predispose people to find meaning in a subject—consider those students who grew up in tough circumstances and were drawn to social and labor history. But there is also surprise: a subject or activity unpredictably captivates—the young woman with no background in science finding her life's work through an introductory class in astronomy. As different as these people are, however, most were in some way searching, exploring, at a transition point in their lives, which opens them to new experience.

Inspiring teachers are hugely important here, particularly ones responsive to nascent interests and with a breadth of knowledge that enables them to make connections that students might miss, who operate with a "if you like x then you might like y" suppleness. Equally important is a student's exposure to different pursuits: to performances, occupational sites, enrichment programs. What opportunities do young people have, particularly young people who are casting about, to experience different ways to use their minds and lead their lives?

We also get to witness people who didn't have the good fortune to be taken with a subject, who weren't engaged with school or had left school, and were bored, felt that, as one person put it, "I wasn't using my brain." The boredom can be caused by school itself, by a bland curriculum and perfunctory or scripted teaching, at times rooted in institutionalized class and race bias. In other cases, people felt stuck in monotonous work and pastimes, a cognitive malaise. They were ready for a change but didn't know how to affect it. For those who did poorly in school, education seems an unlikely option, the classroom fraught with memories of failure and shame. Then someone in their life intervenes or a life event jolts them, and they tentatively enroll in a class or a program. What or who they encounter there is, as we've seen, crucial in inviting them to a meaningful life in school.

We all want to feel valued and respected, and adolescence, developmental psychologists tell us, is a time of especially strong need for acknowledgment and peer approval—and for involvement in a larger purpose.[5] It comes as no surprise, then, that we have many accounts of the light going on in middle and high school. In some cases, these needs are directly expressed as students throw themselves into sports or activities like theater and debate. These pursuits provide a variety of enchantments and also provide order to young lives: practice and routines that lead to getting observably better at something—which brings both the satisfaction of competence and public recognition. Subjects from chemistry to carpentry provide structure as well—intellectual structure and the structure of participation. Tradition is integral to these pursuits, and for some students, involvement in tradition is guiding and gratifying. A student in a wood construction class once told me that he uses dowels to insert shelves into the bookcase he's building because he likes "doing things the old way."

Sadly, these needs can also be denied or distorted by a variety of factors. It might be the school's curriculum and school personnel or the challenges of coming of age in commodified youth culture. There are conflicts within families, and the many forms of bigotry young people encounter as they grow and explore their identities. One of the teachers I interviewed worries about the "everyday melancholy" of some of his students. But the needs remain, and we see troubled students forging connection in spite of distress—Chris Kurosawa pursuing both physics and experimental artistic projects for a teacher who represented a kind of intellectual integrity he craved.

We have powerful examples of the need to be involved in something bigger than oneself, to make a mark on the world. "You can't just simply grow and not help others grow too," says Tiffany Gamboa, the high school student learning about gender differences in economic opportunity. "I want," she continues, "to make some kind of impact before I die." This desire to be connected to some goal or cause can develop over time, as happened with Tiffany, through a mix of life experience, maturation, acquisition of knowledge, and the influence of respected peers and adults. Or it can emerge with tectonic immediacy, as we saw with people whose lives were profoundly reoriented through the birth of a child.

Some young people are drawn to school by the wish to be connected to an adult outside their family who can provide care or guidance. There are many reasons, from seeking advice on issues avoided at home to wanting an anchor in the world of adults because one's family life is in chaos. Feeling cared for can spark a commitment to school, an intimate connection between care and achievement. Several people speak of the responsibility they felt toward a teacher or counselor who did right by them. The teacher or counselor or coach might possess qualities the student admires and wants to emulate: bearing, values, styles of thinking or talking, expressions of race, gender, sexuality, or ability.

In addition to the security provided by a stable adult, school itself provides structure—at the least, food and shelter, which for some low-income students stabilizes their lives. And there is the institutional orderliness of school. Looking back on my own experience, I realize the obvious but consequential fact that Mr. McFarland's intellectual work with me occurred in a place where one accomplishment led to a predictable next level in the opportunity structure. I didn't have that order anywhere else in my life. A future materialized out of senior English.

———————

Students and teachers and subject matter form the beating heart of education, but as my reflection on the place of Mr. McFarland's class in a larger system illustrates, my story and the others are embedded in institutional and policy contexts. An expert on organizational behavior I consulted asked a crucial question: What can schools do at the organizational level to produce more occasions for the light to go on?

The stories make clear the importance of settings that foster interaction in classrooms or workshops but in less formal settings as well: in the schoolyard, athletic field, after-school clubs or tutorials, or just a room open before or after class where students can talk with their teachers about what's on their minds. There is a tendency in some low-income schools toward heightened surveillance, even policing, which undercuts the creation of this kind of humane social space. Ideally, we should consider all school personnel as an interconnected human web, for positive interactions with yard monitors, food service workers, and custodians can make students feel a little more at home in school. At the college level, there need to be opportunities to meet with faculty and staff: tutoring centers, computer labs, programs for vulnerable populations, and clubs and organizations for a range of student interests. Even the physical layout of the campus matters: places to meet and sit, for example, and clearly marked and accessible departments for student services.[6] What does an institution do to create these communal resources and encourage their use?

There are many calls in our time to change the structure of school: the way schools are managed, the organization of the day's activities, the delivery of instruction. Unfortunately, the proposals are often reductive, seeking a structural magic bullet. There has been a lot of attention paid over the last few decades to creating alternatives to large schools, especially the massive comprehensive high school that emerged in the first decades of the twentieth century. In a smaller school, faculty can better coordinate instruction, and students have more of a chance to be known by school personnel. It was not unreasonable, therefore, for the Bill & Melinda Gates Foundation to fund a major initiative to create small schools. But while being small creates the conditions for increased contact and coordination, leadership style, the content of the curriculum, and the skill and values of the faculty also matter. As Deborah Meier, the founder of several terrific and influential small schools, said to me, "You can have crappy small schools too."[7] The Gates Foundation in its own assessment was not able to show significant results, for its focus was on a single structural feature: the physical size of a school.[8] One can make a similar argument about class size. The research consensus is that class size matters, and anybody who has taught knows this to be true. (It is telling that the wealthier the school, the smaller the ratio of teacher to students.) But as with any single element of educational practice, smaller class size doesn't in itself guarantee positive outcomes. If you reduce class size but retain stale curriculum or hire teachers who have narrow notions of ability and learning, then size alone might not make much of a difference.[9]

Perhaps no topic related to structure has captured the contemporary imagination more than computer technology. The computer offers a wealth of possibilities for enhancing instruction, and electronic networks open up abundant opportunities for connection across distance and time for people living in remote areas, who are homebound, or who have family and employment obligations during school hours. Some visionaries propose a more wholesale replacement of the brick-and-mortar schoolhouse with virtual instruction, and we are already seeing various experiments in this vein both at the K–12 and college levels. As one would expect, the effectiveness of computer instruction rests on a number of factors, ranging from the subject and the programmers' skill in presenting it, to the way digital material is integrated into the overall curriculum, to the technical quality of delivery. The students we met offer a further line of sight on these more comprehensive proposals. Their stories are vibrant with human contact, and sometimes it is physical proximity in the classroom or workshop, the schoolyard or athletic field, that enables the initial interaction leading to an educational awakening: an accidental gesture, the halting utterance, the sudden, fumbling need to express oneself. Some of this will be lost through a screen. As we move increasingly toward the use of computer instruction, the quality of machine-human interaction will likely become more sophisticated, so perhaps we can build into the system increased opportunities for people to be heard who are seeking some meaningful connection to school. But we also know from the history of technology that technology can become an end in itself, diminishing the human need that gave rise to it. We will have to be vigilant that computer instruction augments rather than supplants the human core of education.

In its structure and routines, an institution conveys that it operates with a belief in the ability of the people it serves, or a neutral indifference, or, sadly, an expectation of inadequacy and deficiency. This is surely true for schools; you don't have to spend much time in a school to pick up the institutional message. Even if spare, are the grounds well-kept? What's the feel of the place as you walk across campus, as students move through the hallways? What's on display in its classrooms? And if the school as a whole is not welcoming, are there spaces within it that are? We repeatedly saw instances of teachers' classrooms becoming havens for discussion, academic and otherwise. We also witnessed the value of college tutoring centers and programs for special populations. While it is often the case, especially in elementary and middle school, that this sense of institutional affirmation is visually evident in the display and celebration of student work, the crucial elements are not only visual. You can have a school fluttering with banners and splashed with motivational posters that embodies limited notions of ability and limited goals for its students. The classroom where I came into my own had bare walls but was vibrant with talk and expectation.

Studies of organizational change have demonstrated that although the structure of an institution is certainly important, the beliefs underlying the structure are important as well.[10] You can change the structure of schooling, but if you keep in place limiting beliefs about ability, human development, and the purpose of education, then not much will change in the actual practice of schooling. We will change how schools look but not in any deep way how they function.

A major factor in the way a school functions is school leadership, particularly the principal.[11] Running a public school today is especially demanding work, for in addition to traditional responsibilities and routines, administrators must also deal with harsh budget cuts and financial volatility, restrictive federal and district policy demands, culture war flare-ups, gun violence, and more. We have decades of research, however, that demonstrates some school leaders can, in the midst of these constraints, create high-quality schools. Theirs is leadership that welcomes the kinds of teachers we've met—in fact, to the degree possible, seeks them out, realizing that some of them are unorthodox and will challenge the status quo. These leaders have mechanisms in place that enable teachers to learn from each other, either through collaboration or mentoring or through less formal interaction—the kind of thing imagined by Mr. Adams in the previous chapter when he encourages two of his students to become teachers and "come back and start teaming up with other teachers. That's what really changes a school." Of huge importance, these leaders infuse the routines and practices of their school with a belief in the dignity and capability of its students, a belief that is conveyed not only to students but also to teachers who learn powerful lessons about teaching from the way their school is organized.

Unfortunately, many teachers enter school systems where they must work within tight curriculum standards and, in some cases, a highly scripted curriculum. These frameworks and scripts provide guidance, which can be comforting and even instructive for new teachers craving stability as they take on dynamic and difficult work, but the guidance at some point needs to balance with an openness to the life emerging moment by moment in the classroom. Some charter schools with low-income populations operate with an especially regimented curriculum and pedagogy where students follow strict behavioral codes and are required to respond to lessons with brief, disciplined answers. A former student of mine calls this approach "tough love without the love." Imagine what these children come to think learning is, how they define education and their place in it.

Is there in a classroom the opportunity for a teacher to go off script, to improvise, to follow a lead offered by a student's question? There is much talk in school reform circles about "innovation" and "disruption," referring to the large-scale destabilizing of the system. I'm just as interested in small-scale innovation and disruption—those moments where a teacher creatively redirects a lesson, picks up a theme emerging in class, interrupts protocol to hear the curiosity in a student's question, follows a hunch about a child's ability rather than adhering to a diagnostic test. This is the kind of classroom talk and behavior that contributes to the light going on.

Structure at the school and district level is influenced by ideas about structure at the higher systems level. There is in education policy (and in many spheres of social policy) a tension between tight regulation and building "tolerance" (in the sense of "an allowable amount of variation") into the system.[12] This tension plays out, for example, in the creation of curriculum standards at the state level or criteria for teacher certification at the state or national levels. It is also very much present in a current discussion that is relevant to the concerns of this book: college completion.[13] Because college completion rates decline significantly as one moves from elite universities to the local community college, some policy makers are attempting to boost community college completion by mandating fairly structured pathways through the curriculum—in a few cases enrolling all students full time in a predetermined sequence of courses.[14]

One problem with this approach is that not everyone, especially older students, can comply with such a schedule because of family and work demands. And we read a number of stories where people were adrift and searching, took a class on a whim, then took another class, and another. Their path was not linear, had zigzags to it, even breaks as they quit only to come back and try again.[15] Then they encounter that teacher or counselor or subject that makes the difference, that changes their lives.

Some of their experience results from a flawed system (limited course offerings, for example, and poor advising), and making their curriculum more structured and efficient could certainly help. But increasing a system's efficiency in an unequal society will not remove barriers to achievement created by discrimination and vast wealth disparities. Furthermore, we human beings do not live lives of rational choice and unfettered goal attainment. So systems in our country need a certain amount of slack or laxity to meet the wide variety of needs and circumstances of its people, some sort of productive tension between regulation and allowable variation.

This variation requires having "second chance" options available in the system, chances to repeat and revisit school—multiple times, if needed.[16] We saw abundant evidence of the role played by GED programs, community colleges, and workplace instruction that in some cases provided opportunity to learn material one failed or ignored earlier in life. Redundancy is also important here. GED programs, for example, are available in adult schools, community colleges, and some libraries and community-based organizations. Inefficient, perhaps, but each site might be especially suited because of location, personnel, or atmosphere for particular people at particular times in their lives when changes in employment, family obligations, or their assessment of their talents and prospects create an opening.

Education requires structural models that provide form and guidance while accounting for the human propensity to express our ability through the limited options life affords us. At a time when we look for economic-managerial and technological solutions to our educational problems, we must keep focus on the foundational ideas about education that underlie our structural remedies.

———————

Education is a sprawling warehouse of a word, holding many meanings, stacked one on the other. Education refers to a vast multilevel institution, to a field of study, to the outcome of formal study, to the result of experience. It typically involves others who educate, but can also emerge from individual effort. Education is rich in connotation. It suggests competence, expertise, even wisdom. It also suggests advantage. It has an aspirational pull. In some families and social settings, it points to separation, to leaving others behind, and in other cultural contexts, education suggests civility and good upbringing. Many of these meanings emerged in the stories we read.

Of great concern are the ways the meaning of education has narrowed in our time. For many, education has become synonymous with its seemingly endless requirements and obligations, momentous routines, thin on pleasure and curiosity. A number of our attempts at school reform embody a related concern: The reductive technocratic framework that underlies initiatives such as the federal No Child Left Behind Act and Race to the Top simplifies our understanding of education and its many interconnected parts. Thus we try to fix education by focusing on an element or a function of it—testing, for example, or standards, or instructional technology—with the result that the element or function gains outsized importance, consumes our efforts at improvement or reform, at times nearly taking the place of education itself. But testing is a part, not the whole, of education. Likewise, technology can assist or enable certain kinds of instruction, but it is not the equivalent of instruction—in fact, there is a danger that a focus on technology can overtake instructional concerns.

Imagine by way of comparison if our understanding of health and medicine, our very definition of it, was composed primarily of imaging studies, or of blood panels, or of diagnostic decision trees rather than a comprehensive and dynamic model of health and illness. The vital questions at the core of education slip from view: What do we teach, and why, and how do we teach it? What kind of people are we trying to develop? What are the good life and the good society, and what role does education play in helping people attain them? Answering these questions would certainly involve the economic and technological aspects of our lives, but it would also involve so much more, from the challenges and pleasures of using our minds to the search for meaning beyond ourselves. In a truly democratic society, can we aspire to anything less than the development of the full humanity of our people?

I'll return to the definition of education and its philosophical underpinnings at the end of this chapter, but for now, let's take stock of other related keywords: Ability. Intelligence. Potential. Motivation. Character. Academic achievement. The stories we've read involve this basic vocabulary of schooling, fundamental terms used within education and by social commentators reflecting on it. This conclusion is not the place to review the long and consequential history of these terms, but the stories give us a perspective on them and, in some cases, give rise to concern about their commonplace use.

The term that is at the center of education policy and is ubiquitous today in discussions of schooling, on the minds and lips of every school board member, principal, and real estate agent selling parents on the merits of one neighborhood over another, is *academic achievement*. *Academic* refers to the core school subjects, reading and mathematics, and to those subjects identified with the college preparatory curriculum: the physical, life, and social sciences; engineering and technology; and the humanities. Academic subjects are typically distinguished from the visual and performing arts and especially from what came to be called in the American comprehensive high school the vocational subjects: mechanics and woodshop, secretarial science, home economics, and the like. *Achievement* refers to the successful completion of a school task as evidenced by a grade or test score, by the compiling of advanced academic courses, by receiving a certificate or degree. Achievement can also include—increasingly, it seems—certain kinds of extracurricular activities, volunteering, and internships, largely unpaid.

Depending on the context of its use, academic achievement can signify individual or group-level performance (by classroom, school, district, or region) on standardized tests, often of reading and math, or academic achievement can encompass a broader array of scores, grades, and other accomplishments. The pressure on students who have aspirations for college to secure a wreath of accomplishments is intense and likely contributes to the levels of anxiety and depression reported by young people.

When the Light Goes On is in many ways about academic achievement, about what happens to people when school begins to matter to them, and certainly one significant outcome is improved performance. But their stories can help us see the limitations with this crucial term, *academic achievement*, as it is typically understood today.

To be sure, the subjects defined as academic—especially the meta-subjects reading and math—deserve our attention. The problem is that in the American school setting, the *academic* label carries with it a binary distinction—courses not labeled *academic* are de facto *nonacademic*, and the *nonacademic* designation implies lesser cognitive demand and carries less social and institutional status. Entire realms of mental activity are diminished, an erasure of the cognitive content of occupations in the vocational curriculum.[17] A troubling by-product of this diminishment is the cultural construction of the "vocational student" as a concrete thinker, uninterested in and ill-equipped to deal with concepts and abstraction. This person might well be pragmatic, hands-on, and physically adroit but is assumed to be of a different intellectual class than the academic student—an assumption often unspoken. Such a definition will prove to be a formidable barrier as policy makers attempt to revive and improve the current incarnation of voc-ed, called career and technical education. In contrast to this demeaning portrayal of the vocational student, the stories we read reveal similarities in the educational experiences of academic and nonacademic students: both report cognitive as well as emotional engagement, the spark of discovery, the valuing of knowledge and the desire to know more, the relevance of what is studied to one's life goals, and the effect of what is learned on one's sense of self.

As for achievement, one can be succeeding in school by traditional measures—acing that test, getting good grades—and also be exploring and growing in ways not captured by those measures. My worry is that in our time, academic achievement has become such an anxiety-infused scramble that students are motivated to make it as risk-free as possible. Achievement has a finite and conclusive quality to it, bounded, a contest won, a prize. The process that gets you to the prize is demanding and has many rewards—the exercise of competence, praise from teachers and peers—but there is little room or tolerance for trial and error, exploration, a let's-see-where-this-leads inquisitiveness. A number of the stories remind us of the fuller experience of achievement, of its potential dynamism, responding to the allure of a subject or a skill, pushing beyond the familiar, taking a chance, discovering things about yourself as you go.

When the light goes on, people change the way they think about education and consequentially change their behavior. One psychological explanation of this change in behavior is that people develop new goals that channel, direct, harness, mobilize—pick your verb—their abilities and character traits and dispositions toward the achievement of these new, desired ends.[18] Think here of Brad Bowman, the would-be valedictorian, working with heightened intensity on his physics problems. And there's Francisco Estrella, the sharp-tongued, underachieving class clown, who decides in concert with his teachers to become a teacher himself. Driven by the need to understand and define herself, Leigh Masson turns her considerable analytic skills to anthropology and other social sciences to discover her transgender identity. We see in their stories a kind of rearranging and focusing of talents and qualities—quantitative or verbal abilities, quickness of mind, determination—that are in some way evident before the change we witness, though they undergo a transformation of purpose.

But what about those stories, and there are a number of them, where people display intellectual ability, qualities of character (persistence, self-control), and levels of motivation that were not evident before, at least not anywhere near the degree to which they are once the light goes on? It is possible, of course, that what seems like a sea change in ability and performance to school personnel would have been revealed if these people had been given a comprehensive battery of tests and assessments or if we could have gotten close to the daily flow of their existence, perhaps witnessing abilities and dispositions in family life, play, worship, or (if old enough) work that are not displayed at school. We did read about people who had disastrous academic records but were accomplished athletes or kept a home and raised children—activities requiring smarts and commitment. Still, their subsequent achievement in the classroom, at times at a high level, makes one wonder if they possessed an untapped cognitive ability that might well have been unknown even to them.

These speculations take us into the fascinating territory of potential. Widely used in everyday speech and in education circles as well, *potential* typically refers to "currently unrealized ability"—this according to Wikipedia—or, looking to Merriam-Webster: "something that can develop or become actual."[19] An example would be the athletic potential of the fast and coordinated child or, in a somewhat different vein, the academic potential of the indifferent student with high scores on achievement tests. Potential, in these cases, though unrealized, resides somehow within the individual, possibly analogous to a seed or embryo. Given the proper resources and guidance, the chances of this potential being realized are significantly increased. If the person's family, school, or community lacks these resources, our society has a long, though inconsistent, history of attempts to provide resources through an intervention or compensatory program. There is a beneficence to this approach, a desire to develop talent whenever talent is found in the social order—an affirmation of social mobility and a rejection of caste.

The problem with conceiving of potential in this way is that it limits our understanding of potential, leading us in an unfruitful direction as we consider the full range of stories we've read.

As much as developing the potential people carry within, we also create potential. I borrow here from the philosopher of education Israel Scheffler in posing the fluid and emergent nature of potential—that it is not simply a fixed entity or quality that some people have and some don't.[20] Rather, potential can be generated in particular kinds of resource-rich settings and through nurturing and guiding interactions. We have seen, for example, the growth-fostering power of a valued person believing in us, the effect that belief has on our assessment of ourselves and on our imagining of a self that is yet to be. "Potential," one learned scientist tells me, "is our projection of something into the future." We not only develop latent skills and talents through interaction with others, but once developed, these skills and talents also become the basis for entirely new developments, achieved in concert with more knowledgeable others. Consider the astrophysicist Colleen Murphy learning basic math in community college, which enabled her to take algebra and calculus, which established the foundation for the more advanced mathematics she needed for physics. "New potentials," Scheffler observes, "arise with the realization of the old."[21] Along the way, Colleen is receiving emotional support and guidance on navigating the difficult path before her and on ways to compensate for liabilities that might remain from the haphazard education she had before entering college. As she moves through her education, she is able to participate in a range of activities and communities of people who both teach and inspire her. Her goals are reinforced but also embodied as she interacts with others who are living proof that what she imagines for herself is possible. To the degree that we can say that an abstract notion like *potential* exists, it exists both within and outside of Colleen, and of us.

To be sure, the eliciting of potential is not without constraints. All the conjuring and coaxing in the world could not have developed me into a premiere basketball player or, from every bit of evidence I can gather, into a theoretical mathematician or an operatic tenor. Who we are and might become is the result of a highly complex interaction of endowment and environment, nature and nurture. The best of our biological and social theories acknowledge this complexity.[22] What is possible for us is by no means limitless, but when the time and conditions are right, more is possible than we think. Put another way, though our ability is limited by endowment, we can't know exactly what those limits are, both for psychometric and social-political reasons. Thus, there is always the possibility for surprise—and why we should regard ability with wonder and humility. A measure of our educational policies and practices is whether they can honor and generate the kinds of experiences described in the stories we've been reading.

The way we define ability and potential has a powerful effect on our policies for expanding educational opportunity for the less advantaged among us. Earlier I raised concerns about compensatory policies driven by a narrowly individual and internal notion of potential—policies that imply there are these kids out there with latent talent ready to blossom, and that our societal obligation is to identify them and nurture those talents into bloom. But what might happen if we change the goals of our social and educational policies to creating as much as to developing potential? From Horace Mann's mid-nineteenth-century characterization of education as "the great equalizer" to the present, we in the United States increasingly have looked to our schools to solve widespread social problems, particularly social class disparities.[23] School becomes the primary mechanism for creating a just and fair society. This is

an impossible mandate, but what if we even begin to take it seriously? By way of comparison, children growing up in resource-rich
environments—well-funded schools, an abundance of academic
materials in the home, social networks thrumming with educational
advantage—are already living in potential-creating environments. If
we want to establish a "level playing field" for all youngsters, as we
often say we do, then we must begin to face the facts of what growing
inequality means for the educational future of a large number of
our children. For example, there is a 47 percent gap in bachelor's
degree attainment between young people at the top half versus the
bottom half of our country's income distribution.[24]

Educational opportunity depends on more than what happens
within the schoolhouse. Employment, housing, food security,
healthcare, safe streets—these are the social and economic issues
that significantly affect how children do in school. They are the
core problems in the community where I grew up, and in the many
communities in our country that bear resemblance to South Central
Los Angeles. Addressing these problems will require a combination
of resources, political will, an engaged public, and a social policy
driven by generous beliefs about the purpose of education and about
human ability and potential. Such a virtuous combination seems
unlikely as I write in mid-2021, but it has occurred at times in our
past and occurs now in local settings, typically at a community-based
school enmeshed in a network of parents, activists, and social services, constructed of brick and mortar and a faith in the capacity of
its students, an existence proof of possibility.

What to do? As I hope is evident from all we've read, there is no
simple checklist, no off-the-shelf program to make the light go on.
But the stories do lead to some general observations about learning
and teaching and the many needs students carry that can make them

receptive to education. As well, the stories provide perspective on broader institutional issues and reforms and on key concepts—ability, achievement, potential—that inform institutional life. What we've learned doesn't yield a checklist, but it does suggest for teachers, counselors, parents, and, yes, students themselves values and habits of mind and conditions that contribute to the light going on and enhance our receptivity once it does. Let me offer some principles and questions to guide us.

Assume intelligence. Assume people think and derive satisfaction from thinking. People do not want to be bored, to stagnate, to feel dead upstairs. Seek intelligence. Where is intelligence displayed in the particulars of people's lives? And where in all the nooks and crannies of their worlds do the invitations to be intelligent reside: In a school subject? In social interactions? In play? In sports? In the activities of family life? In an interest or hobby, from dance to the study of bugs? In the way people make their way through the day—their skill in living?

Assume a desire for meaning. Assume that people want to find meaningful pursuits, to lead a meaningful life, to matter. What are the sources of meaning in their worlds, from relationships, to religion, to physical activity, to a school subject or trade? And given people's characteristics and interests, what are they likely to find meaningful? Follow a hunch about what might appeal to someone, make an educated guess.

Be alert to barriers to intelligence and meaning. In the school itself, in the curriculum, in its routines and protocols, in the school's "culture"—its shared beliefs and attitudes. What barriers exist in peer groups, in the home, in people's location in the social order? What barriers to using one's mind and finding what matters does someone face because of race or gender or sexuality, because of social class and background, because of appearance or language? None of us can be expert in understanding all these social categories and forces, so we need to consult and confer with others who know the territory, who can guide us toward understanding experience that is not our own.

Be vigilant for what people can do and precise in what they cannot do. Of special interest here is what people can do in circumstances where they are not doing so well in the central task before them, the main event. The boy scraping by in math who is obsessed with basketball statistics; the girl bored in her English class entering spoken-word competitions; the lackadaisical students who move with easy social grace among their peers. What skill, knowledge, finesse, or instinct do these people have that could be nurtured for itself, but also provide a pathway into school? Be vigilant for what people can do, but also be as keen-eyed and as precise as possible about those things that give them trouble. Pinpointing the difficulties someone has with grammar or mathematics or the use of a tool or execution of a physical movement is the first step to helping them do better.

Knowledge is emotional and social as well as cognitive. Acquiring and using knowledge (from knowledge of history to knowledge of woodworking) can be vibrant with feeling: discovery, competence, pleasure, excitement. Knowledge can become a means of communication and connection between teachers and students, parents and children. Putting effort into conveying and explaining knowledge can be experienced as a sign of caring. Knowledge brings people together, the social glue of affiliations and friendships. Knowledge has the power to enlighten and the power to connect.

There are many ways to care. Merriam-Webster defines *care* as "watchful or protective attention to help and protect," and philosopher Nel Noddings has elaborated a comprehensive philosophy of care in education that emphasizes understanding and responding to students' needs in ways that advance their welfare.[25] In common usage, care tends to mean "affection for," and, to be sure, it is good to have a helping and protective regard for anyone learning something new, in or out of school.[26] But it is also important to remember that there are many manifestations of care: care is demonstrated by the effort one puts into helping others to learn; by the way a question is answered . . . and the question after that; through holding high expectations; through the way a teacher or parent responds when those expectations aren't met; through response to error, blunders, bad behavior; by the way one handles one's knowledge and one's authority.

Educating the whole child means educating the whole *child.* We are astoundingly complex creatures. To understand ourselves, we have a tendency, at least in the West, to reduce our complexity: We, for example, think of our brain and therefore our mind as an information-processing computer or as a "meat machine," definable strictly in terms of its organic components. This is the reductive fallacy. It emerges in our schools with a pendulum-swing urgency to emphasize some aspect of ourselves that we believe we have neglected. Because we tend to separate cognition from emotion, we, at times, emphasize one over the other. But the cognitive and the social-emotional coexist in us in complex interplay. Learning is rich in emotional response, and subject matter can be a powerful vehicle for social connection. Similarly, social interaction and emotional sensitivity typically involve reflection and self-evaluation, which are profoundly cognitive acts. This interplay creates multiple and rich possibilities to find a meaningful connection to school—the emotion of a subject; the idea emerging in a caring exchange.

Think of your school as a human system. Try this: For an hour, for a day, let buildings, hallways, yards, and landscape recede and foreground the movement, clustering, and gestures of human beings. See the campus as a hive, a ballet, a scrum. What are the patterns of interaction? Where are there opportunities for students to interact with teachers? With other students around a shared activity? Can you enhance and increase them? Do the routines of the school close down or open up the possibility of human contact? Do the normal and prescribed ways students are expected to interact with staff and teachers enable exploration of interests or discovery of new ones?

Words matter. It doesn't take much to spark or shut down engagement. An observation, a casual utterance, a quick, scribbled comment on a paper. The words have to be based on actual performance, not hyperbole, not groundless encouragement or fake egalitarianism. A few words have the power to change the way people see themselves, for good or ill. On a broader scale, what we say in school and how we say it matters immensely. We are affirming or disrupting a relationship by our bearing, our tone, the way we carry our authority. Our talk, even in reprimand, has a primary purpose: to help people grow.

Listen. We're surrounded by noise, animate and inanimate, by distraction, babble, casual cruelty, enticement. It is uncommon to have someone listen, to have someone try to hear us. "Everyone wants to be seen," said one of the people I interviewed. And everyone wants to be heard. And it is an especially powerful experience to have someone hear what we can't bring ourselves to say.

Be receptive to surprise. We are predictable. We fall into patterns of behavior, routines, ways of being in the world. Others begin to define us by this predictability—and we likewise define ourselves. Change doesn't come easy. But especially during times of development or new environments—though not only then or there—we see or hear or read something that reaches deep within us, or another human being helps us rethink who we are and what is possible for us, or something we ourselves don't fully understand opens a portal out of melancholy or boredom or chaos. This change can happen in and through school. Be ready for it and be on the lookout for signs of it.

No effort at decency is wasted. You might assume intelligence, and do your best to explain your subject, and make yourself available ... and be met with silence, sullenness, even be rebuffed. Still, your decency registers and might be remembered years, decades later, recalled and valued in someone else's classroom.

The perennial challenge facing our schools is funding, the instability of funding and the unevenness of it, inequality in resources locked into the system by a history of discriminatory education, housing, and taxation policy and practice—and at the beginning of the twenty-first century, inequality is worsening. The light can go on anytime, anyplace, as illustrated by the range of settings we've seen—important to remember, for depictions of low-income schools are often one-dimensionally bleak. But budgets matter. Funding for facilities, instructional materials, and special programs, for the recruitment of seasoned teachers and to reduce class size creates more opportunities for students to be seen and heard and to become engaged with school.

There is another kind of educational inequality at work in the United States, one also connected to financial advantage and therefore to social class and race. This is unequal distribution of what we might call philosophical or ideological resources: beliefs about the capability of students to learn, grow, and find meaning, the kind of beliefs held by the educators who contribute to the light going on. Historically, philosophical inequality has been more pronounced the further away students are from the traditional academic curriculum associated with college. Given people's widely varying talents and interests, there is nothing inherently inequitable about students pursuing different courses of study, as long as they have some choice in the matter. The key issue is whether all courses of study—from Advanced Placement English or Physics to a GED prep course— are created and put into practice with the same integrity, the same egalitarian commitment to the conceptual content of the subject, to teaching it in a way that fosters intellectual development, and to guiding students to connect the subject to their own lives and to the world around them.

These philosophical resources are at the core of *When the Light Goes On*, providing a richer and more accurate understanding of learning as affecting multiple dimensions of our lives, not only the cognitive and economic; of teaching as built from the ligature of human relationships; of achievement as reaching beyond one's grasp. Philosophical resources like these emerge from a foundational belief in the capacity of the person being educated, child or adult, that carries with it a commitment to develop in all of us the full range of our potential, cognitive and social, civic and ethical—the beating heart of democratic aspiration.

Along with all the routines and requirements of modern mass education, this commitment directs our schools to honor a wide range of intelligence, to nurture the use of our minds to explore, connect, question—and through this activity to reflect on our abilities. Essential to such reflection are opportunities to think with others, to have our ideas examined and to have them taken up, to use what we are learning to engage the world around us, to cultivate the daily art of leading a thoughtful life.

Understood this way, education can inspire those on the cusp of a career to want to teach, to behold the wonder and power of the work, to think: *This* is what I want to do, to guide people to experience the pleasure of discovery, to assist as they confront their limits, to feel the grasp on one's arm of someone solving a seemingly intractable problem, perhaps for the first time seeing a way forward.

Facing us is the civic and moral obligation to create for a wide sweep of our people an education that can send a probe to Jupiter and help us care for the dying, that enables us to argue in the courts for racial, gender, and economic justice and to create a beguiling fantasy in poetry or film or dance, that leads to a safer car, a rural health network, a yet-unimagined way to heal our divides and live together in peace. These are touchstones as we hurtle into and try to define the middle decades of twenty-first-century America.

ON METHOD

BACKGROUND

Most dictionaries define *education* as an intentional process by which someone provides intellectual, social, or moral instruction to someone else. This process can occur throughout our lives in families, religious institutions, the workplace, or school as others teach us how to care for ourselves, execute a skill, or follow a moral code. And we can use instructional resources to educate ourselves. Many of the phenomena described in this book—the discovery of a subject, the incorporation of knowledge into a developing identity—can occur in any of these locations, but I am focusing here on those instances that emerge or find fulfillment in formal educational settings—schools, colleges, occupational training centers, and educational programs in business and the military.

My focus is on schools and colleges because in the United States they are the primary institutions, public or private, certified by our society to educate. Over the last hundred years, their mandate has intensified as more and more activities and bodies of knowledge—from hygiene to job skills—that were once transmitted through families, churches, work, and civic groups have been moved into schools. And because our country has evolved into a full-blown credentialing society, formal education has gained in social and economic value. We spend a lot of time in school, and our performance has a significant effect on the direction of our lives. These trends bring with them increased scrutiny and anxiety about the role schools play in our nation's overall well-being, and with this heightened concern has come a steady stream of calls for school reform. It is in this context, this historical moment, that I pursued the investigation reported in *When the Light Goes On.*

In line with the managerial-technocratic spirit of our time, contemporary school reforms have relied on various metrics to judge the health of our schools and to determine if a particular reform strategy is successful: scores on standardized tests, completion of courses, grades, the awarding of certificates or degrees, attendance, checklist-style surveys of student satisfaction—things you can count or convert into a number for quantitative analysis. For the most part, there's nothing inherently wrong with such measures, but they tend to be used in expansive ways that invest them with more conceptual and methodological weight than they can carry—for example, using a score on a standardized test of reading or math as the primary measure of learning or making a comprehensive judgment of a teacher's quality by a rise or fall in those scores. This approach to evaluating educational performance misses much of what a good education entails and, perhaps more troubling, over time can influence the way we think and talk about teaching, learning, and the definition of education itself.

I.

The Experience of Education: When the Light Goes On

One way to get us back to a richer and more comprehensive understanding of education would be to draw on accounts of people who had fulfilling educations or, at the least, positive experiences in school. One source could be memoirs, autobiographies, and biographies. For several recent illustrations in memoir, see Sonia Sotomayor's *My Beloved World* and Tara Westover's *Educated*. Another source is educational research. Two current lines of inquiry focused on the kinds of rich K–12 educational experiences that concern us here are "deeper learning and "connected learning." In higher education there is a substantial literature on "student engagement," where engagement is characterized by increased interest, motivation, and effort with accompanying positive emotions such as enthusiasm, even passion.[1]

And then, of course, we could talk to people about their education, exploring what drew them to school or alienated them from it. The advantage of such interviews is that they are interactive, with things the person being interviewed says triggering further questions that can clarify or explore a topic in more depth. The interviewer also sees and hears gestures and changes in intonation—a sweeping of the hands across the chest, a widening of the eyes, a rise or fall in pitch—that add information to what the person is saying. Interviews enable us to understand education holistically as a part of someone's life, the details of how a subject is discovered and the meaning the discovery has, or the interactional give-and-take of a valued relationship with a teacher, or the way one's social world and vocational aspirations are affected by academic achievement.

This book is built from such interviews, but I have especially relied on those cases where people experienced some kind of a shift in the content or direction of their education—an experience I represent with the shorthand metaphor of a light going on. I knew from my own time in Jack McFarland's twelfth-grade English class and from many years of teaching and research that this transitional experience, this shift in the meaning of education, can happen in a variety of ways, can occur when a person is doing relatively well in school and encounters a transformative subject or teacher or can occur with someone in crisis. It can occur quickly—the student entranced by an introductory astronomy class or cosmetology program—or gradually, over time, with stops and starts, involving multiple subjects and teachers.

These experiences are especially valuable because they foreground the process and purpose of education. There is a before-and-after quality to the transformative experience that increases its salience to the person involved (and to others) and therefore, it's reasonable to believe, makes it more available for reflection and scrutiny.

Selecting the Participants and Interviewing Them

There are several ways to select participants for a research study. Probably the most well-known is random sampling where participants are picked by chance—so if I were using that approach here, people with a wide range of educational backgrounds, lousy to excellent, would have had an equal probability of being chosen. But because I was interested in exploring a particular kind of educational experience, my selection process was "purposive"—I was attempting to find people who fit the criteria I just outlined.

But though I had criteria in mind to guide my selection, I wanted to gather a wide range of ages, education levels and interests, and personal histories within those criteria. I also wanted a diverse group in terms of race/ethnicity, gender, social class, and sexual orientation. With these twin goals in mind, I began selection by tapping into my own rich network of friends, past students, and other teachers and educational researchers. And they in turn referred me to friends, relatives, or students of theirs. As I was about three-quarters of the way along and seeing gaps in my population of interviews (for example, underrepresentation of a particular racial or ethnic group or field of study), I focused my search on those categories. The final one hundred ranged in age from seventeen to seventy-five, and occupationally ranged from students to retired professionals. Approximately 45 percent identified as White and 55 percent as persons of color. The male to female ratio was about the same, with two participants identifying as transgender and the rest as cisgender. Though some participants had solidly middle-class socioeconomic backgrounds, the sample skewed toward people from working- and lower-middle-class households.

I was able to conduct 70 percent of the interviews in person, in my office at UCLA, in my home, at the educational institutions people were attending, or walking and driving through their neighborhoods. I'll discuss the neighborhood interviews shortly, but in all other cases, the person being interviewed and I sat alongside or across from each other at a small desk or table, the audio recorder between us. As part of a parallel research project, I was joined for twenty of these interviews by one of UCLA's talented graduate students in education, Joy Zimmerman. The in-person interviews lasted about one hour on average, and all took place in Los Angeles County.

Roughly 30 percent of the people I interviewed lived beyond Los Angeles or outside of California, so I conducted those interviews by phone, constraining somewhat the spontaneity of the exchange and removing my observation of gesture, though not intonation. These interviews also averaged one hour in length.

To get us started, whether in person or by phone, I typically asked people to tell me about their educations, beginning at whatever point made sense to them, whatever stood out when they thought about their time in school. Though I had some general questions in mind, given the purpose of this project, I did not follow a fixed protocol because I wanted the flexibility to pursue an emerging line of thought as I tried to understand people's experiences of education and the meaning they attributed to particular events. I did ask clarifying questions and often would return to something mentioned earlier, asking people to offer additional details, or to describe as best they could how they felt, or to tell me what else was going on in their lives at the time. And these questions would lead to further recollections and clarifications.

Let me say a word about the chapter titles and themes and how I placed people in them. The chapters are not meant to imply a neat category scheme. Life is too messy for that. The person encouraged back to school by a loved one (who I place in the "From Life Lessons to the Classroom" chapter) might also have had a dreary time of it in school—and thus could also be included in chapter 6, "Becoming Smart." I placed people where I did based on what they emphasized in their interviews, what they thought was most important about their experience in school.

The Traveling Interviews

Researchers doing qualitative work have long known about the power of place to evoke memory, emotion, insight. I certainly found that to be the case when I was studying good public school classrooms for *Possible Lives*. I learned a great deal about the local significance of education by talking with teachers not only in their schools but also in their homes, in the shops and restaurants they frequented, and along the streets they walked and drove. Accompanying interview subjects to get their experience of their everyday environment has come to be known as the traveling or "walking" interview.[2]

The interviews I conducted while driving and walking with participants through their neighborhoods were preceded by sit-down or phone interviews that took place anywhere between two weeks to six months earlier. Because I grew up in Los Angeles, I was familiar with the areas we traversed, and I augmented my knowledge by reading the history of those areas before revisiting them with the people I interviewed. Both this knowledge of place and what I learned from the prior interviews gave me questions to ask during our journeys, but as with the sit-down interviews, I let the people I was with set the physical and experiential itinerary. Typically we started at their childhood home and finished at their high school. The accounts of their schooling and coming of age were consonant with what they told me during the stationary interview, though they tended to provide more detail to places and events discussed earlier, they recalled new events, and certain sites evoked a noticeable emotional response not evident in our earlier conversation. I audio-recorded the interviews, which lasted between two to four and a half hours.

The Accuracy of the Interviews

Self-reports of events in our lives can be inaccurate, subject to the vagaries of memory, and influenced by current events and circumstances. The credibility of participants' accounts is supported by changes in traditional measures of achievement that accompanied the transformations in attitude and behavior they reported to me: attendance, grades, courses taken and completed, and certificates or degrees granted. And in every case where I was able to speak to teachers, counselors, family members, or peers of the people I interviewed, all confirmed the participants' increased engagement with school.

Another dimension of accuracy, of course, is whether my rendering of the interviews conveys the lived experience of the people I interviewed. I was able to have three-quarters of the people I interviewed read what I wrote and got their approval, sometimes with corrections of facts I got wrong and sometimes with a comment on the phrasing I used to describe a particular event or feeling. I would then revise my text, often in concert with them. One-half of the people I interviewed, sometimes as part of this review process and sometimes spontaneously, sent me emails or letters with further information or participated in follow-up interviews, in person or by phone.

Anonymity and Writing

Given the sensitive nature of some of the material in this book, I guaranteed anonymity to the people I interviewed. Except for Jack McFarland and a few high school friends, all names are pseudonyms. And in a small number of cases, I changed minor details about people's backgrounds (e.g., their father's or mother's occupation) or neighborhoods (e.g., the location of a landmark) to further protect anonymity. None of these changes alter the overall accuracy and meaning of their stories, and all were approved by the participants.

To further protect anonymity, I generally avoided physical description of the participants. Midway through writing the book, I began to realize—amplified by several readers' comments—how much as writers and readers we rely on descriptions of people's faces, bodies, and clothes. I hope I'm able to convey the vibrant humanity of the people I interviewed through gesture and the qualities of their speech—intonation, rhythm, timbre—and, of course, through what they told me about their lives.

II.

Self-Study: Senior English

My former teacher Jack McFarland and I wanted to understand with as much specificity as possible what happened in his senior English class that contributed to my transformation from a drifting adolescent to a captivated young person headed to college. What made the light go on for me?

We were fortunate to have a number of artifacts to aid inquiry: books he assigned, essays I wrote for him or other teachers, my class notes, my report card, his grade book, the school yearbook and other memorabilia, and photographs from the time. In addition, I interviewed several classmates and visited my high school.

CONCLUSION ▪ 233

I had half of the books from 1961 to 1962, some of which I had underlined, written in, or dog-eared the pages. In all but one case (Racine's *Athaliah*), I was able to locate used copies of the editions we used. I also had the final drafts of the essays we wrote, which included a grade and Mr. McFarland's comments, and one earlier draft of a long essay on Joseph Conrad's *Nostromo*, a novel I chose to read for Mr. McFarland's elective course. Finally, I had my class notes for senior English, neatly recopied, the recopying an indication of my seriousness about the class and a significant change in my schooling behavior.

I did not keep any of the many mimeographed quizzes on the contents of our books or on the lists of new words drawn from *30 Days to a More Powerful Vocabulary*. Fortunately, several quizzes were reprinted in the program for one of our class reunions where Mr. McFarland was being honored.

I had essays from two other classes that were valuable for comparison. Two short essays were from junior English, which represented the clichéd and superficial written work I was doing in the year before Mr. McFarland's class. And I had six essays written for civics, a course I took at the same time as senior English. My report card displays three grading periods per semester, leading to a final semester grade. For the first semester of civics, my grades read C, B, A, with a final grade of B; the second semester reads: A, A, A, with a final grade of A. The civics course was heavy on reading and writing and became a platform to apply the skills I was developing in senior English, an indicator of what educational psychologists call *transfer of training* and today would be viewed as an example of *deeper learning*.

I relied on our class yearbook and a smattering of other high school memorabilia, such as programs from football games, to provide information on class composition, senior "most" awards, and the like. I also had a number of photographs of me and my buddies. I interviewed two of these men to get their memories and impressions of Mr. McFarland, his readings and assignments, and the dynamics of senior English. I also used my classmates as sources to verify or correct my recollections. Last, I went to my high school, walking the perimeter of the campus and across the central courtyard, eventually finding the window of the room that was probably ours or that had the same layout. It was the weekend, so I was able to look in on the room for a long time.

All this material formed a small archive of my time in senior English that provided a good deal of basic information, from the names of fellow classmates to graded essays. The archive also triggered a range of emotions, another kind of data about my experience in Mr. McFarland's class. I was using objects and verifiable information to pursue the elusive content of memory and feeling.

But it was the conversations with Jack McFarland that converted the archive fully into inquiry. Rereading the books, examining the papers, and going over them multiple times helped make our recollections of senior year more specific. What did Jack know then, let's say, about *Macbeth* or about Shakespeare more generally? How did he prepare—he said he was reading feverishly to keep a few weeks ahead of us—and what didn't he know how to do? And based on what I marked (or didn't mark) in my copy of *Macbeth* and what I wrote about the play—based on this evidence and our discussion of it, what can I surmise that I knew about *Macbeth*? Of equal interest, what did I seem to know how to do—and how might I have defined knowing? Did I know *Macbeth* when I knew the characters, their basic motives, and the plot? From all I can tell, that would have been my definition of knowing in the eleventh grade, before Mr. McFarland's class. Jack and I were able to trace the development of a richer sense of knowing over the nine-month span of the essays.

Self-Study: Going Home

As is true for all the participants' stories we read, my transformative educational experience is located in a larger life history. I wrote about this history in an earlier book, *Lives on the Boundary*, so I already knew from the writing a good deal about my past and the past of my forebears, including the history of immigration, of industrialization, and of Southern California, particularly Central and South Central Los Angeles. For the present book, my research focused on understanding everything I could that might have contributed to my experience in senior English.

I had been going back to my old neighborhood many times since moving away in my early twenties. While writing *When the Light Goes On*, I visited the area right around my former house eight times, driving and walking the streets, looking for landmarks or remnants of them, and documenting the changes wrought by economic and demographic shifts. I spent time on my block, noting where each of the businesses and homes of my childhood were located: the garage with its two hydraulic lifts, the Mexican restaurant, the hobby shop. When I could do so without being intrusive, I would linger in front of my old house, trying to picture the interior, particularly the bedroom and small dining area where I read and wrote for Mr. McFarland's class. I also had photographs of my house and the adjoining buildings. These were a great help in recollecting place, but standing in front of 9116 S. Vermont Avenue heightened the emotional memory of what transpired there in 1961–62.

The few artifacts I had from those years—a star atlas, the M volume of the *World Book Encyclopedia*—provided detail to recollection, but what proved to be a great asset to memory were the artifacts I could buy or find in the library: model airplane kits and the magazine for amateur astronomers, *Sky & Telescope*. It is one thing to write from recollection about ineptly assembling a balsa wood model airplane, to remember that it was a difficult task, and that I did not enjoy it. But it is quite another experience to write with a similar model kit spread out before me, matching the many pieces to the unfolded plans, starting to assemble one part, a wing or the fuselage, recalling the tedium blended with a creeping awareness that this model was utterly beyond me, sitting at our gray Formica dinner table in the broader hopelessness of our spare little house. These artifacts—and all the artifacts I used for this book—particularize both the content as well as the feeling of memory.

Self-Study: The Local Library

Though I had been going back to my old neighborhood, I had never revisited Mark Twain Library. The library was ten blocks away from my house, in the same location as in the early 1960s, but the building was new—yet some books and the adult fiction and nonfiction stacks themselves were from the time I was there. I went to the library three times, browsing the stacks and reading and writing. I interviewed the librarian, who showed me documents and photographs related to the library's history, going back to its origins in 1927. Particularly on my first visit, the old reference books and wooden stacks evoked strong memories and feelings, but it was also evocative over all three visits to watch young people using this library today, a new generation, with new reference technologies, and new hopes, finding their way with books.

Self-Study: Another Set of Eyes

During one of my trips back to my neighborhood, I brought with me Roberto Alfaro, the young man from El Salvador who we met in chapter 7 as I retraced with him the geography of his schooling. As a further check on my perception of my neighborhood, I wanted a different set of eyes. I learned as I toured Roberto's neighborhood with him that he had a keen perception of the nuances of urban landscape. Though he now has a college degree and is on a professional career path, as a young immigrant Latino from a working-class community, he is much, much closer than I am to the current realities of an area like South Central LA. What would he see and understand that I would miss?

There was a good deal that we both observed and discussed in similar terms, from the absence of fresh produce, to the mix of well-kept and run-down houses on any given block, to the proliferation and meaning of auto repair shops and decrepit motels. Though I conceptually understood observations he made about race—race and poverty, race and violence—I, of course, could not share in the experience from which his observations emerged. What was powerfully enlightening to me, given my purpose for asking Roberto to accompany me, were the things we both saw, but that Roberto saw more sharply or with a different emotional reaction. He was alert to indicators of vitality and survival. He could tell more quickly than I if a store we were driving past was closed down or just closed. He spotted right away a sign on a building indicating subsidized Section 8 housing. And he speculated on how many people might be living in a particular apartment, given its design and location in a complex. As we traveled, I noticed that when Roberto talked about houses, it was with a special kind of appreciation. My old clapboard house had been stuccoed over, the patchy lawn replaced with concrete, no greenery—to my eyes, a colorless shell of a house. When Roberto and I first walked down my block and I pointed it out to him, he said, with full heart, "Oh, it's still beautiful." No matter what state it is in, a house is not an apartment. Roberto's comment gave me a fuller appreciation of an important event of my childhood. When my mother was finally able to scrape together a down payment on the house we were renting, it must have anchored her when so much else was becoming unmoored.

Self-Study: The Role of the Participants

A word in this context about the interviews.

First, the traveling interviews. Though my primary purpose in conducting these interviews was not to aid in the recall of my experience in my old neighborhood, as I accompanied my participants through the low-income communities where they grew up, some of what they told me and what I saw resonated with my early life: specific reactions to school subjects and interactions with teachers, but also the look and feel of small, modest houses tucked along side streets, the ma-and-pa businesses with hand-lettered signs in the windows, my participants' reflections as we retraced their walks to school.

And all the interviews held the possibility of resonance as people discussed classroom activities, their conflicts and desires, moments of insight, and the solid feeling of being valued by a teacher. A young woman praises her high school English teacher for showing her class how to make a timeline out of a jumble of events "to see the bigger picture." An only child describes her mix of frustration and guilt in caring for her chronically ill father. A student from a poor community tells me with conviction, "I really wanted to go to college and be somebody." These moments both provide evidence to support claims I'm making and also take me back in time.

III.

Reading Books with Jack

I've described the way Jack McFarland and I attempted to systematically investigate my experience in his senior English class, but I would be remiss, I think, if I didn't try to also convey a sense of the experience itself of engaging in such a project with the person who taught me—the weight and the pleasure of it.

Here's how things typically go when Jack McFarland and I have what he calls our book club of two. We read the edition of the work we read in his class, though sometimes, as with Cervantes, Jack also recommends a new translation he likes. We speak by phone on Sunday mornings. I'm in a room that has bookcases along three walls with decades of books, including those from senior English and college, lined up alongside small plants, stacks of warbly mixtapes, and many snapshots: a one-room schoolhouse I wrote about, the diner in Pennsylvania where my father met my mother, friends with children who are now grown. The calls last about ninety minutes, and I record them. This conversation is followed up with shorter calls or an exchange of postcards as further thoughts and questions come to us.

These conversations allow me to experience again—though from a very different vantage point—some of the qualities that a much younger Mr. McFarland brought to senior English. There is, for example, his erudition and attention to scholarly detail. Sophocles wrote about ninety plays, seven of which have survived, and Jack read all seven before our discussion because he wanted to put *Oedipus the King* in the context of the other plays. Though we read the translation he assigned in 1961, he kept another edition by his side because he thought the footnotes were superior.

During the first few years of the project, I consulted with thirteen educators and non-educators to sharpen my work with my former teacher. What would they want to learn from such a collaboration? What were they curious about? In addition to whatever else they wanted to know, everyone asked about the nature of the interaction between us. Is Jack still the teacher, they wondered? Who sets the agenda and poses the questions? How do the conversations feel— what's their emotional quality? Are we equals?

At various times over the length of the project, Jack and I have talked about this unusual thing we're doing, its ease and enjoyment and how lucky we are to be doing it. We shift in who takes the lead, and though I have a number of questions to probe what made the light go on for me in his class and what he thinks I learned, neither of us lay out a grand plan for the conversation, allowing it to go where emerging topics take us. Because I'm audio-recording, I do pay attention to the recording device and to time. But I've discovered that letting the conversation unfold provides information of a different kind about what might have happened in senior English as well as about the significance of what is happening now.

In trying to answer my consultants' questions about the nature of our collaboration, Jack finally compares his side of it to a walk with a friend who is calling his attention to things he might not see on his own—and the delight he feels "as my little line of thought gets diverted" and he has to think intensely about an emerging topic. For me, there's a reciprocity in these discussions that in itself is pleasing and is unlike so many intellectual exchanges where institutional roles or personal needs lead speakers to grapple for advantage. What happens with Jack is qualitatively different. To be sure, Jack and I have our disagreements, but even then, our discussion feels like we're lightly tossing to each other something that is both of great value and familiar. "Listen to this," I might say, offering an observation in response to a point he made. And he, in turn, might admit, "That's a good way to put it," or "I hadn't thought about it that way," and then sees where my idea takes him. Back and forth. An inviting rhythm.

In addition to our dive into the past, there is a "presentness" to these conversations that paradoxically can be revealing about the past—as well as offering its own immediate rewards. I am surprised by the degree of emotional response I have, even to the most distant of the books from senior English—to sections of *The Aeneid*, for example. Of course, I'm able to read a work like *The Aeneid* with vastly richer comprehension than I could at seventeen. Furthermore, I am not under the gun of a school assignment and struggling simply to understand what's going on. And I am much older, deeply absorbed in life and closer to death myself. There is as I read a raw immediacy in Queen Dido's anguished love of Aeneas and in Aeneas's grief over the death of his father; so, too, in Macbeth's famous soliloquy upon learning of his wife's death, leading to the despairing pronouncement that life "is a tale / Told by an idiot, full of sound and fury, / Signifying nothing." I've taught the play and know the passage well but this time around feel the chill of emptiness, choke up and shudder as the death Macbeth has set in motion collapses in on him, utterly alone, speaking his own "last syllables" into the final hours of a life that has lost all meaning.

In the twelfth grade, reading *The Aeneid* or *Macbeth* was pretty much an isolated task, lying on the bed or sitting at my desk, me and the book, trying to figure it out, a page or two of notes from Mr. McFarland's class as a guide, my mother somewhere else in the house, making dinner or watching TV. Now I read not only with a long history of books and conversations about them within me, but also in anticipation of talking about what I'm reading with someone who is embedded in the social fabric of my life. In the final act of Chekhov's *Three Sisters*, a play resonant with the weary sadness of unfulfilled desire, the middle sister, Masha, must say her last goodbye to Colonel Vershinin, with whom she is hopelessly in love. In one production I watched on the internet, Kristin Scott Thomas, playing Masha, grabs Vershinin's lapel, pulls it back, and buries her face halfway inside his overcoat, closer to his heart. Chekhov's stage directions have Masha sobbing, so Ms. Scott Thomas's move came either from the director or, more likely, from her actorly instincts. The gesture captured more than all the words around it the intensity of Masha's sorrow. I couldn't wait to tell Jack about it.

Over the time Jack and I were rereading old books to find clues about my experience in his class, the reading began to take on a life of its own. Jack's intelligence and passion create a kind of literate force field, drawing you in if you are anywhere near it. I am reminded of that summer after senior English when I threw myself into reading the books he only had time to mention. As was true for some of the people I interviewed, I was becoming aware of how much more there was to know, and I was hungry to know as much of it as I could.

Decades later, I'm caught up again in the power of Jack's enthrallment with books. As our project of reclaiming the past was drawing to a close, neither of us wanted to let go of it. So Jack and I kept on reading, opening up the fiction I've bought or have been given over the years but never had the chance to read, books embedded in memories on the shelves in this room where Jack and I on Sunday mornings have been exploring my earlier awakening. Here's Tim O'Brien's novel about war, *The Things They Carried*, the first chapter listing in cold detail the tangibles and intangibles a foot soldier carries, from a rifle and grenades to a pocketknife, body lice, superstitions, and fear. And close by sits *Under the Feet of Jesus*, Helena Maria Viramontes's lyrical story of a migrant worker's daughter, her harsh coming of age in the unforgiving agricultural fields of California. All these stories stacked up, closed, rousing to life again as Jack and I keep reading. Will I ever stop learning from and with this guy?

As long as we're both on the planet, I suspect I'll be getting letters written in the free-flowing script that once guided me toward college, letters recommending a new writer Jack's discovered or a fresh translation of an old one. And I'll want to tell him, pick up the phone or a pencil and let him know about the girl, Estrella, whose birth certificate is folded in an envelope under a plaster statue of Jesus, or a scene where an actor buries her face close to her lover's heart.

A vital claim in *When the Light Goes On* is that transformative experiences in one's education change what's possible further down the road of development, affecting not only economic and social mobility but also other spheres of existence, in ways not always predictable. This rich, long arc of influence is evident in the stories of the older people I interviewed, and it is certainly true for me. One of the teachers I consulted to guide me and Jack as we undertook our self-study wondered if our exploration, in its detail and intimacy, enabled me to make a kind of peace with that awkward, searching youngster leaning apprehensively over a book at the desk his mother bought for him. Was I able to pull up a chair and sit alongside him, as I have done with so many students over the years, watching and listening as he gets the first taste of the immense possibility that is opening up before him paragraph by difficult paragraph—and clasp his shoulder for sticking with it?

THROUGH LIGHT AND SHADOW, BY POWER OF OPPORTUNITY AND EXPERIENCE

P ropitious, the decision by Mike Rose to grapple, later in life, with the phenomenon of light in educational experience, wisdom, and understanding, time-tested, at his call. Fitting that a son of Italian immigrants, an educator and a writer sensitive to the murmurs of the mind, would become a Caravaggio of educational research, a scholar equal to the task of translating light and shadow in education into words. Objectively, light belongs to the natural world, but it also resides in social life. It may travel at mind-boggling speeds through the vacuum of space, but on earth and among humans, Rose reminds us, the light does not go on in a vacuum; it depends on opportunity in the social environment. Across millennia, we, the denizens of the planet, have given the natural phenomenon of light a dwelling place within what we call our "being," our "hearts." Where and how might one find this peculiar kind of light? How does one learn to detect it? Listen first, we are instructed, to the narratives of people whose educational quest is punctuated by adverse circumstances, setbacks, openings, and breakthroughs. Alternately, look to where

intellectual challenge, structure, and kinship exist in symbiotic relation. There, asserts Rose, you may find educational desires being
fulfilled. There, I imagine, you may find fortune and observe the
metaphorical spark we all carry within being transformed into a
kind of candle, one that complains against the wind when it senses
itself about to be quenched.

What kind of book is *When the Light Goes On*? It can be, I think,
a handbook, a vade mecum—from the Latin, meaning *go with me*—a
thought companion, an observational consultant, a soon-to-be dog-
eared field guide. One that may help you catch sight of other ways
the light goes on. Go with me. Where might you go? Places, the
crucibles where sensibilities and skills are developed and teeming
with life, are indispensable in learning how to recognize, describe,
and explain the phenomenon of light in education. Perhaps a perch
at evenfall? But after you have read the chapter from Victor Hugo's
The Hunchback of Notre Dame—"A Bird's-Eye View of Paris"—in
which there is no dialogue, only a fanciful vision of his home city
as an "enormous tortoise," the medley of steeples and monuments
transformed into tiaras and pastries. In other words: test the approach locally. From high up, as one by one the switches are flipped
to fend off the darkness, imagine your city or town as a place where
the appetite for light both rages and is satisfied. Ask yourself: Where
might one observe the emergence of this educational light?

People, meaning-oriented human organisms capable of all manner of good, afflicted with the capacity to harm, blessed by evolu-
tion or their maker with the power, among others, to think, play,
wonder, and envision. Rose limns Jack McFarland (and others like
his beloved high school teacher) into literary existence for us to
consider the kind of person it takes to help others in their pursuit
of light, meaning, and purpose. (Contrast McFarland's temperature
and temperament to the rigidity of Mr. Gradgrind in the Charles
Dickens classic *Hard Times*.) Along with the hope that you have had

at least one educator like McFarland in your educational career, it is beneficial to note that he is an environment unto himself. (Educational scholar Ray McDermott wrote of persons both as environments and creators of environments for one another.) What kind of an environment ought an educator strive to become? Patient, flexible, pliable, curious, clement . . . the line between personality and avocation seems designed to be smudged. With Rose's inquiry in mind, the designers and organizers of educational environments can also be thought of as the electricians, maintenance people, and trouble-finders (and, unavoidably, the occasional trouble-makers) of those same environments. Metaphors multiply possibilities; they broaden the visible spectrum of human potential. At our finest, educators are the night-watch folks, people tasked with keeping the light on for the next person who is curious about what it means to study, inquire, communicate, and learn. If, as Rose insists, a focus on how learning is lived helps us develop a binocular vision of social life, then we cannot forget that the electricians of educational environments are also seekers of light. When the light goes on for someone, when we contribute to the light turning on, we usher into existence relations of mutuality.

Rose did not explicitly set out to write a moral treatise on education. Nonetheless, the implications regarding the light of educational experience and our common humanity sit patiently, waiting to be addressed. A central premise of this book: no matter the history of complications and disappointments, even the once-discouraged and half-broken can participate in and benefit from educational experiences designed to energize the light within. Proficiency affects who we are, Rose declares, as do the explorations and defeats that punctuate the landscapes of our lives. Mercifully, the latter do not disqualify us from the dignifying experience of once again trying to produce light.

Let's loop back to the opening sentence of the book: "Education is human work with human beings." Generative and generous human labor for the benefit of self and other. Not a regimen of instruction guided by, in Rose's words, a segmented model of humanity, which would amount to training for humanoids, but a vibrant process through which the elements of our humanity can be quickened and entwined. Education as movement toward wholeness. Whether arrived at via religious or secular tributary, this egalitarian notion—all can be made whole, everyone can potentially recoup some of what has been lost, each one of us can bring forth a new self—merits meditative pause. Through light and shadow, by power of opportunity and experience, we cause the human personality to flower and add to the running list of all we have been and will become over the life course. Rose's examination of the features of profound participation in the lives of others and his sense of the responsibility of bearing witness to that involvement positions us to nourish the "growth-fostering perception" he holds as vital in understanding when and how the light goes on. Owing to his discussion, I think it fitting to reimagine the activity of creating educational environments where people can experience the light going on as not only a notable interpersonal phenomenon but as an inescapable duty of social life.

—Manuel Espinoza

AN ACKNOWLEDGMENT

I t's a warm evening in August as Mike and I sit at his dining room table. Having assisted Mike for several years on this project and many others, the hours of diligent work in this setting are familiar to me. The Santa Monica breeze is playing with a wind chime from his patio and bringing some much-needed relief through the open screen door. Mike flips back from the end of his nearly two-inch-thick, clip-bound manuscript and sets it on the edge of the table. He pulls his glasses off and flips them back and forth against his hand before laying them on top of the title page of this book. He turns to me and says, "Now that's a good day's work, chief," the underlying joy in his tone conveying the deeper message. It had been an enormous journey—from intellectual conception, conversations with his friends and colleagues (often hosted by the Galley, Mike's sole restaurant of choice and backdrop for decades of cherished moments), interviews with hundreds of humans whose stories were carefully collected and explored, hour after hour of diligent and careful writing, to weeks of edits and revisions. Now the very last citation was finished. This book—the message Mike was determined to send out to a disheartened world—was complete. Meetings with several publishing houses were already booked, and Mike was illuminated with a contagious excitement. The only remaining writing for *When the Light Goes On* was the acknowledgments section. And he cherished this task.

We are still reeling from the cruel turn of life that happened a few days later. On August 15, 2022, this wonderful human left our world. In the weeks that followed, I, Dr. Christina Christie, Dr. Manuel Espinoza, and other close friends and colleagues came together as we began to process the shock and immeasurable sadness of this loss. But we were also grateful to be holding the words Mike had so carefully crafted. In the darkness of grief, this book became a hopeful light—a way to give the world one last conversation with Mike Rose.

If Mike were still with us, this section would be a thoughtful acknowledgment of so many, many individuals who have been a part of this work. He would have included everyone, making sure each person felt that warm recognition—the "I see you" that Mike was so very good at delivering. It would go on for several pages with genuine and heartfelt appreciation, a testament to the kindness of an esteemed scholar and professor, the thoughtfulness of our friend. While it would be presumptuous to even attempt a compilation of the names Mike would have included, we hope to act in his spirit of generosity by saying this: You were important to Mike and essential in the process of creating this story about the transformative power of education. Whatever your part—a phone call, hours interpreting handwritten edits, an email with your thoughts about a section, a photo of your classroom or desk, the dinnertime chat in the Galley, a thoughtful discussion while he took his evening stroll, or some seemingly small moment that Mike remembered, included, and followed up on—he valued it. He appreciated you.

—Carmel Wright